DIARY OF DECEPTION

DIARY OF DECEPTION

SAUNDRA STONE

Library of Congress Control Number: 2005908333
ISBN: Hardcover 978-1-5992-6711-1
Softcover 978-1-5992-6710-4

This book was printed in the United States of America.

To order additional copies of this book, contact:
Xlibris Corporation
1-888-795-4274
www.Xlibris.com
Orders@Xlibris.com
29570

DEDICATED TO:

All the guys I've loved before
I traveled in and out their door
So glad they came along
I've loved them, right or wrong
Yes, all the guys I've loved before.

The winds of change always blow
This is something we all know
They carried me away
Yesterday and today
With all the guys I've loved before.

A Special Thanks

I would like to thank my best friend, Marsha Brooke, who entrusted her work to me for finishing. This work was overwhelming at times as she presented it to me on about 105 scraps of paper, which I had to put in order and add to the many pages she had already written.

We both feel that ***Diary of Deception*** will prove to be of value to sexual addicts and women who just can't seem to say "no" to a man.

Saundra Stone

PART ONE

By

SAUNDRA STONE

CHAPTER ONE

May 16, 2002
Crestfield Hills, Illinois
(40 miles west of Chicago)

This is not a simple, ordinary Biography, so if you think it's going to be one of 'those,' you'd better stop reading now. I'm not even sure if it will end up tucked away in my drawer somewhere, or if I will save it as reading material for my golden years. But I probably won't be around to read it then anyhow, so I won't worry about that now. This is a true, down-to-earth, naughty, risqué story of my encounters with obstacles and problems and I will tell it like it is, has been, and will be.

I suppose you might say it is premeditated that I plan on having a nice cold beer in a frosted mug after work today because it *is* my 34th birthday and this provides a good excuse for me to stop for "just one drink." So what's the big deal? I haven't had a beer in six months.

The big deal was that my third marriage almost broke up six months earlier, but Carl (my husband) changed his mind when I promised I'd never touch the stuff again and wouldn't start running around as I had, since the beginning of our marriage. I guess when I drink, I flirt, and one thing leads to another and that man is added to the collection of those I have slept with. But after working with the mentally ill day after day for fourteen years, plus the forty mile drive each way, I like that tall frosty beer. I also like sex.

When arriving at work, all the other registered nurses started bugging me. They knew my past history quite well and everyone said, "Surely you will stop for one drink tonight, Marsha. After all it's your birthday and just one won't hurt you."

"Sarcasm" filled the air. I'm sure they all knew I couldn't stop with just one drink. I certainly knew it. I didn't have any friends at work to accompany me, so I would go alone and enjoy myself. I had learned through the years that there was nothing or no one as evil as a nurse. They are back stabbers. They talk pleasantly to your face and then stab you in the back when you walk away. Bitches, all of them, and no way did I want one of them to go with me anyhow. But I must admit they had the office decorated and nice gifts for me when I walked in today. I knew they were up to something,

When driving home, I asked myself once more if I really wanted to stop, for there was still time to change my mind. I knew myself and didn't understand some of the things I did. Once I started drinking, and a man approached me, I had to go home with him for I was one of those women who couldn't say "no."

"Hunks," that's what I called them. All of them are sweet in one way or another. Either they had neat, sweet blue eyes or muscles galore, or nice butts. (The first thing I notice on a man is his butt.) If it's well-rounded, he is automatically the one I pick. No flat butts were noticed by this gal.

Then I noticed his wedding ring finger. If he wears a wedding ring, I really go wild because through the years, I learned that married men understood married women so much more than the single ones did. They knew we have responsibilities and couldn't stay out all night. The single ones just couldn't get that in their heads.

I kept driving and decided to stop at the bar on the left side of the highway. It was a dinky place, set way back from the road, almost like it was trying to hide from the world. It called to me, "Marsha, Marsha, come on in. We'll buy you a birthday drink."

I pulled into the parking lot with my radio blasting away, my hair completely wind-blown, and of course my red convertible top was down. That's the only way to go!

I had to laugh as the place was called "Moonlight Inn." The name just didn't fit the joint. When walking in I spotted my barstool, alongside the wall, and waltzed over to it, counting my steps, "1-2-3-4-5-6-" I picked that spot because if I happened to get looped, I could just lean against the wall for support. Also, I was able to see everyone who entered and just maybe husband number four would venture in the front door.

I sat thinking of how I had everything in life since I came to Chicago from Alabama. What a difference it was. I loved my aunt and lived with her in the downtown Chicago area, which was a little too close to work. My first two doctor husbands worked with me there and that's the reason I moved forty miles west to Crestfield Hills, Illinois.

So what did I do after those two bitter divorces? I married a dentist, which was going from bad to worse. But at least with Carl, I didn't have to work. That makes a hellluva difference to a woman. It puts a whole new light on the subject. I work because I want to.

My closet is full of designer clothes now, many with tags still on them, and it's full of coats, shoes in every color, and designer accessories that were an overflow from my dresser drawers. I want for nothing, except sex, which my husband didn't give me six months ago and won't give me now. So I began to "fool around." Man, did I fool around!

I was so deep in thought as I sat gazing into space that I didn't see the hunk come and sit on the barstool next by me. I lost count of my drinks as we talked. When I told the bartender that voices from inside the bar called me in, telling me the bartender would buy me a drink since it was my birthday, he smiled and thought that was funny, but he brought me one. Both he and my new friend alongside me wished me happy birthday.

My new friend and I danced together, and I sang and danced on the bar. They all sang "Happy Birthday Marsha" and my friend and I made several trips to the back seat of his car, which also had a cooler full of cold brews.

We went back to the bar and drank a couple more and I vaguely remember smoking a cigar and five of us played strip poker. I looked at the clock which told me it was time to get home. I never even asked my friend his name.

I drove home, trying hard to stay within the lines of my lane, and as I walked in the back door, the clock in the kitchen told me it was 5:00a.m. I was so loaded that I could hardly walk. Carl was standing there right in my face, tapping his foot. I ignored him and went to bed, not needing a lecture on my birthday.

~~~~~
~~~~~

CHAPTER TWO

May 17, 2002

I got away with it last night. I sit here writing in my diary, which I plan to start doing again on a daily basis. It has been a long dry spell, with nothing written for six months and now, here I am starting up again. Some nights I will write more than others, as I did before. But let me tell you, I am going to be one helluva happy old lady, laughing when I sit back and read this diary and remember all the exciting things I did in my middle age years.

Every time I go out with someone new, I like to write about it and describe him. Of course he must like sex, and I tell of his favorite positions and describe his size (both length and width), not that I measure it but I have had enough men in my life (approximately 500 in 16 years), and I'm not bragging here. This is something I am not proud of, but nevertheless it's a sad fact of my life.

I go out looking for husband number four is because I believe that sex, is the most important part of marriage and I honestly can't live without it. I have to get it somewhere, right? My husband is "perfect." He doesn't smoke, doesn't drink and always wears black shiny shoes and black socks. Never have I seen him in a pair of tennis shoes or shorts. He's a dentist, and always wears a suit, is regimented as to scheduled chores, and only goes shopping on grocery shopping days. I go crazy because he just wants to sit and watch television every night and I never watch it. I am not even familiar with the programs that are on.

Plus he never wants to entertain and doesn't believe in birthdays. "What's the big deal?" he says. "It's just another day." I don't feel that way and had a ball at my celebration and don't even know the name of the guys I drank, danced, ate, and slept with. What did it matter? In fact there were three guys besides the one I went to the car with. And I don't know their names either.

Yes, I did make it to work this morning. It took about one hour to revive myself and catch my breath but I made it to North Park Rehabilitation in Chicago, which is really a halfway house instead of a nursing home. Everyone calls it North Park Rehab, and I am the charge nurse. Its hard dealing with mentally ill patients because of all the attention they demand. But the physical side of it isn't too demanding, as they do their own care.

Anyhow, I did make it to work, but I was slightly late. It was not a good day and I knew that there would be a drink stop once more on the way home.

The bar where I stopped today was called was called "Evergreen" and the outside was actually painted green, with a green bar, green booths, and green candles on all the tables. Every available spot had a potted evergreen, decorated with white lights. There were no other lights on in the place, and it was kind of neat.

I found a barstool by the wall and tapped on the green bar top for the bartender, "I'd like a tall one in a frosted mug with a slice of lemon. And you can call me "Princess Marsha."

"Please remember that I like my beers with lots of foam and they must be in a frosted mug." He just looked at me when he brought one and it did have the foam. It tickled my nose as I drank it.

Within ten minutes I felt the tap on my shoulder. That's usually what they did when they wanted your attention. In a way I hated it, but I loved it.

"Hi, my name is Geoff. Do you suppose you could give me a ride home?"

I explained that I hadn't even finished my second beer. "Well hurry up." was his reply. I drank it down and we headed out to my car. How the hell could I say "no" to this man? But he didn't have to boss me like that. He looked innocent enough, and just might be my next husband, my "Mr. Perfect" who would have nothing to do but make love to me all day; therefore I had to be nice to him.

So I hurried with my drink and asked the bartender to save my stool. "I have to take a chauffeur break here. I'll be right back." He told me that he would watch my spot and Geoff and I walked out to my car.

Geoff didn't try any fast moves, and I thought he was an okay guy. But when we got to his second floor apartment, I found out otherwise. Once inside his place he immediately grabbed me and planted a messy kiss on my unsuspecting lips before we even took off our light-weight jackets. That certain word, "sex," was written across his forehead and one could tell that by the look in his eyes, even before he said, "Let's do it honey."

And we did. Afterwards, he went to sleep right on the dirty kitchen floor where "we did it" and I was left with the familiar empty/nothing feeling. He passed out and I went back to the bar.

The bartender grinned at me—he knew what I had done and sure enough, he saved my barstool for me. He glanced over at my messy hair and messy clothes, and whispered, "Did you have fun?" I just smiled at him and shook my long, blonde curls. He brought me a cold, fresh, beer in a frosted mug.

I began singing, quietly at first, but it gradually became louder and louder and everyone at the bar looked at me questionably. One guy said to another, "She must be crazy," and I would have to agree with him. The next thing you know, I was out on the floor dancing with an imaginary partner. He kept stepping on my toes and I began pounding on his back like I was playing the bongo drums. I bumped into someone playing pool and made him miss his shot and he gave me a dirty look.

I waltzed over to the music machine and put more quarters in; I just had to hear more of bluesy blues to put me in a good, party, wonderful mood.

And then I heard it, a barely audible 'ping' telling me that my attitude and personality would be changing and I would be 80% Roxanne and only 20% Marsha. The Roxanne side of me was wild and crazy, and I have to admit that when we got together, there was more fun and excitement. But it also spelled TROUBLE in capital letters.

Someday when I sit on my front porch laughing as I read from this diary, it will be mostly because of the things *we* did together. I will laugh my ass off (LMAO for computer people here). The trouble we found ourselves in without even trying was amazing.

You should see me now. I write in this diary in my work room, or when Carl isn't home, as it's no one's business what I write. Such a good feeling—Yes, I am WMAO (writing my ass off) for all the Dell and Gateway Computer Operators out there. (Personally, however, I am not partial to the makes of computers.)

Oh what a fun night it turned into once Roxanne entered the picture. I ordered another beer and started dancing faster than I ever had, twirling while spinning my arms and snapping my fingers. People began clapping, and the pictures on the walls began jumping around and it worried me that they'd fall off their old rusty hooks. I blinked my eyes as two pictures started doing the twist. They actually touched each other on the sides and everyone laughed as the music became louder. I saw a tiara fall from the ceiling and land on my head and suddenly they all called me "Princess Rock."

I slowly felt my body going back about seventeen years. I was so much younger and so attractive when I was between marriages and free. I could do as I wanted with no man around permanently. Somehow they bugged me during that period of life (between husbands two and three). But I had my fill of men by that time. I remembered that when I did marry Carl, it seemed that one husband and one boy friend didn't cut it for me. I had to have one of each and a spare (the proverbial bird in the bush story).

I straightened the tiara that fell to my head and remembered that ever since I was a little girl there was a man in my life. It started with my stepfather but I won't go there now.

I finished my beer and bowed to my handsome prince, who came out of nowhere to dance with me. "Are you my husband number four?" I asked him and the bar patrons laughed. They thought I was joking, or talking to myself, because my Prince was invisible.

For the past few months I'd been hearing voices in my head more frequently. They speak loudly and clearly to me. I'll clue you all in right now: I know that I have a mental illness but I'm afraid to have a Doctor put it in words. I don't want to hear those words.

I am noticing different things and it worries me. For one thing, I repeat a lot, in case you haven't noticed yet. Please forgive me for this. The voices spoke now.

"So get off your butt and go look for him. He just might be here now waiting for you. Don't waste time with an imaginary prince."

I didn't like voices telling me what to do, but I did look around to see if the wavering throaty voices knew what they were talking about. At the same time, since they had upset me, I spoke back to them: "Shut up. Shut up. Leave me alone."

Once again, the patrons stared at me.

I decided to be quiet and act like a lady and make that psychiatric appointment as soon as possible. Something was wrong with me. Hell, the mind is part of the body and sometimes needs a doctor's attention just as an ear or toe. I couldn't put it off. So what if a nurse had to see a shrink? But the more I thought about it, the more I decided I just couldn't pick up the phone and make that appointment.

I got up and walked across the gritty floor to the music machine. I stepped on fucking popcorn and chewing gum and almost fell but I did make it to the jukebox and played four songs by Gary Moore. What a group!

After dancing a bit, I went back to my barstool, and as I walked, everyone watched my long golden curls and big boobs bounce. Once again, everyone stared. I evidently was putting on a show for them. So what if I was over thirty and still liked long curls? And so what if my boobs were 36D? I was 5'6" tall and weighed 135 pounds. That didn't make them too big for the rest of me, did it?

(I write more in my diary today than other times. Maybe I do this because I am just more wordier or maybe more has happened in my life and I am getting caught up on paper tonight. Or maybe it's because there is no one at home to listen to me talk, so I put it on paper.)

The place became wild. Others evidently liked Gary Moore too. People began tapping their feet as the trumpets became louder. The walls were vibrating with pictures dancing once more and customers began pounding their beer glasses, cans, and mixed-drink glasses on the bar. A few of them were tapping both feet in rhythm. The place was up for grabs. The hand clapping and stomping grew louder. I twirled, waltzed and then hoisted myself up on the bar and stripped—down to my next-to-nothing lace panties. I had just enough beers to do my strip dance performance.

Then the party became even louder and the place was alive with laughter. Roxanne and I loved it. The bartender put a bucket by me, for a joke, but people came to throw coins and bills in it.

I dressed, and when I sat at the bar and began tapping it with my mug, Mr. Bartender brought me another drink which I didn't order, but it was fine with me if he kept them coming. I had no complaints whatsoever.

The old player piano began playing a waltz which provided quite the contrast with the blues on the jukebox. The entire place rocked. Man, I savored every minute of the activity and wished I could bottle it and take it with me.

Roxanne grabbed an imaginary partner and the four of us were doing the mambo. Of course patrons would only see me, as Roxanne and the two guys were invisible, but Roxy and I were having a blast. My skirt was too tight, so I took it off to dance.

As I sat down, I said to the bartender, "Hey, honey, bring me another beer." I knew it was Roxanne talking, as I don't call complete strangers "honey," not even bartenders. By now Roxanne had completely taken over.

"Thanks, baby." That was the next thing I said to him.

I couldn't believe how I was talking and my face turned a brighter shade of crimson with both comments to the bartender. The walls began to close in on me with the floor coming up, the ceiling coming down, and all the barstools spinning. I headed for the front door to get some fresh air. But the entire room was filling with fucking white feathers. I squatted beneath my barstool. Can you imagine what Carl would say if he saw me in a bar, without my skirt on, squatting beneath a barstool, with fucking feathers all over the place?

"Let's all get out of here. They are closing in on us and coming to take us away." The bartender quickly ran over to assure me that everything was fine. "There ain't no feathers in here." With tears in my eyes, I got up and I thought my days of hallucinations and delusions were a thing of the past. So what was going on now?

I felt the tapping on my back and turned around. He wore no wedding ring and was tall and muscular. His teeth and smile were passable and I gave him a "4" on the proverbial scale of 1-10.

"Would you like to see my new apartment?"

"Sure, if you buy us another beer."

"Us? I only see one of you."

I didn't feel like explaining about Roxanne.

"Sure, I'll buy you a couple of beers." What could I say? I drank one beer and was just about half way through with my second one and in a gruff voice, he said, "Hurry up, you're wasting my time. Let's get going."

"Don't friggin rush me." I took my time and finished my second beer and then he pointed out his car and we walked towards it. He didn't even help me as I stumbled to get into the damn vehicle and head for "who knows where" because once more I surely didn't pay attention as we drove.

The clock on his dash told me that it was 2:03a.m. and I knew trouble was in store for me once again. I could feel it. I wanted to jump out of the car but wasn't sure where I was. This jerk smelled of garlic, stale beer, and pizza and I knew he wasn't my future husband, my "Mr. Perfect." He was silent as we pulled into his long driveway. So why the hell did I keep wasting my time like this? I knew already that I didn't like this loser.

This time it was me speaking, not Roxanne. "I don't know you well enough to go to your place." (Roxanne would just have gone.)

"So why the hell did you come with me in the first place if you weren't expecting and wanting a quickie? Come on, Miss Priss. We are here. So get your skinny ass out."

I was looped and couldn't move so he started yanking at my arms and pulling my legs, saying, 'I've got the hots for you, so let's go.' Come on. Come on." He pointed upwards and said, "That's my apartment."

Then he dragged me, and I fell, and the jerk stood there laughing like a moron hyena (and those are the worst kind)! I don't know how I managed to get into such predicaments but I certainly did.

We were in his apartment and he undressed me piece by piece and seemed to enjoy it. He then planted slobbery kisses on my lips and began to undress himself. I had to laugh because his manly organ was no bigger than my little finger (minus the fingernail) and I had to turn away and stop laughing—such a sight! I know they say size doesn't have a thing to do with it, but it does!

He began pulling his organ and trying to stretch it to have sex and asked me to help him. I knew what he meant and there was no way I would do that. "I just want to do intra-course. Help me, please?"

Once more I had to turn away to keep from laughing. Why didn't he just come right out and say, "Let's fuck?"

I wanted to run, but he seemed to read my thoughts and informed me that it was the woman's job to make the man hard.

Then he added a few choice words and tried to have sex but there was no way he could begin to do it—the noodle was limp.

"I guess we might as well get going, 'cause you aren't doing me a bit of good.' Both of us are failures, because neither of us can do intra-course."

He drove me back to the bar, and I headed for my car. Enough was enough for that day.

Why is it that we never learn from our mistakes? I surely didn't. I had every intention of going home, but spotted the small bar and really did want one more drink in spite of the late hour.

Sometimes a woman, like a man, just longs to sit in a place and meditate without someone bothering her. That was the case with me when I saw that particular bar.

I ordered my drink and sat and savored it. I was tired, and it was late, but what the hell. I ordered another. Then I felt the tapping on my back and was certain. I just knew this time it was my special man. We smiled at each other as he sat by me.

~~~~~
~~~~~

CHAPTER THREE

May 17, 2002

His clothes and body were covered with a thin layer of powdery film, similar to what a construction worker might accumulate after working all day. He was muscular, probably from working long, hard, hours. When his arm accidentally touched mine, I quivered inside. But I looked down and saw the dirt beneath his fingernails and it was a total turn-off. You know how nurses are about clean hands!

"How about it if we finish these drinks and I take you for a little ride?"

"I'm happy just sitting here for now."

And I was. The bar was almost empty, and the bartender was having a cigarette. I loved listening to the quiet. It was a clean bar, with freshly washed floors and the liquor bottles were neatly lined up in front of the sparkling glass mirror. There was not a speck of dust on the mirror or anywhere else in the bar.

But then, I had a special feeling about this man and I had to finish my beer and go with him. I knew it, "Sure, let's go." It was Roxanne who spoke that time.

"Okay babe. You name the place and I'm ready," she said. Sometimes it is easier to go and avoid conflicts and arguments, instead of doing what you want.

I was still in the mood for excitement that night, as if I hadn't had enough already.

I was dizzy when he put his arm around me, and almost pulled me over. 'Damn it. I had better not screw up my last chance of the evening.' That was my thought of the moment.

"Three strikes and you're out, Marsha."

The voices were passing this little hint along as friendly advice this time. I was in the mood for excitement and figured, 'what did I have to lose.' There was whistling and gurgling in the pons of my brain or was it the inner mass of my brain fibers? I didn't know. But I could feel my gray matter shrinking and becoming numb.

"Honey, I have a place that my old lady doesn't know about. Are you up to going there with me?"

"Yes," I blurted out.

We hopped into his little red truck. It was a foreign job and once again, I didn't pay attention as we drove.

He gave me a rub down as we drove and it told me that I had something to look forward to once we got to his place. I kept thinking that the girls at work always talk about construction workers and said they were good for going that extra mile. Man, that sounded too good!

I made the mistake of bringing up how dirty his hands were and his reply was, "What the hell do you expect. I just got off work." I didn't mention them again.

Soon he pulled into a disaster looking driveway with beer bottles, cans, and empty liquor bottles all over. He told me they were from the people downstairs. But I didn't believe him as there was grease on the handrail going to his apartment. Both his living room and kitchen were a mess. I had picked another slob, another loser.

The couch was all torn up, and papers covered the rug. He said they were on the floor so people wouldn't see the dirt. And he was serious. He told me the couch was torn up from the cat, but there was no longer a cat. It was so dark in the room "because all the lights were burned out," so we went to the adjacent room.

In the kitchen he made us drinks and he poured something extra into one of them. It was a powder but I couldn't see exactly what kind or how much he used as he stood in front of what he was doing.

"I only drink beer."

"This is a special drink for a special occasion." He handed me a dirty, greasy glass, with lipstick on the outer rim. No way could I drink from it. The grease almost made my hands slip and drop the friggin thing.

"Drink it, dammit." No way did I like the way he talked to me.

"I'm not thirsty, dammit."

"Drink it anyhow, dammit."

"Okay, dammit."

The first swallow was the hardest. The second wasn't quite as bad. The third was taken with a big gulp, as I help my nose and almost choked, but then I felt fine. So fine! It relaxed me from my spiked hair to my curled toes. I was limp.

And after finishing it, I felt like a new person. (a Roxanne) I stood up and stretched. Then I stood on a chair, lifted a leg and twirled, almost falling, I did a graceful princess climb to the top of the old gas, Servel refrigerator. (vintage about 1956) and lay there amongst the bananas. Soon I started throwing the yellows to the floor.

He walked over to me and I wasn't sure if he was going to pick up the bananas, kick me in the butt, or take me back to my car. But he picked me up from atop the refrigerator, kissed me, and we headed for his bedroom.

No way could anything in the world bother me at that point. I remember singing and humming, softly at first, as usual, then it became gradually louder. He kissed me on the cheek, told me to be quiet, and said, "I knew you'd like this, honey. Let's try out the new bed." He then put my hand on his dick, and the desire to lie next to him grew stronger.

"I don't know what the hell you put in my drink, baby, but thanks. It reminds me of Morphine and cocaine." I meant it, and didn't even tell Roxanne to shut up because I didn't know if she was talking or if it was me!

A girl never knows what is going to happen when she picks up a guy at a bar. You are at his mercy. Chances are you had too much to drink or you wouldn't have gone with him in the first place. I liked what I was doing, but hate myself for doing it. I mean, I liked going to those hunks' bedroom, but I hated the fact that I was in problem situation again. I didn't know how this one would end up, maybe just like the others—a big nothing and waste of time.

He was gentle and loving and things looked promising. Maybe tonight would be the night.

He massaged my legs, my thighs, my calves, my back, my neck, my front (all of it) and then the kissing started. He didn't miss a single spot on me. Not a single one!

Gradually he became slightly rough then very rough, then came the poking, probing and pinching. He pinched my nipples and twisted them. Then he jammed three fingers at once up my twat, and I wanted to scream. He probed around up there as a doctor would. Next he brought out strange, unusually shaped objects that he used to poke me in every available orifice. I couldn't see what he was using and putting in me but that "poker" was rather large.

He had chains on my hands and feet and they were wrapped so tightly that my flesh was being cut. I passed out, either from the drink or the pain, or both. I was at his mercy.

But once again, I woke and looked at the clock. His evil face then moved, blocking the clock so it was out of my range of vision. But when he walked over to the dresser to stop the terrible noise, I saw two things: A movie projector which was focused directly on my crotch and the machine was clicking because it had reached the end of the roll of film. That's what he turned off.

And the second thing I finally saw (which made him unusually angry), was his clock that told me it was 5:20a.m.

He began clacking his dentures, growling, and snarling. I said, "I have to go. I have to go."

"No way can you drive."

"You will spend the day here."

There was no way that I could tell my husband that I was going to spend the night and day at another man's house because of being drunk and drugged and that I had wrists and ankles cut up and bleeding because of the chains he put on me. Can you imagine?

He did help me out to his truck and drove me back to my car and as I got out, I said, "Call me, I'm in the book."

It had to be Roxanne talking because after being chained down and treated as I was, there was no way I would go out with him again. And he wouldn't even tell me his name when I asked him five times earlier. Yes, five times with no answer. Plus, I had to worry about him drugging me again.

I don't remember driving home or approaching the driveway and surely don't remember a car pulling in behind me. A man got out and walked over to me and said, "By the way, my name is Hal Myers. Remember the name because it is going to make you famous. You are going to be the biggest and most famous porn star of the century."

"Well thanks a lot for finally telling me your name and what the fuck do you mean about me being a porn star?"

He laughed as if he thought this was funny. "Just wait and see, Baby. We'll watch the movie together when it comes out. You were great."

I don't remember parking under that tree. But I did. I then looked back at it and said, "Oh my God." I had a hard time getting out of the car. I fell on the ground, got up, wet my pants, and fell in the grass again. This completely dirtied my uniform. I got up and listened to the stillness. Not a sound was heard and the sunshine in the sky was bringing us a glorious day, and I don't remember ever feeling so good—all over.

The house looked so white, but hadn't been painted since I lived in it. When was it painted? And the shutters were painted a fresh, bright, green. The birds were singing louder than ever and the butterflies were abundant. The crickets chirped "Hello, Marsha."

Then I saw "it" which answered the many questions I had. "It" was the purple fringed magic carpet from girlhood days. It rescued me when I was in trouble in my younger years, about twenty-five years ago when my stepfather chased me through the woods after drinking his moonshine. The carpet had carried me home this morning while in my car. That's all I could figure out. It probably had told me, "I'll take you high, over houses, and trees, away from problems, as I had done so many years ago."

I walked back to the car and saw that there were no keys in the ignition, and I hadn't taken them out of my purse. I searched in my purse and found them, buried. They had not been used this morning. I returned home by the power of the magic carpet. No car was driven because there surely would have been an accident tonight. The carpet saved me and "it" also sobered me up with the fresh wind blowing on me as we traveled. I shouted, "Thank you Magic Carpet." I watched it roll up and lay next to the garage. It didn't move after that. I hadn't been hallucinating and I was far from delusional, but then, I had been drugged. Was I really sure I saw that Magic Carpet as it had been so long since it was a part of my life?

The purple fringed carpet had been on my car hood and was now alongside the garage rolled up, and just staying there.

There was no way I could go to work. I knew it. It was almost 8:00a.m. and by then, I knew Carl was waiting for a good fight and argument which would take up a helluva lot of time.

The air never felt fresher. The dew on the grass sparkled. I counted steps to the back porch: "One-two-three-four-" There were squirrels everywhere. I kept in step with the violins in the background of the orchestra. "Six, seven, eight—I am late."

I began praying that Carl was asleep. He had to be asleep or at work. The positions Hal had me in, plus the drugged drink, plus the late hours, plus my friggin job worries were making me crazy.

"Nine, ten, eleven, twelve, thirteen—" How far must I walk to get to the porch?

"Fourteen, fifteen, sixteen, seventeen—" I could feel trouble and problems in my bones. I saw the porch finally, and hoped the rabbits on it wouldn't trip me. They were running all over the friggin place.

I prayed again. "Please God, let Carl be sound asleep. He is my man. I love him. And that is the truth. In spite of everything, I love my man."

"Eighteen—nineteen—twenty—twenty-one" (I wondered why I had to count everything—Every friggin thing.)

I wondered if I was going to get an infection of some weird variety from Hal's dirty hands; maybe I'd be another AIDS statistic. God forbid. Hell, I'd fooled around with enough men. Maybe God would punish me. My senses were numbed, big time. I probably tried too hard once again to reach a climax and should have just relaxed and let the drink do the work. Maybe it would have happened. Yes!

Suddenly I was depressed. I hated myself and my life. I was a slut. A dirty slut. I didn't deserve Carl. I began singing and twirling. "I'm no good. I'm no good. I'm no good. I'm no good." I then fell, just as I was climbing over the first step. That's right; I was climbing over it, not onto it. I suddenly felt like crap. I made it to the top step and was ready to open the door when I dropped my keys. Damn.

I bent over to get them and fell backwards on my butt and sat there. It felt so good that I stretched out and began singing.

"Twenty-two, twenty three, twenty-four, twenty-five—At least I'm. alive."

"I'm going away with the winds of the seven seas.

Pass the pepper and let me sneeze.

I need to go, come home, change and went.

But out of shape I am bent."

It felt so good lying there, but I had to get up and call in sick. I had to hurl. I stood up and held on to my keys this time and that's when I saw them. Shoes. Shiny black shoes. Stockings. Black stockings. And then I looked up into Carl's face. I smiled. He didn't. His arms were folded and he had a look of extreme displeasure on his face. I knew his every move by heart.

I, his "good-for-nothing-wife" slowly walked past him and into the house. He followed me and got up into my face.

"Coochy coo," I said to him as I tickled his chin. He didn't say a word.

"Happy birthday to me." Did I ever tell you that you had a nice ass, honey?"

Damn, Roxanne was still with me, but I had to laugh. We actually said these things to my husband.

He glared at me and seemed to look straight through me while he slowly walked in my direction, with his face right up in mine, and ever so slowly, I felt my butt, along with the rest of me, sliding downwards until I hit the floor.

Swisssssssh!

The roller coaster had come to an abrupt stop.

~~~~~
~~~~~

CHAPTER FOUR

May 18, 2002

I opened my eyes, probably six hours later and hurried to the phone to call in sick. Talk about sarcasm at the other end. Fuck!

Then I crawled to the bathroom to hurl, big time. I pulled myself up on the bathroom countertop and looked in the mirror at "her" who sure wasn't me. The one in the mirror had long black hair with lots of gray and dark circles under her eyes. Her eyes were brown and mine were blue. Had I gotten that old overnight?

Did the friggin drink do it to me? Then I went back, sat on the floor and hugged the porcelain bowl, suddenly my best friend. And I vomited and did it again and again. I thought that was good as all of the drink was sure to be out of me by then. "She was in the toilet bowl, looking at me, and I wanted to scream, so I did. I had such long beautiful blonde hair, not at all long, blackish-gray and frizzy. What was happening to me? On the way out of the bathroom, there was no one staring back at me in the room, so that made me feel better.

I made it to bed and ran my tongue over my teeth, but they were all gone. I looked in the mirror and once more, screamed. And no fairy had been in the house to leave any money under my pillow.

Glory be. Shades of the past! The purple-fringed carpet was on the ledge waiting for me. But I had planned to go to bed. I knew that I had to shower first, as I smelled of Hal. I couldn't seem to get the smell from my clothes or skin. The mentally ill say you rot from the inside, and that's what I thought was happening to me. They also say all your teeth fall out and that also described my situation.

As I walked to the shower, I noticed that the nerve endings at the bottom of my brain felt tangled and the misfiring; neurons were driving me crazy. The strange sensation in my feet told me all my toes were twisting and the tendons in my knees were out of sync with my heartbeat. The itching over my entire body was like insets crawling, and I knew I needed another drink. The hell with my nap.

Somehow Carl entered the house before I heard or saw him. I heard Silent Night playing on the organ and it wasn't Christmas and we didn't have an organ.

The Master's voice spoke: "So where have you been all night, my dear? Why was your uniform so wrinkled and your panty hose dragging, with only one shoe on? What happened to the neat, meticulous wife I married? You reek of another man's perspiration and something else. Go take that shower, and wash out the tub. No way will I stand in another man's sperm."

I couldn't believe my ears. He was screaming at me—he had never done that before.

"How do you think it makes me feel to know that I give, you everything I possibly can, and then some, and you still aren't satisfied?"

"And somehow you have fallen behind in the housework area. I can tell by your tiredness and the look in your eyes that you are out screwing around every night. You don't have to say a word, because no explanations are necessary."

I looked at him with a facial expression that was entirely blank. We both knew what he was saying was true.

"Marsha, as far as sex is concerned, you knew when we married that I couldn't and wouldn't give you "that." I think sex is messy, ugly, and a waste of time. My first wife lived without it and so can you."

"Oh, you are right, but remember you didn't tell me until after we were married, on our wedding night. If you had told me sooner, my dear, I wouldn't have married you."

He didn't like the words I had said, and I did feel guilty of being bitchy, but they were true and why shouldn't I let him know. He then struck back with, "I'm not even going to comment on your comment. You make me sick. I sure picked a winner of a wife this time, Bitch." He then stormed out of the house.

May 19, 2002

It was an uneventful day at work and Carl didn't come home yet. He doesn't really get home as early anymore. I began to wonder if he had a girl friend but I doubted it. I decided to call my friend Saundra and see if she wanted to go to a movie, but she already had plans so I went driving to a new bar.

I don't know or remember the name of it, but I had four beers and Roxanne flirted with the bartender. His name was Al and he liked me. He told me the bar closed at two and asked if I would come back. I told him I would and without

Carl hearing me, I put on my long sweater over my sexy gown and sprayed on some special $200. per 1/2 ounce special perfume. We had sex in the storage room and he asked to see me again. I said yes. And I probably will. No, Carl didn't hear or see me come home.

May 20, 2002

I do not feel well today. I will see my doctor. She keeps saying nothing is wrong with me, but I have extra-sensory perception and know there is. They just aren't telling me something. Otherwise I like Dr. Louise and think she is the greatest. After I saw her, I stopped at a little bar for just one drink, as my stomach was churning. The beer was great. It has always been my drink of choice. When the handsome hunk tapped me on the shoulder, I refused to have him buy me another drink. I would not go to his apartment; I just did not feel up to it. But the quickie in his back seat was fine as we listened to his stereo.

I never use protection when having sex, and know I should. But somehow, it seemed like too much work, and besides, what man always carried a rubber in his pocket? So I just did it, carefree and loose and knew somehow that I would never catch anything.

May 21, 2002

Thinking back six months ago, I knew I was heading in the same downward direction. Back then I would go out with a new man that I picked up in a bar and stay with him about three hours, then find another hunk go with him, and have sex in his car, and then find another to watch a porno flick with. I usually didn't get home until 8:00a.m.

But I had sense enough to stop when Carl threatened divorce. And things had started out again, just as they were that time—ever so gradually. What happened then, as you will see just ten pages back in this diary was that one of Carl's friends spotted us coming out of an XXX movie in the early a.m. That did it.

At that time, as I remember, I was seeing about thirty-five men per week and it was only when my job and marriage started going down the tubes that I decided to turn over a new leaf. But here I am again. I try, but can't help myself.

May 22, 2002

Well, I have to start looking for my new man again. Carl and I aren't speaking and I expect him to mention divorce at any time now. I try to avoid him when home and just go to bed with the covers over my head and one eye sticking out to watch for him.

I woke up today and thought about things and realized that I should play the "good little wife."

Did you ever have the feeling that you didn't know who you were? Think about that one. I knew I was a wife and a RN, but never knew when I walked into a bar if I'd be a dancer, a singer, or a princess. My co-workers noticed mood changes and said I was day dreaming all the time. They told me to come down out of the clouds.

Today, I woke up as a dancer. I wasn't scheduled to work, and stopped at a bar as I was desperately in need of a drink. I wore a yellow dancing dress, my favorite color, with a full skirt and a top cut slightly too low. My two huge boobs were exposed and today once again, I was in the mood for action. I actually looked for Roxanne. But I'd make sure I didn't get a hangover and would only go with a guy if he was a perfect specimen of manhood. Know what I mean? He had to have a bulge in the right place to interest me, honey.

I checked my make-up, drove to the bar and gradually got out of the car, elegantly, slowly, and gracefully, as maybe "he" was lurking in the parking lot. That's the reason I twirled as I walked in. It made my skirt blow up in the wind and showed off my perfect legs.

I walked nine steps in the gravel, and then I was in the paved parking lot area. I counted and walked up seven steps. I snapped my fingers the entire time and the humming grew louder. The old brass door knob turned slowly and suddenly, there I was.

I loved the smells—Old familiar smells. I smelled burned popcorn, stale beer, sausage sandwiches and pizza in the microwave. And I can't forget the smell of hot dogs and stale cigarette smoke, and the odor of rancid, spilled whiskey and Bloody Marys that had left a tell-tale reddened area on the floor. Nor can I forget the odor of feet that needed a good washing, in their old tennis shoes, with dirty stockings. One thing I was blessed with was a good nose.

I twirled and didn't care that everyone stared at me. I twirled to the end of the bar with butt shaking and boobs bouncing. I leaned up against the wall, chewing the taste out of my gum, and spit it out in a nearby napkin. I then started giggling, for no reason. I didn't know what was wrong with me. I tapped three times on the bar and Mr. Bartender noticed me, and of course I ordered a tall beer in a frosted mug. Once again the foam hit my nose and as it did, I laughed. It was at least 1/3 foam, a perfect specimen! I began my customary day dreaming and didn't even see the bartender place the second drink down in front of me.

I began to shout loudly at the laughing voices in my head telling me a joke and everyone in the place looked at me. Then I began to cry, and the voices in my head snapped me out of it. My laughter was wild. They all probably wondered what I was laughing at, but they didn't hear the voices that I did:

"Fuck a duck. Fuck a duck. Fuck a duck."

It just cracked me up. The bartender came over to me and asked if everything was okay, and I told him, "fine and dandy, like sugar candy," and he scratched his head and walked away.

I felt the tap on my shoulder and the kiss on my neck tickled. "Hi, you sweet thing. Do you wanna?" The next thing you knew I hopped into his old rusty truck and went to his apartment. His rusty old Ford truck jingled and jangled down the road and there was not a word of conversation all the way to his apartment. He didn't even tell me his name but then I didn't tell him mine. But we both knew what we wanted.

He got right to it, wasting no time, with not a bit of foreplay, not even a kiss and I felt "used" as we drove back to the bar. He dropped me off at the door and took off. I had completely satisfied him but I had an "empty" feeling once more.

When I walked back into the bar, I had a big bad buzz going on in my brain and body. I walked in this time, to the end of the bar, with only the three B's moving: Boobs and Butt. Everything else was stiff. It took me a long time to learn that trick!

It was getting late and I was loaded. When I looked at the clock, I began singing, "Hate late, hate late, hate late."

"Forget the singing; forget looking. There is no one here. Get your ass home where it belongs."

I knew I had to get going and couldn't be late again. I walked out to my car with a flat tire and "he" walked over to fix it for me. I thanked him in the back seat of his car and all is well that ends well. Rather boring day.

May 23, 2002

Work drove me nuts today. I don't know why patients stand by the window talking to someone outside when there is no one out there but it happens three times a day (at least.). Today, one was telling off-color jokes. One was walking around nude and I had to tell her to get dressed. Howard was dressed in a silk gown with heels and fancy nylons and I made him change. I had to go outside and tell Nancy to wear heavier clothes if she was going to be making a snowman but when going outside; I realized that she wasn't making a snowman after all. It was May and she was just sitting in the sun.

Then I realized that I had locked my key in the med room and no one had a key to that room but me. The voices were loud and clear:

"Go get your car keys; they will work."

I laughed, but gave it a try and they did work. I got some prescribed narcotics that were in the lock box, and when I told the nurse coming on the next shift, she didn't believe my car keys could open the medication room door. She tried them and they didn't work, and she told me I was imagining things again. I could see the purple fringed carpet flying off and knew my answer.

It had been a wild day and I realized the need for a beer stop, in fact it was a matter of life and death today and I looked forward to it.

One of the patients threw a beer can and hit me in the head. Another was having serious behavior problems and I had to get three people to hold him down to give an injection of Haldol, a major tranquilizer. I goofed and instead of giving two milligrams, I gave him ten and it took four hours for him to snap out of that little nap. No, I did not report it. Bad nurse! Why did I decide to work at a Psychiatric Facility? I will never know.

I found the little rustic bar as I drove home. The boonies are loaded with them. I parked my car and walked sixteen steps to the back door, and found my preferred bar stool against the wall, vacant. I claimed it. Eleven minutes later, I could feel the tapping on my shoulder, and what a hunk he was. There was not an ounce of padding anywhere and he wore a wedding ring. He was the one. I knew it. "Mr. Perfect" had arrived. He had a well-rounded butt, with a bulge in the right place and jeans that were so tight it looked like his butt was ready to break the seams. He had a sun-burned face and bright blue eyes, with sparkling teeth and when he came over by me and kissed my cheek after tapping my shoulder, I felt my heart pounding.

"Hello babe can I buy you a drink?"

"Sounds good." I explained that this body had to get home to fix my husband's dinner and he understood.

"Let's finish our drink and let me take you for a ride in my two-week-old Chrysler convertible." I did see it pull up in front of the bar and it was dreamy.

"By the way, my name is Fred. My friends call me 'Fearless Fred' because of the things I do."

"So what do you do?"

"Everything, baby."

"So what does 'everything' include?"

"Everything you always wanted to do, any way you wanted to do it but were afraid to give it a try."

Roxanne spoke up.

"That gives me a lot of requests, honey."

"Life is too short not to do what you want. So just do it. What's stopping you?"

"Oh Mr. FF." I shouldn't have flirted with him but I knew it was Roxanne. But still, it was me.

He looked like a jolly, fun loving hunk, and when I asked again what the "special of the day" was, we walked out to his new Chrysler.

"Come on. Get in." I did, and he asked. "You want to know what I would like to do today, so you can join me?"

"Well, tell me first."

"Well, here goes: I get in this car, close the doors like this, and proceed to turn the stereo on. And at once, my song, 'The Stripper' begins playing. "Like this?" He played it louder. "Does that tell you what my special of the day is?"

"See, I play this song and strip. Down to nothing. Then when I come alongside a truck and the guy looks down, you should see his face. And if a woman is with me in the car with the top down, the driver's expression is even funnier. I just keep driving like nothing is unusual. I then pull into the gas station and signal for someone to come over. I try for the little old ladies. They scream the loudest. So do ya want to do it with me?"

"No, that doesn't sound like my cup of tea. Or bottle of beer."

"Wow, what a pretty car you have." I had to change the subject so I told him this once more.

"Yes, and it's customized."

With that, I heard my door slam shut and knew I was locked in. I didn't like that feeling. But I still maintained the feeling that this had to be my man because anyone who drove a car like this couldn't be a bad person.

I saw immediately what he meant about a special car, because everything was customized, and in various shades of red. There were red throw pillows and red covers on the seats, red fur on the steering wheel and even a red pair of dice hanging from the mirror. But he didn't look the least bit like the furry dice type.

The speakers blasted "The Stripper" and he began stripping as I sat in awe. First off were his shoes, then off with the stockings, then came the trousers, then his shirt, then his under shirt, next came the jockey shorts, and his gold watch lay on top of the pile. "Come on, get with it, babe."

"I told you 'no.' But Roxanne started to unbutton my dress. Then she began to pull it down.

"Stop it, dammit." I was talking to Roxanne but how could I explain that when he asked who I was carrying on the conversation with.

I felt as though I was suffocating in a sea of blood, locked in a main artery with no means of escape. By then he was completely nude and Roxanne reached over and rubbed his chest. He was then kissed on the right hand side of his cheek by her and he didn't mind it one bit. I pulled away and he said, "What's the matter with you. Why start something if you don't finish. Quit pulling away."

She rubbed his thighs and between his legs and reached higher. I pulled her away.

"Don't stop."

She then kissed his thighs and started at his chest and worked her way down. I pulled her away.

"Damn it, what are you doing?"

How could I ever explain Roxanne to anyone?

"Well, do ya wanna?"

"Do I wanna what?"

"Strip."

"No way."

He reached behind the seat just as the bus passed and I almost passed out and almost pissed in my pants at the same time.

In huge letters with the picture of a naked woman who had only a towel covering her, I saw the sign:

PRODUCER
HAL MYERS
HITS IT BIG WITH NEW PORN STAR
MISS MARSHA B.
IN HER FIRST HOT FLICK
"WHAT A PERFORMANCE."
DON'T MISS IT
BUY THIS VIDEO TODAY!

~~~~~
~~~~~

CHAPTER FIVE

May 24, 2002

I read it so fast that I didn't see all the details of my picture, but maybe that was meant to be. All that covered my body was a towel. I felt myself turn a ghastly shade of pale and F.F. said, "What's the matter?"

I couldn't answer but that was okay because I didn't want to tell the guy anyhow. "I feel faint."

It appeared that he hadn't seen my picture. Thank God.

"Why do you look so pale? Is my dick that ugly that it makes you want to faint?"

"Do you want to sit here and look at my dick or do you want to sit on that bench over there? If I were you, I'd choose my dick to look at and maybe stroke it a little, and I bet you anything, you'd like to sample it too. I'm not afraid to try anything. They don't call me 'Fearless Fred' for nothing."

I had to push the billboard from my mind temporarily. My heart pounded and I felt as though I was going to start hyperventilating. How the hell could Hal make, develop and advertise the video so soon? I had to talk to that jerk. But the important thing of the moment was to get away from this naked man and his ideas.

"Come on baby. Undress. Try it—you will love it. It makes you feel so good and so free. Try it just once for me and you'll want to do it more." With that, he took off my skirt and blouse. All I had on was a bra and panties.

The woofers were blasting to the high heavens, and he stood up on the seat, with nothing on, and flaunted his naked body. I had to steer because he evidently had forgotten that he was the driver. It was a nightmare Everyone was looking at *me* as if I were telling him to perform his act and they stared at me with only a bra showing. Roxanne was laughing her head off. I was so upset that I began to laugh hysterically too.

I knew that I had to come up with an escape plan but my nerves were jumping out of my body. My hands and legs began to tremble. I was all hyper and scared to death. I really got into a mess this time. Both F.F. and Roxanne were fighting me and there were friggin billboards all over town.

I toyed with the door and found that if you pushed the handle all the way forward, it would unlock. I did, and held it in that position so I would be ready to make my move when the time came. My move was to get out of the car, then roll down in a hilly area by the forest preserve where we happened to be. Once down the hill, I would button my blouse and put my skirt back on the correct way. My senses told me that Mr. F.F. wouldn't try to follow me. After all, he was naked and the traffic was heavy duty. What naked man would leave his car to run after a woman in heavy traffic?

"You look like you are going to have a convulsion. Relax. Watch this." He began fondling his dick and it became erect and then he told me, "I want to take you to a movie."

"With no clothes on?"

"Yes."

"Did you ever see Oliver Twist?"

"No."

He turned "The Stripper" louder and began fondling his personal parts. Sure enough, it stood up and began to twist. Nothing else on him moved.

"Now you have seen Oliver Twist."

Roxanne laughed. I didn't.

"Would you like to see some more of his tricks?"

"No thanks." I was serious, determined, and upset. I think he knew it.

F.F. suddenly put the top of his convertible down for some reason and the windows closed automatically. I held the door handle, wondering what the hell was going on.

He was silent. All of a sudden, my seat went backwards into a bed. I could barely reach the door that would allow me to leap to freedom. The odor of marijuana coming from the vents was so strong that it caused me to relax completely. That along with the drinks did me in. I don't know how long I slept, but when I woke up, I was completely undressed. I don't know how long I was like that or what had transpired when I was out of it.

"Beautiful. Beautiful. Beautiful." That's all he said.

The clock on the dashboard told me it was 7:00p.m.and that meant Carl would be home and wondering where his dear wife was once more. Damn, I was getting too old for this crap. I knew it was time to make my move.

As he told me his plans of what he intended to do with me, I knew it was "now or never."

"This smell ought to put you in the mood, baby. Inhale it. Smell it. Chew it. One way or another, hon, you are going to enjoy this little party with me. And then we will take a naked jog. No one will know you because I brought you a bag to put over your head."

I released the handle, and began to roll down the hill. I didn't know where I was but did know that he wasn't likely to jump out of his car and follow me. At least I hoped not.

As I rolled down the hill covered with soft vegetation, at least my partially naked body wouldn't be all scratched. But my thoughts became more jumbled. I wondered where I was, how I managed to grab my clothing, how I would put it on, what I was going to do, and whether anyone other than me would read my little diary. Heaven forbid. If I were to write "Private" on the front, that would be all the more reason for someone to snoop, so all it says is "Marsha." I sure would have things to write in it tonight. And I intended to write everything, "for posterity."

If ever I needed a man, I needed one then—to guide me and show me the way.

As Fred pulled away from the stop light, I neared the bottom of the hill but heard him yelling, "Come back. Come back. The fun is about to begin." His voice faded All was quiet.

Someone warned me that this forest preserve was dangerous, and I seemed to remember reading about and seeing something on television about it. Maybe I would be another statistic for whatever it was. Then I remembered. It was the area where women were beaten, abused, and two were murdered. I had to find my way out yet I couldn't go back and risk meeting F. F. I just didn't want to see him following me, with Oliver flopping in the breeze. I walked faster, looking for a way out of the wooded area and then I heard the footsteps following me. I finished buttoning my skirt and blouse and thank goodness I still had my shoes.

I walked faster, they walked even faster. I stopped, they stopped. I felt a tap on my back and then heard two deep roars of laughter. There were two of them. But I couldn't turn around and look. No way. Then I heard more laughter and three voices. I almost fell to the ground. This was the exact area where the women had been raped. But maybe they didn't want an older woman.

There was heavy breathing behind me and it grew closer. I still couldn't look back. I could feel the perspiration dripping down my back. Fright. I had a tremendous fright.

I could hardly focus my eyes with the impending dusk. I kept falling and began to cry. Time seemed to stand still, and I fell again. My knees and arms were scratched and sore. Was this all for real? It seemed too real not to be real.

Minutes later, the men began pulling my long hair. They each pulled it and laughed, and I finally fell to the ground.

One of the men said, "Hey Baby, wanna screw?"

They all laughed. I finally looked at them and I'm sorry I did. One was tall, very tall, with no hair and no teeth. The pants he wore looked so dirty, and there was a strong stench of urine and whisky along with ripe shit. Another man was short and very fat, with gray hair and bib paint pants, once white. He looked as though he hadn't washed or shaven in weeks and smelled the same way as the first man did. The third man was of average height, with crossed eyes, no teeth, and ratty looking jeans and tennis shoes. Evidently homeless, they surely didn't make any effort to find shelters to clean themselves and freshen up. I didn't know how they could stand the smell of themselves and each other.

When I fell again, there were five guys who stripped me of all my clothes, and said, "Who wants to go first?" Once more I was naked.

Then about ten more men appeared out of nowhere, all saying, "me too, me too."

They argued and somehow, I grabbed what clothing I could and ran. I didn't know where I would hide, but I saw a clump of bushes and hid behind it. I sat on some sticks with sharp points along with some hard rocks and fought back a scream. I had taken a helluva chance. I waited.

They looked for me, and headed right for the area where I was hiding but by then it was dark and they staggered, bumped into each other, and cussed but they couldn't see me. I was sure of that as I lie there, naked and shivering with tears in my eyes. I dare not move and somehow managed to put on the two articles of clothing I had grabbed. It was the dress and slip. I had no shoes, panties, or bra. Even my purse was left behind and had approximately $60.00 in it plus my address, credit cards and complete personal identification.

I stayed put for a while and finally stumbled around for the longest time and fell repeatedly. My feet were wet and I noticed part of the wetness was blood and my arms were also scratched and bleeding. I couldn't stop the tears and didn't know where the hell I was going.

I stumbled upon a new type of terrain and discovered it was a path. I had no feeling in my feet but I knew it was a well-worn path. The only problem was that I could hardly see it in the darkness. Maybe it was a lovers' path leading to a secluded romantic area but I doubted that. Not in those woods. Then it might mean it lead out of the woods and back to civilization. If only I could see it better.

I heard the most wonderful sound, it was a miracle. "Thank you God," I prayed. It could hear cars which meant there was a road ahead of me.

But I worried that Fred would be looking for me and try to pick me up. I had no idea how far I was from the point where he dropped me off. I could have been walking around in circles.

But a car stopped after a while and a manly voice said, "How about a ride, honey?"

I walked closer to the car and saw he was dressed in jeans and a light flannel shirt. He wore huge boots and wore a man's wrist watch.

And then, and then (excuse me for the excitement here!) I saw two little boobs beneath the flannel shirt. It was a woman, not a man. My heart was no longer heavy nor was my brain tormented when I saw the pony tail and noticed the lipstick.

"Hi, I'm Cynthia."

"Hi, I'm Marsha." I looked her over, wanting to believe she was a woman, but knowing myself as I did, doubts appeared in my mind. I know she was a lesbian or a vampire. But I had to trust her at this point,

"Honey, whatever are you doing out so late in these woods? Just look at you. Oh my God, you were beaten, too. It happens in these woods everyday. Don't you read the papers?"

I told her the entire story, even the part about Oliver Twist. I had calmed down a bit and we both had a laugh out of that one.

She floored the gas and we got out of that area. What must she think of me, after telling my story? I wondered. The heebie-jeebies took over again when I heard a man's laugh. I had never seen such a manly looking woman. She asked if any landmarks looked familiar and I told her no, and that my car was parked at "Jim's Joint." I told her that I didn't have the foggiest idea where I was but was so glad that she came along and rescued me.

When stopping the car at the next intersection, we both saw the billboard and I can't describe the look on her face. Cynthia rolled her eyes at me and said, "Oh my God, I can't believe it."

My picture evidently was all over town and I wonder what Carl must be thinking.

I always wonder what Carl must be thinking, which makes me wonder what I must be thinking when I go out on him. I really love him, and I honestly mean that, but why is my behavior so wild, wanton and disgusting?

She didn't say another word, but kept driving as I finally did see familiar terrain and I told her where to turn and where the bar was.

We parked her car about two blocks away and I gave her my car keys. No way did I want to go over and get it. Besides, she had suggested, that I allow her to go get it as her height was 5'10" and she looked more "manly." "I'd scare the shit out of anyone who saw me. Now sit here and relax."

It was about 11:30 and Cynthia returned in my car. "Yes, he was there, and he took one look at me and disappeared into the bar like he was in the biggest hurry to escape from me. I think he believed I was coming after him."

Something strange and different had happened to me that night. First I had the bad time with Fred but it turned out okay because I met Cynthia.

Very seldom do you "click" with a person as I did with her and I believe she liked me too.

She said, "You know Marsha, we have a lot in common. I don't have time to go into it now, but I will at a later date. I just can't believe how we went through similar situations and I also had three marriages. I ran around on all three, but no more marriages or men for me. I'll tell you all about it sometime. Do you have time to stop for a cup of tea and a piece of cake? Sweets are my weakness. Can't you tell?"

By then it was 1:00a.m.and this would mean another late night, but I promised myself I couldn't let it get too late. "Yes, sure I can stop. It sounds like fun." It would be so nice to have a female friend besides Saundra, even though I could always depend on Saundra for anything.

I looked and felt crappy and combed my hair. Cynthia gave me some sun glasses to cover up my reddened eyes and messed up make-up. I began to cry.

I let loose and cried like a baby. "God is punishing me. This is his way of punishing me for my behavior."

"Ah, don't talk like that. Don't keep putting yourself down. You are a good person. I am a good judge of character and I happen to know you are A-1 and that's pretty darn good. You just have the same basic problems as I do."

"You know what, Cynthia?" I have a good husband and all I do is cheat on him. He's my third husband and I can't help the way I am. I have only one female friend at work, but I will let any man take me to his apartment. I don't know what's wrong with me. My own husband doesn't really know me and that I lack the ability to really be intimate with anyone. Sex is the only intimacy I know and I share it with every man I pick up."

Tiredness had begun to set in but I didn't want to leave Cynthia. We talked about love, life, sex, and work. She told me that I had to learn to gain genuine interest in a person, talk to her, and share my thoughts and secrets to have a true friend. I thought about that, and she was correct. The magic word for friendship is "trust."

She explained that, "with a one-night stand you build up self-confidence, share feelings, and temporarily gain the friendship with a man and sex makes that friendship even closer. The next thing you know, he is gone, but the memory is so good that you go out and do it again the next night. Once again you felt confident, but when he is gone, it's like you have an empty spot left, so you repeat the process over and over. This fills the void that was left from something gone wrong in childhood. Maybe, your parents didn't show their love in the right way. How was your childhood?"

"I can't talk about that yet, but when I'm ready I will."

It grew later and later and I told her I had to get home. She told me that the last thing in the world I should do was to get Carl upset with me and I agreed.

"Cynthia, you sound so professional and I don't want to lose you as a friend. Let's exchange our names and phone numbers and do this again."

"For sure."

I got out a piece of paper and wrote my information and she handed me a card which explained her feelings and knowledge about life.

Cynthia Connors, Ph.D.
Psychiatry
Consulting and Clinical Services, Ltd.
Adult and Adolescent Behaviors
9-408-295-7112

The clock on the dashboard told me it was 3:15am which meant we'd unknowingly talked the night away but for some reason I didn't feel guilty or really care this time. I believe my meeting Cynthia, an aftermath of meeting Fred, was meant to be. I believe both of these happenings were pre-determined, not at all left to chance.

~~~~~
~~~~~

CHAPTER SIX

May 24, 2002
Later—Home

Yes, I was completely happy driving home. I had a new friend and knew somehow that she would end up being more than just an "ordinary" friend. She was special. I pulled in the driveway, smiling, and danced up the steps and on to the porch.

Once again I was met by Carl and had to explain that I was out with a girl friend. I didn't tell him about the woods and almost being killed. I didn't know that the spot I was in was called "Lo-life Haven." Only two people had ever ventured there and lived to tell about it. I would make number three. But how could I explain the whole long story to my husband, going with Mr. F.F. and all that? So I took his verbal abuse. We didn't speak the rest of the evening and once more, I had a lecture on "If you want to stay married to me—"

May 25, 2002

We were still not speaking, except to say, "Pass the coffee," or "Pass the sugar." The necessary words for daily living were the only words spoken. I busied myself around the house today. I got caught up on weed pulling and laundry. I thought about getting a gardener next summer. Pulling weeds was hard on my nails.

I called Cynthia and we did go out for coffee. She suggested that I begin seeing her as a patient the following week so we could get to the bottom of things and I told her that I would think about it.

May 26, 2002

Still not speaking to my husband. It is hard living in the same house with someone and not speaking.

May 27, 2002

I stopped for a drink, and then made a terrible mistake of going to the bathroom and leaving my drink on the bar. I was talking to a guy who told me his name was Ben and I believe he put something in my drink when I went away from it, even though he said he'd watch it. I didn't taste anything but when I walked out the door to go to Ben's place; I couldn't feel the front steps or the concrete sidewalk. We went to his place, and I don't remember a thing after that. He drove me home in my car but I don't know how he got back to his car. All my money and credit cards were gone and I had just received new ones. I had no idea what his last name was, and I called the bar and was told by the bartender and several patrons that they had never seen him before either.

May 28. 2002

At work today, after I did my fifth monthly summary, I made a promise to myself that I would try harder to be efficient at work, do more with my patients, and also keep my house in better order. I would be more loving towards Carl even though there would be no response from him. Also I promised that I would not go to bars anymore, alone, with guys, or at all. I didn't think Cynthia would go with me, but I wouldn't even go with a woman because I know she would end up leaving early, leaving me there alone, and I would just go off with some guy.

I vowed to drink only at home and believe me that would be hard to do. I talked to Cynthia on the phone and we stopped for pie and coffee. We talked about men and I found out she looked at their butts first and we both liked the same kind. Once again she assured me that my problem began as a child, and that we were going to "dig" until we pulled up the roots. I don't think I would mind digging with her, as she was easy to talk to and no matter what, I would make it in to see her the following week.

(I just don't feel good. There is a ringing in my ears and those voices don't stop. I ache all over, but don't think it's arthritis. Something is going on in me and I wonder what I am supposed to do.)

June 4, 2002

It was my first visit to a "shrink." It was one thing to have her as a coffee-date person, but somewhat demoralizing to see her as a patient. But her office waiting room was comfortable and her receptionist was warm and friendly. Her inner office looked just like her—neat, perfectly groomed—and everything carefully picked. Her black leather furniture was very expensive, anyone could tell. She had white shag carpeting and glass coffee tables and end tables with black vases, white flowers and ferns in hanging baskets. I stood in awe and commented to her how beautiful everything was.

"Why not lie on the couch, Marsha. Grab a few throw pillows and lie down. Just put yourself in a blue void in space somewhere. I happen to know you like blue."

I did just that and surprisingly, it was relaxing. Imagine, me, relaxed in a shrink's office, on a couch, no less! But she was a friend shrink so that was okay.

(I write in my diary here sometimes using quotes. I don't know why. I guess it's to break up the regular paragraphs and continual rambling. Bear along with me. Maybe I am writing a book but probably don't know it yet.)

When she explained once more about digging, I told her I really didn't like digging as I was afraid of what might be uncovered. Sometimes in life we have secrets or events that we don't care to remember, and in my case, I put them on a back burner, way in the recesses of my brain caverns and they are hidden from the world. Also they are buried so far back that even I don't think of them. And now Cynthia wants to start digging. Then she informed me that she was going to record our session. At first I didn't like this idea, but if Hal had recorded a video, I guess she could record a digging.

We talked about the usual things like the weather, jobs, our past experiences with men, and she told me that she didn't date anymore. Evidently she is still in love with her last husband but she drove him away with her running around. Then she stopped talking about personal things, apologized to me for taking up my time and even looked like she had a tear in her eye.

"Marsha, first of all, I want you to get a life other than working. Find a woman friend or two and go out with them once in a while. Go to movies, and go shopping with them. We know it's more exciting to be with a man, but give it a try with a woman friend."

"I will try it out with a woman." (I will find a class or two to take just for the fun of it. This will be my new goal.)

I asked her if she thought it was possible to have a man as "just a friend" and not have sex with him. She told me it was, but in my case it would be very hard. I explained that I wanted to have Carl as a friend, and we weren't having sex. I then cried and explained how I didn't want another divorce.

"Marsha, it's so hard to set boundaries on that kind of relationship."

I told her I was aware of that but that I was thinking about just being nice to Carl, so he would put divorce out of his mind. I explained that I definitely needed him for security reasons and didn't want to be alone in life.

I told her that Carl could be unkind and insulting at times. "He always makes fun of what I wear, when I am alone, at home. Why do I have to dress up to lay and watch television? So what if my dress is orange and I wear a red belt with a green feather behind my ear. I am sorry, but people may think of me as a little eccentric but who wants to be normal? I don't. Besides, when you think about it, what the hell is "normal?"

"You know, Cynthia, I would like to adopt a child or two before I am too old. It would be quite a change for me, but that's what life is all about—changes. We change our job, hair color, husbands, buy new cars, and change make-up colors. Why couldn't I change from being a nurse to being a Mother?"

But I also told her that if "Mr. Perfect" came along, I would be long gone from my marriage. She didn't comment on that and deep down inside I knew it just wasn't right to use Carl for my own needs and leave him if someone better came along. I wasn't a cruel person, but I think in life one has to look at their own needs first. Hell, knowing me I'd stay with Mr. Perfect and have Carl on the side. (Dr. Cynthia wrote a lot on her legal sized pad that day.)

It was at that time that Dr. Cynthia asked me to keep a personal journal on my feelings. My first thought was "Oh no, not more writing," but I agreed. She wanted me to enter everything, including my feelings, thoughts, and what I did during the day.

(Oh, I love to write—and have just tons of empty diaries waiting for my scribbles.)

June 11, 2002

My next visit to Cynthia was on the following Tuesday and at least I knew more about what to expect. I was familiar with her personal mannerisms and we had a good doctor-to patient relationship.

She asked how I felt and I told her. "I feel weak, depressed, lonely, insecure about the future, and tired of doing without companionship from my own husband. He still isn't talking to me and can't warm up to me. I keep hearing friggin voices and organ music. I've had it with my life. I don't know why the hell I was born. What does God expect from me? I brought my journal and you will see that this has been a depressing day."

"Marsha, don't feel worthless, insecure, and wonder about your reason for being on earth. The Lord created us all for a reason. You may not know it now or even in a year or two, but someday you will. Just remember that each of us has a special reason for being here. Each of us is special to Him and we must learn to love ourselves and strive to find out why we were created and put on this earth."

"Well, I certainly don't love myself as you will be able to tell when you look at my journal. I guess I was put on this earth to be a 'helper'. I'm a nurse, and a helper to satisfy men I just walk around in circles accomplishing nothing. That's the story of my entire life."

"Marsha, you have to gain more self-worth and more self-esteem. Something along the line destroyed all of this. We are going to recover the positive and do away with the negative."

I told her that the only thing that builds my self-esteem is sex and when it is over, I fall back into the blah area as I have a "nothing" feeling. It's a 'no orgasm again' feeling.

"We can't cover everything in one day, but let me just touch on this subject. Marsha, women don't always have orgasms, but feel content just holding and being close to their man and satisfying him. But once in a while, they need to have an orgasm just as a man does. When we never have one, it's called 'female orgasmic disorder' which could stem from a number of things."

"I know. I feel content just holding and being close to a man and satisfying him. But once in a while, don't you think we need to have an orgasm just as a man does?"

"Marsha, there are things such as hormonal changes, approaching or going through menopause, lack of emotional closeness with your partner, boredom, monotony, sameness of positions, tiredness, nerves and so many things that can influence having or not having an orgasm."

"Marsha. Just remember that you are young and have everything going for you. You are an extremely pretty woman and you are intelligent. One has to be intelligent to become a registered nurse."

"But I am tired of my place of work, tired of being a nurse, and tired of living. Sometimes I just want to die. I have mood swings, where I am so happy one second and down in the dump pits the next minute. I see and hear things that aren't there. Like I hear squirrels talking to me and imagine people are all staring at me, and imagine I weigh 300 pounds and see myself in the mirror as old and wrinkled and with gray hair."

"Well, Marsha, let's get into this a little deeper next week."

"In the meantime, I will have gone to bed with at least eight new men. I can't help myself. I honestly have tried, but can't stop."

"Oh Marsha, I wish we had more time today. I have a test I want you to take. I think you have a—"

"A what?"

"A—we'll talk about it next week."

"Just tell me what you think I have. We don't have to get into it today."

"I think you have a slight mental problem. Don't worry. It's nothing serious and there are tons of medicines out there for problems. Let's get into it next week. Bye for now."

"You can't leave me like this. What do you think I have? I am schizophrenic. I know that."

"No, you are not schizophrenic and we will talk about it next time."

Just like that, she was dismissing me. I was pissed.

I remember just getting up and leaving at that point. I didn't pick up any book list or anything. I just left. I made my mind up today, while driving home, that I wouldn't go to bars anymore. Let the men find me because no way was I going to go looking for them. In fact, I planned to have a shopping day, and it would be every Saturday. That way I'd go out for about three hours and Carl wouldn't suspect a thing. I'd make sure I had something to carry home in a bag.

Each week I'd head for a different shopping mall. I smiled to myself. I didn't have to look for men in bars. They would find me and tap me on the shoulder. I'd play a good little wifey and a good little nursie and a good little shopper and Carl would love it.

~~~~~
~~~~~

CHAPTER SEVEN

July 13, 2002

There was no doubt about it. Starting today I would go out days instead of nights. There would be no protective veil of darkness as I entered the malls. That meant anyone could see me, but then, I didn't plan on having anything to hide.

I fortified my body with Ativan and Klonopin (anti-anxiety medications) and left the house, floating because I took three of each, and said "no" to my three cups of breakfast coffee.

It was great walking through the shopping mall today, and after walking around for an hour or so, I decided to stop in the little coffee shop for coffee. I missed having it at breakfast. I put my purchases on the floor and after only three minutes, I felt the tapping on my shoulder and heard a soft "hello there" spoken by a man. They had the same way of messaging women as did men in bars. I acknowledged him, noticing that he was clean cut, with blue eyes and blonde hair, neatly pressed shorts and a blue checked shirt. He wore a wedding ring. He had to be my Mr. Perfect.

His opening line was the same, "Gee, you look lonely. How about some company?"

"Sure, but I have to get home soon."

"Me too."

We sat and drank our coffee and he asked, "would you like to go for a walk afterwards?"

"After what?"

"After we finish our coffee, silly."

The restaurant smells were great. It smelled like freshly baked cinnamon rolls and coffee brewing, but most noticeable was the 'clean' smell. It was heavenly compared to bar smells.

We both enjoyed the freshly brewed coffee and bear claw rolls.

He asked what I thought he meant about going for a walk and we both laughed. So we walked and walked. And then guess where we went? Anyone reading this? Bet you can't guess!

We went to his apartment. That part of being a man never changes. No. I didn't get his name. Sometimes names don't matter to me, I guess. All I know is that he lived in a little cottage on the lake and I don't even know the name of the lake.

He has finesse, stamina, strength, and everything necessary to make him a good lover, but I still wasn't satisfied afterwards. His body was super great and just being near him made me happy. We had sex three times and could have gone on and on all afternoon and all night, but it was getting late. Besides, his wife was due home any minute. He got three gold stars in my little diary.

I drove home to an empty house and wrote in my Dr. Cynthia diary. How could I explain my feelings—confusion, contentment, guilt? I didn't know.

When Carl came home, I took him out to dinner and sat next to him. He shoved me away with his elbow. "Give me room to breathe." I had to explain my feelings on that one too. I felt pissed on and discouraged as the tears welled up inside me, and I decided that if he could play that game, so could I. Marsha Frosty would be my new name. No more trying. So why did I even feel guilty about going out on him? I don't even know.

July 20, 2002

The following week, I was just perusing all the store windows, decorated for summer, and someone tapped me on the shoulder. He told me his name was Gene, and asked if I'd help him pick out a suit. He wore a wedding ring so I agreed. He asked me to go in the dressing room with him to check it out.

I asked him what "it" was. Yes, this was Roxanne's day. I could see that. He then held me against the wall and I knocked the chair over and made a tremendous noise when I hit the floor, pulling him on top of me. We had three store personnel in there checking to see if everything was okay, and we told them everything was just fine. We both laughed our asses off.

Afterwards, we went to his apartment and made love four times and he asked to see me again. Gene was married, but his wife was out shopping and due home any minute. For some reason, thinking the wife would come home any minute made sex more exciting for me. I always wondered what I would do in such a case.

(He asked if he could see me again and I told him "possibly." If we happened to run into each other, he would see me, right? So I wasn't lying, right?)

(I would like to mention here, if I didn't already—I forget things more often now that every man in the world is "good" in one way or another. He is good looking, has a good body, good manners, good stamina, a good—working-man-thing, or nice butt!)

Gene got three silver stars that day. He was one of the most tender men I have ever met. We had sex in four positions, and it was great. His mood was happy-go-lucky, and it transferred to me which lifted my spirits.

July 27, 2002

I had shopped and dropped in a coffee shop, and could hardly hold my head up when I felt the pinch on my arm. That was something different for me. His name was Roy and I found out we had many mutual interests. He was rugged. He was neat. His teeth were perfect, (possibly his wife was a dentist!) and his butt looked sweet. I could tell that he wasn't a womanizer and I was beginning to find out that men in coffee shops were more sensitive than the ones I found in bars. The coffee shop guys had feelings, and I actually began to enjoy writing in my diary and journaling for Dr. Cynthia.

I still saw her every week and she wrote a lot on her legal sized yellow pad but never condemned, and just kept repeating that the two of us had so much in common. She still wanted me to work on my self-esteem and I did pickup the books she suggested. Since I had been talking so much about the guys in the coffee shop, and my own things, I temporarily forgot about what she was going to tell me on June 11. I told her that for sure I was going to hear about it on my next visit which would be in one week. She agreed. I remember going shopping to kill the depression.

I met a new man in the elevator. He kissed me and I kissed him back. He gave me a little feel and I gave him one back. We enjoyed the people watching us. The door opened and I went to the left and he went to the right.

When driving home after meeting a new man in the malls, Carl never asked questions. He saw my shopping bag and smiled and it was so simple. Almost too good to be true.

July 29, 2002

Well, this was the day to see Dr. Cynthia. I asked her what she thought my diagnosis was and she answered with, "Marsha, I'd like to ask you a few questions if you don't mind. I found this psychiatric journal and the questionnaire will confirm my suspicions, I am sure. Then we will talk about diagnoses."

"What do you mean, diagnoses? Do you think I have more than one problem?"

"Yes I do. Now hold on, don't go getting excited yet."

She pulled out the questionnaire from her papers, and asked me the questions which I thought were stupid. She didn't know, but I also recorded this session. I will now play it back so I can read it when I am old and gray, but I will write it for you:

> "Do you sometimes feel that others once in a while think of you as slightly eccentric?"
>
> "Yep. They all tell me I'm crazy, goofy, nuts."
>
> "Do you have little interest in getting to know people?"
>
> "Yes. I don't like meeting new people. Just men."
>
> "Do you have the idea that people are talking about you behind your back?"
>
> "I know they are. All of them."
>
> "Do you have the feeling that they are all staring at you?"
>
> "I know they are."

(The questions didn't make sense. What was she trying to prove?)

> "Were you ever sexually abused as a child or adolescent?"
>
> "I refuse to answer that one." (I wasn't quite ready for that one.
>
> "Have you ever stayed in a romantic relationship after it became abusive?"
>
> "Yes. I do it all the time."
>
> "Do you often find yourself preoccupied with sexual thoughts and day dreams?"
>
> "Yes. With every breath I take."
>
> "Personally, do you feel that your sexual behavior is not normal?"
>
> "Yes, but I can't help myself."
>
> "Do you honestly think you could stop the behavior?"
>
> "No. I tried over and over. I can't stop the search".
>
> "What search?"
>
> "The search for Mr. Perfect, my next husband."

"Does your sexual behavior make you feel bad?"

"Yes. It makes me feel guilty."

"Do you ever feel like you are someone else?"

"Yes, sometimes I feel extra happy and like having fun. Then I call myself 'Roxanne.' Sometimes I see an image of me in the mirror and it really isn't me. The one I see has dark hair with gray. I don't know who she is or where she came from."

"Do you ever feel like someone is following you, checking up on you?"

"Yes, and my husband has done that in the past."

"Do you ever feel that friends or co-workers are not loyal or trustworthy?"

"Yes. Didn't I once tell you that all nurses are backstabbers? Do you know why? What they see in their work is the most intimate side of life and living, so they tell the most intimate secrets about you and add a little negative flavoring to them."

"Do you sometimes feel that people 'have it in for you?' Know what I mean?"

"Yes, everyone does have it in for me, everywhere."

"Has your sexual behavior ever caused problems for you and your family's relationship?"

"Yes. My husband knows and is going to divorce me. I don't know when, but the time will come."

"Have you ever sought help for your sexual behavior?"

"Yes. I am seeing you now and read self-help books every chance I get."

"Have you ever worried about people finding out about your sexual activities?"

"Yes, I think everyone in the world knows and feel my life is an open book."

"What do you like most about cheating?"

"Thinking about it, planning what I'll wear, the part before I actually go out, and getting home safely."

"Do you hide some of your sexual behavior from others?"

"I try like heck. No way do I want them to find out at work if I can help it. But I know they all do know."

"Have you made an effort to quit a type of sexual activity and failed?"

"I never quite get to the stage of trying to quit. Even when I didn't drink for six months I still fooled around. I think the two were connected."

"Have you ever found yourself in more than one relationship at a time?"

"Hell yes. One at a time is too boring."

"Have you ever felt emotionally degraded because of your sexual behavior?"

"Hell yes. All the time. Especially when driving home after fooling around."

"Have sex or romantic fantasies been a way for you to escape your problems?"

"I think that's why I indulge. It makes me forget everything but the joys of screwing."

"Has your sexual activity interfered with your family life in general?"

"Yes. My husband is upset. I think that's because he knows he can't do it and I have to go elsewhere. I think in a way he's jealous of my lovers."

"Do you find it hard to be emotionally close to other women?"

"Sure do. I have one female friend at work and you. That's all. It is impossible for me to get close to women."

"I'll be right back, Marsha." (She then left the room. Finally, after all those questions. I had no idea what conclusion she would could come up with the information I gave her.)

She walked back into the room and told me the news: "Marsha, it may have seemed like a dumb little test but it sums up what I did suspect."

"You know addictions come in pairs. Like the drinker who is a gambler. We both knew that you were a sexual addict, and an alcoholic, but you have a schizotypal behavior problem. It's just a slight mental problem, and you are manic depressive which goes along with it."

"Unfortunately, a sexual addiction is one of the most serious types of addictions out there. It can cause the ruin of individuals, marriages, relationships, and jobs."

Why did I feel relief then? I guess it was because I found out I was not schizophrenic. But then, she was still talking about what I did have.

"Marsha, one in four American families has a mental illness of some sort and we must acknowledge it. You may ask for a definition of mental illness. It can be defined as 'a group of disorders causing severe disturbances in thinking and relating which diminishes one's ability to cope with normal demands.' When symptoms interfere with an ability to be satisfied and effective at work or school, and in personal relationships, it's a good idea to seek professional help as you are doing now."

"Anyone who suspects they or a loved one has a mental illness should contact their doctor, psychiatrist, mental health clinic, or hospital as soon as possible."

I knew she was getting impatient with me, but I just had to ask. "What are some of the symptoms of a schizotypal personality?"

"A person with a schitzotypal personality shows oddities in the way they dress, talk, and in their behavior."

"They feel that they have magical powers that can predict what people are going to say before they say it. They have tendencies to become very happy or very sad with no forewarning."

"So far it does sound like me."

"They have speech oddities such as frequent digression or vagueness in conversation, meaning that they have problems in thinking and perceiving. They also show isolation, hypersensitivity, and inappropriate emotions. Sorrow hits them harder and can seem devastating. However, it is believed that the disorder is defined primarily by cognitive distortions and that affective and interpersonal problems are secondary. Yes some of the symptoms of a schizotypal personality disorder most certainly can resemble those of schizophrenia and there does appear to be a hereditary link."

"Will mine develop into schizophrenia?"

"I don't think so. Did anyone in your family have a mental illness?"

"No."

"We have good medication that will help you. It's not like ten years ago."

"Marsha, we have to get busy and study your early childhood years and I think you should visit your mother to see if she has some answers for you."

"I'll help all I can, but you have to get on this problem right away. So let's get together again next week and talk some more."

All of a sudden it hit me. I had to get out of there. I'd never go into a bar again and on the way home, I planned my next shopping spree, said goodbye and left. I went straight home, and hopped into bed.

August 3, 2002

I did my Saturday day thing and met Randy who just dandy, and that's the best way to describe him. He had a certain way of walking and talking and carrying himself. He rolled his eyes at me and I melted. He wore a wedding ring and had a nice behind. We had coffee and then went to a motel. That was different, but he told me his wife was at home. We spent three hours making love and he had a couple of original "Randy Positions" that I describe in my little green diary. He left to go home and then I went back to the mall to buy something to take home in a shopping bag and at the check out counter, I felt something similar to a tap on my shoulder. I was almost too tired for such "nonsense" but turned around, met Tom, and he wore a wedding ring, so we went to his house.

Oh, he was a good sport but when he pulled his pants down, I noticed he didn't have a substantial sized "man tool" and he told me it didn't work. He told me that he hadn't had sex in so long, that he forgot what it felt like. I did feel sorry for him, and as tired as I was, I worked with him and it for over one hour and ended up rating him as a "6" on he scale of 1-10. He thanked me over and over and over and begged me to see him again. I promised that if it was possible, I would surely see him.

Yes, I had two men that day, one who could and one who couldn't. I was relieved to return home to fix dinner and relax in front of the television.

That night I had tortured dreams, with men chasing me in dark woods and feathers filling the entire room and I woke up screaming. Carl simply said, "Shut up," and then rolled over and went back to sleep.

August 6, 2002

It was not Saturday, but I met Ted at the drug store and Roxanne flirted with him. She walked up to him and started rubbing his legs and inner thighs and I told her "Stop it, stop it." The man looked at me and asked who I was talking to. I told him that I was talking to myself and he said, "More, more, more. How about some more!" (He liked to be rubbed!) I went with him to his apartment. We had sex six times in two hours which is extremely difficult for most men and women too. (And the one who liked to be rubbed, didn't carry a rubber.) I wondered if he took the Viagra just before going to the drug store just in case. Or if he just happened to pick me because I had "that certain word" written all over my forehead. It was unbelievable that we didn't talk, didn't kiss, and I never found out his name. I didn't tell him mine either. We just had sex and rubbed.

August 10, 2002

The following Saturday. I met the man of my dreams while shopping. His Harley was parked just outside the window where I was sitting and sipping my tea. He waved to me, then came in telling me that I looked lonely. His name was Pete and he was neat! I asked him if he would take me for a ride on his bike and he agreed. After we finished our tea, we walked out to his bike and I hopped on behind him. I will admit that my arms were slightly too firm around him and I sat a little too close. But he smelled so good, with his cologne, a slight musky odor, and a slight odor of perspiration. He wore no ring and we drove on the highway for a while and then to a building not too far away and he told me that he'd take me to his apartment if I wanted. I agreed.

There was a mural on the stairway wall of a huge Harley Cycle, and once in his apartment. I noticed how everything was related to what I later found out was his favorite thing: *Harley Motor Cycles.* We drank beer from Harley mugs while his dog named "Harley" looked on and together the three of us looked at his Harley scrapbook. It was full of friends that rode bikes with him, trophies that he had won, and memorable scenes from the various cruises their Harley group took. I listened carefully to every word he said and I sat on a chair with his leather jacket hanging behind me.

He asked me to accompany him to South Dakota this year for the big rally and then we went to his room and made love. He was a practiced lover—in fact, one of the best I have ever known. He almost took me to the top of the highest mountain but just as I was about to reach it, his old Harley dog barked and I fell down that mountain. In the scrapbook was a picture of a girl on a Yamaha, and I asked who it was, and he told me: "Oh, that's Tammy, my ex-wife."

Afterwards, he drove me back to the mall, and I really hated to see him go. Hooray for Harley! Pete was so good that he rated five gold stars.

Something was mumbling in the background. I couldn't make out the words. Finally I did. Suddenly a cold, clammy feeling came over me.

"Marsha, something very different is going to happen to you within a few days. Avoid it if you can. But we can't tell you what it is. Stay in the house. Be careful, we love you."

August 11, 2002

I proceeded with caution. I was only outside for ten minutes. I didn't answer the phone.

August 12, 2002

As of Monday at noon, nothing unusual had happened. I wondered and waited. The day passed, and I continued to be restless. I would be so glad to stop at the drug store to pick up my prescription, and then go home, make some popcorn and sit and watch television with all the drapes pulled and the doors locked.

I walked to the pharmacy counter and asked for the bag with my three prescriptions. It was ready, and I paid for it, turned around and suddenly had a dizzy spell. I fell right into the arms of the most beautiful man that I had ever seen in my entire life.

PART TWO

Dear Diary,
What is wrong with me?
Dear God
Please help me.

CHAPTER EIGHT

August 12, 2002

"Pardon me, I am so clumsy."

"No, pardon me. I was standing too close."

Our conversation ended there, but not the sight of his well-rounded butt or the smell of his expensive cologne. His dark hair and brown eyes haunted me as I turned into another aisle, where I kept hoping that I would run into him again. And sure enough, he jokingly bumped his basket into mine in the vegetable aisle and laughed.

"Hey, you," he said.

"Hey, you," I repeated with a grin.

"Oh, I see you like green beans, too."

"My favorite."

"Mine too."

As I passed him, our arms accidentally touched and we just stared at one another (already, that certain chemistry was there), and then we smiled and continued with our shopping.

Once we finished picking up what food items we needed, we checked out and who do you suppose was parked right next to me in the parking lot?

"I can't believe this."

"Me either."

We exchanged small talk. He told me that he was convinced something had brought us together—"It's fate, my dear."

He looked at his watch and asked, "I don't suppose you have time for a cup of coffee?"

I knew that no matter what time it was, I'd find time to have that cup of coffee with him. I put my groceries in the trunk and hopped into his car. We went to a cute little restaurant that looked more like a small, white cottage.

We talked about our jobs, our spouses, and how close to each other we worked. I told him that I was a nurse and he told me that he was a marketing consultant for a manufacturing company.

Little did I know at that moment how our accidental meeting at a pharmacy counter was going to mark the beginning of my travels that strayed from the straight and narrow paved road of life onto new side roads, dusty gravel roads, hills and valleys, and places where I had never ventured before. Those roads would wind, twist, turn, and run though dark forests before finally ending up on the main highway again. My life would never be the same.

The day was breezy, warm, and perfect in every way. The restaurant had frilly Priscilla curtains, fresh flowers on all of the window sills, and waitresses in black uniforms and crisp, white, lace—trimmed aprons. John held the door for me as we entered and he held my chair as I sat. We were side by side so we could both watch the ducks out on the water.

They floated on the calm, clear pond and left pencil-thin trails as they skimmed along the clear, blue water beneath the weeping willows. I'll never forget the beauty of that day with the shining sun, and ducks quacking, and John holding my hand and looking into my eyes.

The weeping willow branches were a soft shade of green, and barely moved in the gentle, summer breeze. They drooped, almost to the ground as they surrounded the entire lake.

The beauty of those leaves can't be described. I breathed deeply of the fresh air and was completely relaxed. The heavenly feeling of having John at my side, plus the beautiful surroundings, put me in another world.

I felt like a princess with him sitting next to me. He was such a handsome man with a firm body and the special designer suit that he wore looked so good on him. His cologne fragrance lingered with me for the rest of the day and night. I closed my eyes and inhaled the scent, as it proceeded to arouse me in certain ways.

Evidently the waitress saw something in our eyes and kept refilling our cups of coffee in order to let us prolong our visit with each other.

Afterwards, we walked outside and sat on a bench on the other side of a huge tree and we were in our own private bubble, watching the trees and ducks.

He continued to stare into my eyes, and I knew he wanted that first kiss as much as I did. He held me so tightly that I thought I would break in half.

Finally, John's eyes looked down and he said, almost in a whisper, "Marsha, I hate to leave you but I must. I have to get home, damn it."

"I understand. I must go, too." I knew what would happen if I came home too late, with the look of a far-away-dreamer. Carl would begin to wonder, what I'd been doing. I certainly didn't want him checking up on me.

We drove back to my car and John opened the door for me to get in, and suddenly he swept me off the ground, and held me in his arms and the kiss he planted on my lips left me speechless. I didn't even know my own name.

We exchanged e-mail addresses, and shortly after arriving home he had already sent me a message:

Marsha, oh Marsha
I have to see you again. I will call you in the morning.
Love,
John

That was all he wrote, and I read it over and over. I had to be careful. I had just met him and didn't want to scare him away. Yet I was an adult and knew what I wanted and I promised myself that I would be patient. I meant it, I really did. I wrote back:

John,

It is so good hearing from you.
I will wait for your call tomorrow and I'll be ready.
Thanks for today.
Love,
Marsha

Some of John's fragrance rubbed off on me when he was so close, and before I went to bed that evening, I rubbed against my pillow and placed the pillow next to me as I slept, pretending it was him. I had only known him for two hours and I was madly in love with this man. I felt myself going back to my teenage years and know for certain that I had a smile on my face when I went to sleep that night. I couldn't help but wonder what a handsome, elegant man like John saw in a simple nurse, dressed in a white uniform.

Somehow, the night passed, and I dressed in a new nursing uniform especially for him. I thought of him all morning. He called and asked me to meet him at noon.

August 13, 2002

At work, the hands on the clock didn't move. I stammered and stuttered and didn't get my medication passed on time. The patients complained. Finally it was almost noon and I went to the bathroom to put on fresh lipstick and comb my hair. I was ready to see my dream man and my heart was fluttering.

Within minutes he parked his car and I was ready to walk over to meet him, for when your love is fresh and new, you just want to sit and hold each other. He surprised me by locking and getting out of the car, and walking towards the restaurant.

Talk about disappointment. I wasn't the least bit hungry, I just wanted him to hold and kiss me and maybe do a little touching here and there. But reluctantly, I joined him, wondering if he saw the disappointment on my face. "Let's go, sweetheart. I'm starving."

Maybe I was Roxanne, just thinking of sex. I don't know how I managed to eat a thing with all the fluttering around in my chest and stomach. He lowered his head and spoke to me in a whisper:

"Hon, I'm married but I don't love my wife. I probably like her because we've been together for so long. But there is no love. I need a companion in life, and I think you just might fill the bill."

I reached over and held his hand and told him that I was in the exact situation. Then once again I wondered if I had said the wrong thing and if I had in fact, said too much. He then told me, “But I don’t want to change my status in life. I have five children and don’t want to leave my family or home.”

I sat and silently wondered what he was trying to tell me. I thought it was a little soon for a man to speak those words. After all, it was only the second time we were together and those thoughts never even entered my mind.

“It seems that you need a friend just as I do. I think we’d be good for each other. You could be my nurse, and I’d be the doctor and examine and kiss every inch of your body, and manufacture a problem for you.”

I could tell him what my problem was without an examination. In fact all he had to do was look at my forehead to see the words written there.

I just floated on air. I really cared for this man. After finishing our meal, we went back to the parking lot. “Come on over to my car,” he said.

“Okay,” I tried to say nonchalantly. Once in his car we just sat and listened to a romantic c.d. on his player. Then we shared our first passionate kiss and it seemed to last forever with neither of us wanting it to end. We knew then, after kissing, holding, and caressing that we were made for each other.

One could tell this man was practiced in lovemaking. But then, so was I. When we kissed, I heard buzzing, saw fireworks of every color, and realized he was holding me tighter and kissing me harder. I promised myself that I’d see this man as often as possible. I knew he was my “Mr. Perfect” and hoped he would realize it soon.

August 16, 2002

My mind had been working overtime and I just couldn’t concentrate. I knew I’d walk over burning rocks or in three feet of snow to see him. We stopped for coffee after work every day and I felt our love growing more intense. Every day I felt new, revived, and younger.

August 18, 2002

Nothing mattered but John. I began to live and breathe for him. Yes, it was fate that brought us together. We were both desperate and found each other to fill a certain void. “It was a miracle; hon. Just you stay away from drug stores and don’t fall into anyone else’s arms like you did mine.”

August 21, 2002

I don’t know why it took so long, but we both knew it was time for the next stage in our relationship. We both had thought about it and I didn’t know why we hesitated. It was probably the fear and just not knowing what our spouses would do if they happened to see us coming out of a motel. He finally looked at me and asked, "Should we give it a try?"

I answered with the loudest "Yes" that was ever heard. He just looked at me, held his ears, and said, "Oh my!" (I believe Roxanne was the one that gave him that answer.)

The motel was in the middle of nowhere. We wouldn't run into anyone; I was sure of that, and it was early. I could always say that I had to work overtime and so could he. We could foresee no problems. We weren't hurting anyone, and just wanted a couple of hours with skin on skin. So what's wrong with that?

It was a completely happy and satisfying union and we couldn't get enough of each other. We spent four hours there, had a cup of coffee and sat in our room holding hands. The motel furnished coffee and we sat with next to no clothing on in our room, as we fondled each other. We kissed every inch of each other's bodies.

I was completely happy as I reached the top of the mountain for the first time in my life, then soared up to a cloud, then slowly floated down and later soared to the mountain top again. I couldn't believe anything could be that wonderful. (These words were putting it mildly.) The fireworks continued for hours, and I had tears in my eyes when we finally had to part.

August 25, 2002

I am sorry for skipping days here, but John is all I can think about. I have no energy left to write. I see Dr. Connors, and those meetings go fine. I no longer need tranquilizers but told her of my guilt feelings towards Carl sitting alone at the kitchen table when I come home, knowing what I had been doing with John. But I sweep it from my mind as I didn't want to start with those feelings already.

Dear Diary, what am I going to do?

~~~~~

August 27, 2002

Our feelings continue to grow. They seem to get stronger every day and at certain times I'd blush like a little girl. We both found out what we had been missing as we had admitted to ourselves and the entire world that our finding each other was the best thing that either of us had ever experienced. Our lovemaking was never rushed as we believed in long foreplay and we certainly tried to get each other aroused thoroughly before making love.
~~~~~

My happy glow was noticed by those at work. Dr. Cynthia noticed it and just smiled, but Dr. Louise remarked, "I have never seen you look so happy and content in the last ten years since you've been my patient. What's going on, Marsha? What's your secret?" I just smiled. I wasn't telling anyone my secret.

I loved John but it still hurt to think of Carl home alone. You might say I was "torn."

September 1, 2002

By September 1, things were getting mutually serious between John and me. We talked about leaving our spouses and families and just going away together. "I know I told you weeks ago that I wouldn't change my status in life, and that I like my wife too much to leave her. But honey, things have changed. I just want to be with you."

I loved the idea and my heart beat faster, but a few days later as I drove home, I realized it just wasn't feasible to leave Carl after living with him for over fourteen years. You just can't do that. Maybe you don't love your partner anymore, but you still liked him or her and were friends and it was a comfortable feeling that you shared.

And I thought of what it would do to John's children and his wife. I put myself in his wife's shoes. When I arrived home, tears ran down my face. Why did life have to be so rough?

The gossip was hot and heavy at work as someone had seen us together somewhere but John continued to meet me after work for coffee. Then, when he walked to my nursing station later that day (a surprise visit) everyone stared as he kissed me. It was as if they all knew everything that was going on in my personal life.

After work, we went for coffee and stopped near a cornfield to hold and kiss each other and then made love amongst the cornstalks. We continued to talk about everything, and I slept with a pillow between my legs that night. Oh how I wished that pillow could have been him.

September 5, 2002

It was raining, and on rainy days we just sat in the car kissing and acting like teenagers, but we had to constantly watch the clock and not fall asleep in each other's arms. I always kissed Carl when I got home, even though he didn't return my affection. But at least I felt good knowing I tried, as maybe my showing affection would prevent a divorce.

September 6, 2002

I know what I am about to say will sound mushy/crazy, but remember, this was my first real affair and even at my age, it reminded me of being a silly teen-ager again. I always have had one-night stands and never knew little intimate details of the man I was with. But with John, I knew every inch of his body.

As much as I enjoyed being with John, the favorite ending to this story is creeping home to Carl as the hour grew later and later, knowing that one more time I made it without being caught.

My life with John as a husband would be a dream come true, but a dream was all that it was. He'd never marry me. He'd never leave his family for me. But he was still with me in my thoughts, every minute of the day.

September 8, 2002

Nothing new at work and nothing new in my life with John or Carl. John told me that he was in love like he never had been before and we had to do something about it.

September 11, 2002

If you only knew what John's kisses did to me! And it was the first time I ever felt so completely in love, so fulfilled, and alive which was something really new for me.

September 14, 2002

John was out of town and didn't call. I miss him. He will return tomorrow.

September 15, 2002

John didn't call, but I figured he was unpacking and getting reorganized.

September 17, 2002

I couldn't concentrate at work. Everyone was whispering about me and I didn't know why. Then he called and said how busy he had been. I was just thankful that he called. He asked me to go out for coffee with him after work and I was excited—so excited.

September 18, 2002.

John met me two days now for coffee, and we held hands as we walked, but I wanted to make love and he said there wasn't enough time.

Carl asked why I had been so depressed lately and I told him, "I miss having my beers."

I began to drink at home. If only John would ask me to a motel so we could be alone and comfortable without people staring.

September 20, 2002

The past two days, I felt a real need to be near him—our naked bodies touching again, and I wanted to call and let him know this. But I decided to let him call me and then maybe I would tell him my feelings.

September 22, 2002

I watched my bank balance decrease. I was spending a fortune on my nails, hair, and clothes. He called and talked for all of three minutes but didn't mention seeing me. It's funny, but never once did this man tell me I looked nice, no matter what I wore or how long it took me to dress up for him. If only he'd notice me.—All my designer coats and shoes were purchased for naught. Fuck it.

When we did get together, we were in our own comfortable world, isolated from cares and problems, tucked away somewhere between blankets. It was good to have that complete naked body contact again.

John never mentioned the two of us going away again, but I accepted that as it wasn't practical or feasible anyhow, even though I once thought I would like it. Evidently he feels the same way.

September 23, 2002

We began to meet twice a week. We didn't believe that we were hurting anyone; our spouses didn't know so how could it hurt them? I don't know about John's wife, but Carl trusted me. This made me feel even worse: if someone trusts you, at least you should allow yourself to be worthy of that trust. The problem was that I was addicted to John's loving, and he was addicted to mine. We were so good together. Know what I mean?

September 26, 2002

I longed for John to give me candy or flowers, but he was just using me for his own pleasure. I began to see that. It hurt and I felt cheap. I was pretending that he changed his mind and did care for me, just because we started seeing each other again. I was only fooling myself. I still loved Carl. Damn. I was confused.

September 30, 2002

Things remained the same at work. The mentally ill patients drained me, making me more tired, and I decided that I was getting too old for psychiatric nursing and started thinking of changing jobs. I didn't do justice to my work and felt guilty about this, too. And then, on top of it, John began talking of all the things he did for Norma, his wife. We still saw each other twice a week, but our "together time" had gone from approximately 2-3 hours per day to 1 hour.

He took Norma to the "See Food Restaurant" and they had lobster. He never took me out for lobster. Why didn't he keep his damn big mouth shut about what he bought and where he took Norma?

He took her for Sunday drives, bought her ice cream, genuine pearls, diamonds, expensive jewelry, and new kitchen appliances. He never even helped pay for the gas that I used to drive to his house. He bought her car and paid for the gas and she drove all over the countryside.

But he did call me when he wanted sex. I was his "call girl" meaning that he would call me and I would meet him. I have to admit that I was getting sick of it. We were down to meeting once per week now.

And then came the afternoon that I saw him coming out of a motel with another woman. Talk about hurt! Later I saw him driving around with someone new, and it looked like he had his hand up her skirt. I dried my teary eyes, but when I got home, Carl asked, "What's the matter? Why are you crying?" He was satisfied when I told him that I had a bad day at work. What would I do? I would still see John when he called me. No matter what.

October 5, 2002

Another hurt today. I was having coffee with John and he was giving me a sob story about not having sex with his wife for seven years. He said she just didn't like it. (So how does he happen to have a three year old son if they didn't have sex for seven years? Give me a break!) I told him I was in the same boat, that my husband never wanted it either. And then he answered: "Yeah, you should have seen her the other night when I tried to reach over for her, and she pulled away."

So I caught him in another lie. But then, should I really mind? After all, I wasn't his wife and she had given him five lovely children. I had seen their pictures. What really hurts was that I saw him with three other women in his car holding them all so closely that I thought they were glued together.

Then came the sex talk era. All he talked about and thought about was sex and sex positions and sex toys. It was a turn off for me. I was just a toy, for him to play with when there was no one else around. I was a "Better-than-no-one" person and I believe he only called me when he had no one else. I began to dislike him. We went to motels for a couple of hours a couple of times per week and got right down to business. There was no foreplay anymore, and he didn't try to satisfy me. I was merely an object for his pleasure. The trouble was that I still loved him.

Today on the way home from work I stopped at a different type of bar, one in an exclusive hotel in Chicago. Soon an elegant appearing gentleman in a blue suit came up to me and inquired whether I was as lonely as I looked.

I agreed that I was lonely, and we had four drinks and then he invited me up to his room. His room turned out to be an exclusive suite, where you walk into a meeting room, equipped with a bar, refrigerator, and microwave. Beyond that was an actual living room, with a bedroom to the side. We made love for two hours and it was great.

His name was Andrew and we stopped for steak and lobster in the hotel dining room and had a bottle of champagne. All I could thing about was "What am I doing with him if I love John and I'm married to Carl" I would have to call my shrink in the morning and ask that question.

Carl believed me when I came home at 9:00p.m. and told him one of the nurses didn't show up for the second shift. It was just too easy!

October 10, 2002

I called Cynthia and asked why I couldn't just be with one man and she told me that my addiction was becoming more serious. I explained my latest activities and she said I'd be better off just sticking with Carl.

She told me that I had a love addiction, and that I was in love with love and that every man I met, I seemed to become deeply attached to.

She said that real love isn't based on one night stands or knowing a guy for just three months. She knew all about John and didn't think that it would work out for us. "He's different. John's a womanizer and would never be happy with one woman, so don't waste your time on him."

We talked it over thoroughly, and I do understand now where she is coming from.

October 11, 2002

My mind is going crazy. John is calling me by other women's names. He told me again that he likes my big brown eyes and they are blue.

Dr. Louise gave me a prescription for stronger tranquilizers. She told me I no longer looked happy, and had reverted back to the old Marsha. She said I could take them more of the stronger tranquilizers, up to four times a day. I also went back to the same hotel and met Andy once more. We talked and shared beers and it was relaxing—I put John out of my mind. If he could erase me, I could do the same to him.

October 12, 2002

I began taking still more tranquilizers, plus I had sleeping pills. I didn't realize that I was digging a deeper hole and burying myself more. I walked around in the fog during the day and really didn't think much about John. What would be would be. I had seen him three days in a row walking around with different nurses. Yes, I did still care. Damn it, I couldn't fool myself. I really did love the bastard. He started yesterday and today being cooler in attitude towards me. He asked me out to coffee and I told him that I was busy. I couldn't see the writing between the lines. Damn. I was a dumb broad.

"Marsha, no matter what this man says, there is no future for you with him. No way will he leave his wife or family for you, so accept it. He's only using you for playing games."

I already had realized this. His kisses had grown cold and less frequent—his kisses now were like little chicken pecks. The calls and e-mails gradually stopped and I couldn't imagine who his new "special person" was.

October 14, 2002

I realized today that he had more than one special person. But I should have realized that a man who cheats on his wife will cheat on his girl friend too. Right? In my opinion he was a bigger and more serious sex addict than me, for sex addicts come in many shapes and sizes.

Than began the "Excuse Era." Every day he had a new excuse for me, something Norma wanted done or something the kids needed. I spent the nights crying the past week and I was going to work wearing sun glasses.

When we did talk, his voice lacked luster and enthusiasm as it once had. Now only monotone, dead words echoed in my ears. Why couldn't he tell me, "Gee, I wish we could be together instead of being with the family?" But, no. Never. Not once.

Now don't get me wrong. I realize that a man's family comes first. But what about "the other woman" who gives of herself, lets him use her and does things that the wife won't do? Doesn't he know I have feelings too? "Fuck, fuck, fuck." I have feelings and lots of cares and concerns he doesn't even seem to give a damn about, but he won't give me a chance to express them, but he expects me to have broad shoulders and listen to him.

Meanwhile, the wife gets all the attention and the "other woman is left by the wayside." Shit. Can you tell how angry I am today? Evidently I have served my purpose and he doesn't give a flying fuck how much we shared or how much he once cared for me. "Just toss me aside like a dirty piece of laundry, for someone else is getting your kisses and loving now." And I didn't even get a decent "good-bye." I do wish he would tell me good-bye instead of letting me raise my hopes.

I think the worst thing is to pass him on a Sunday drive with another woman who isn't his wife. Who do you tell? You would only hurt him if you told his wife. And I love him too much to hurt him that way. How do you think I feel knowing his hand is inside her skirt, hoping he will get lucky? He would never tell me, and I can just hear him now:

"Oh Jill, I'm so horny. I haven't had sex in ten years." You know that just the day before, you had relations with him three times and he told me at that time that he hadn't had sex since we were last together. I knew better. I know all about his sex drive and know he has a super big one, but then, so do I, but I can wait. He can't.

It was costing me $15.00 to drive to his town, just south of Chicago, and it added up. It was at least $60.00 per week—just for gas.

It is so good to finally be able to put all this on paper. I had started a diary again, for I am a talker, writer, and a bad girl with much to tell. I am not able to stop my actions, no matter how hard I try. I had hopes of growing old and sitting on the porch in my rocker and reading of all my adventures. But only I know how I feel and know I will never make it.

I was so tired one night, and just wanted to take a short nap as John did, before we went to dinner. I woke up in time to see him put his latest advertisement on the web site, using my lap top. (He surely didn't sleep very long.) I waited and watched as he was in another world, not dreaming I was awake. Hurriedly and frantically, these are his words:

> *People say I'm very easy going. I exercise three times a week. I believe sex is an art, and when making love to a woman, every part of her body*

should be touched and kissed. I please my partners by G spot massage, and oral stimulation at the same time to do the trick.

The trick is varied positions as I please her other ways. I love sex, but am not looking to change my status, even though I am not happily married. I am open for new experiences as variety is the spice of life and makes life interesting. I prefer one on one, but a threesome can be beautiful. I love to share, touch, breathe, and express my feelings in all ways possible. Your wish is my command.

Partner must not be afraid to express her feelings. Sex is especially beautiful with someone watching. I love long foreplay and plenty of time to tantalize. My favorite thing is to have someone watching while three of us make love. I work in Chicago and could get away mornings, afternoons, or any evenings or weekends. Your time is my time. John123

What really got me is that he says he can get away any time yet with me he always had a curfew. I found out he is on six web sites.

The next day I saw him walking down Randolph St., arm in arm with a nurse from work. She is the same one that used to stare at me and give me dirty looks and I can't help but wonder how much she knows and what he has told her about me.

I saw him later today holding hands with another woman, and kissing her right on the bridge over the Chicago River. It felt like someone ripped my heart right from my chest and threw it on concrete. I couldn't catch my breath for a while and I'm glad he didn't see the tears flow as I watched the two of them. There was hot and heavy gossip, meant for me to hear as I walked out to my car to go home after work. "Yes, he put a rose on her steering wheel and a box of candy alongside the glove box. He is such a cool man."

I couldn't help but think how he never bought me roses or candy and felt the pain rip through me. I don't think I'll ever forget what he's done to hurt me.

I did stop for a drink, but sat at the bar, as I was a complete mess, crying my eyes out, and no one approached me. I went home early.

October 16, 2002

I began taking a bottle of blackberry brandy to work and sneaking drinks now and then. A couple of times patients asked me if I was drinking and I told them, "No, it is just teaberry gum." When I think about it now, I wonder why I didn't just say, "It's none of your fucking business."

Oh yes, after the Brandy, I usually popped three Klonopin, and not the 0.5 mg. size, either. Talk about a buzz. I sure as hell didn't want to be caught by Delores Norton although some of the nurses knew.

John told me had another business trip to make. He told me he would be gone one week and could we see each other when he came back. I wasn't too sure of how to answer him. Sure, I wanted to see him, but I was tired of his making a fool out of me. I knew he was taking someone with but didn't even cry. "I'll think about it," I said and patted myself on the back for this one!

He had so many business trips when we first started going together, and I managed to get away with him some of the times. When I couldn't go with him, I'd call him in his room. He talked freely. Now I'd never do that because I never knew who'd be in that room with him. Oh yes, I knew all his tricks. He'd talk to his girl friends via the computer in the hotels but he never had time to send me an e-mail and never called.

He'd call nurses at work, trying to disguise his voice. How dumb did he think I was? I was the one who happened to answer the damn phone, and I sure knew his voice.

I can't bring myself to tell this man goodbye. I still love him and probably always will. He has made a groove in my heart that can't be filled.

October 19, 2002

Today I saw him with a woman in the same restaurant we went to that first day. They left there and I followed and sat behind them at Belmont Harbor as they enjoyed the view from the same bench we used to sit on, watching the boats, only weeks ago. I felt insecure, not knowing what I should do next.

(It seems that at the end of the day I write more. I am more relaxed and so anxious to get things off my chest. It just isn't healthy to keep it all inside.)

My paranoia, negative self-image, and self esteem are existent within me. Strange sounds bombarded my brain and the hallucinations are multiplying, I feel as though I'm running on electrical current and need a new fuse.

For days and weeks now, the voices are returning, louder, more garbled, and not making sense.

My work is suffering and the director of nursing gave me three days off without pay because I forgot to give medication to one person, gave the wrong medication to another and missed doing two treatments. I drank in the kitchen at home, in the bathroom, and in new bars. I have been averaging three men a night and the strange thing is that I don't enjoy it.

The voices were getting louder and yelling at me. But I deserved it. Why was I sacrificing everything, ruining my health and going broke buying gas to go to and from Chicago twice every day, not only to work but to pass his house in hopes of seeing John? Why was I destroying the relationship that Carl and I once had for one with John that could never be?

His wife! Now that's a story. She had it made from the time she picked him to be her husband until the present day. She has her own housekeeper, a laundry lady, a masseuse that visits her three times a week coming to her own bedroom so she doesn't have to drive to or from the massage parlor. Norma has clothing galore, jewelry, but most of all she has John.

He gives her anything she wants or needs and she doesn't know the meaning of the word "work." He takes care of her quite well, even gives her an allowance equaling more than I make on my job. And according to him, she doesn't even offer a kiss. Bull shit. And to think I was dumb enough to believe that at one time. She is one bitch that lives like a queen. Sure she knows that he is a cheating bastard, but she also knows what she has and therefore can't and won't leave him.

When you think about it, I am somewhat in the same situation with Carl. He gives me anything and everything I want and need. Surely a woman my age could forget about sex and be satisfied with rest of the luxuries. But like John, I was out looking for something I evidently didn't get at home. When I think about it, he is a bigger sex addict than I am. And when John and I break it off completely, they won't lose a thing. They will go on just as they were until he finds another.

Yes, John was actually dumping me which was something I never expected while Carl didn't even have an inkling of what I had been through.

Unfortunately, there are so many eager women out there, just waiting for someone like John, but here I am, feeling used, worn out, depressed, and ten years (at least) older. Men seem to improve with age. Not so with women.

I'd like to interject a few words here for the women of these men: Why does it seem that in marriage one of the two people invariably cares more for sex more than the other? Can't you at least "fake it" and do what he wants instead of driving him to another woman to fulfill his needs? With all the women out on the prowl, you'd better take a second look at that handsome, man you married, the one who caters to your every fucking whim, because where would you be without him? He will eventually find a new woman who will certainly treat him well, do what he wants, and scratch his itch. Don't fool yourself. Probably she is out there waiting for him right now, under the bushes. He waits till you go to sleep and then meets her, just as he met me. She will also know how to treat him and he will be completely happy—for a while—but I sure as hell won't tell her that it won't last forever. Let her find out as I did.

I begin to lie wake nights, just staring at the ceiling. What the hell was I going to do? I couldn't make a decision. Perhaps I should talk to John and ask what his plans were. Maybe I should just tell John that I love him and leave Carl. No, that is something Carl would never do to me. I finally made my decision.

October 23, 2002.

I told John that he had my permission to live his life however he decided, but to leave me out of it. He was gone almost instantly, without an argument. Evidently he didn't care as much as he said, because there was no hesitation on his part.

But I had become dead inside and felt like an empty shell. What the hell was I going to do without the cheating bum? Once a woman knows good sex, she finds it extremely hard to leave it all behind. Carl and I had so many years of sharing and companionship, and I had only known John for a few months. There was no comparison. I just wanted to stay married, to have a male companion that I could trust. Besides, I didn't want to start over with another man and another bag of problems. God, I only hoped it wasn't too late for Carl to change his mind and decide to stay with me.

I tried everything to please Carl. But at the same time, I missed sex without John—such long, cold nights. I couldn't even reach over to touch Carl's warm body. I had to stay on my own side of the bed, as that was one of his rules. I didn't feel like going to bars again. I just wanted to make my marriage work.

They say everything happens for a reason. What could these reasons possibly be? Maybe God wanted to show me what complete fulfillment was, and he did, for a while. But then why did he take it away?

Maybe God realized that an affair makes a marriage stronger, and it does. Why? Because you don't realize how good and comfortable things are at home until you have the affair and compare.

For example, Carl doesn't mind seeing me without make-up, or without fancy new clothes. As John commented once, he gives his wife so much money for clothing, and she always looks fashionable. Carl never gave me money for anything I needed as I worked, although he would buy me a new car every year and any special clothing I could not afford. I made money by working, and it was all mine, to spend as I liked. I feel comfortable in my home, but John's has slate floors, no carpeting, just expensive oriental throw rugs and genuine leather furniture. But you know what? It feels cold and uncomfortable. Carl and I have made our home a cozy retreat over the years.

Yes, John is just about running out of time. Too many years of fooling around—too many women and one of them will eventually make serious trouble for his marriage.

(I guess this is another wordy night for me. Sorry.)

Many women would say a married man is better to fool around with because they happen to be married too. "Married men won't jeopardize my marriage."

Others would say, "After hot dogs, you want steak for a change. A change never hurt anyone."

Yes ladies, the fun is super and the change in diet is great, but unfortunately they don't last. So wherever you are—STAY. "The New Lover" will just use you. Believe me, there are no exceptions.

Ask yourselves these questions if you dare:

> **Where does he spend his weekends, holidays, and time away from work?** (He's probably with his family or perhaps with another 'special someone').
>
> **How do you know for sure that he'd be true to you?** (Remember that he cheated on his wife and what's to prevent him from cheating on you?)
>
> **Why do you take all the wear and tear of sex from a man other than your husband?** (And there is wear and tear related to having sex. Think about it).
>
> **Why do you spend the money, time and travel expenses, yet still have stress that you will get caught, or stress that you wouldn't have if you had stayed at home?** (He just wants a good lay, and he really doesn't care about you and doesn't give a flying fuck about your stress. His brains are not in his head—they are in that other head below his navel).
>
> **Do you really want to hurt yourself by hearing of the gifts and things he is buying for "her"?** (Hell no! If you're like me you have to work your butt off for the money you spend. I don't work in an assembly line, but I work my butt off as a nurse. His "wifey" sits home and eats bon bons).

Am I bitter? Hell yes. It isn't fair that this bitch he married gets everything he has and he takes her out to eat at least four times a week. And what does she do for him?

So what does one do? She stays with what she has as she knows him. This eliminates work and unnecessary planning, moving, and anguish over leaving and starting over. She doesn't hurt her husband who has given her so much He has been true to her and she should do the same to prove she is worthy of his love.

John was a spoiled little rich boy, stubborn and used to getting his own way. He is number one in his book but no longer does he hold that position in mine. He told me that he was going back to an old girl friend that he really loves. God bless him! But dammit, did he have to drop me—on my head? He needs three or four women at one time to satisfy him, but I only need one to satisfy my needs and give me what I want. One good, loving, considerate man at a time satisfies me (along with one in the bushes just in case). Thank you, but John would never fall into a monogamous category.

Thinking back on my affair and thinking in general, I believe women use good sex outside of marriage as an escape from something that is not so good at home. Men do it because other women are a non-stop curiosity/thrill/wonder object, which they must chase until they catch and then try her on for size. She flirts and smiles at him and he runs after her until she is caught. Show me a man who isn't horny all the time, and you can bet he is gay.

But if you're like me, even though I felt better without him, the activities with him continued for a while. I couldn't just make a clean break instantly. It was fun to go to a new motel, but on the other hand, there is nothing as wonderful as being in your own bed with your husband lying beside you. Infidelity breeds confusion and confusion breeds stress, and it is such a sick situation you could kick yourself in the ass for ever starting looking at other men.

When you are out in the middle of nowhere, what do you do if your car breaks down? Who could you call? How could you call your husband and tell him you are stranded in the back row of a cornfield in Whereani, Illinois at 3:00a.m?

When I called it quits and made it final (finally.) I felt better mentally and physically. I had my phone number and e-mail address changed and broke off all old ties which allowed me to feel like a new woman. But, needless to say,

When I work the night shift I think of him.
When the phone rings mysteriously only one time at midnight,
I think of him.
When the phone rings mysteriously at noon,
I think of him.
On summery days when I see little ducks,
I think of him.
When I see Priscilla curtains,
I think of him.
When I get a whiff of a certain manly cologne,
I think of him.
In the fall with leaves on the ground,
I think of him.
In the winter when the first snow falls,
I think of him.

In the car when I cry,
I think of him.
When I see couples going into a motel, or
sitting in a car kissing and holding hands,
I think of him.
In other words, I miss him day and night.
The pain is terrible.
Like a knife cutting into raw flesh.

(Thinking back on things now, the time I spent with John was not equal to that which I spent in hatred, disgust, and misery with myself. Yes, there were some times when John made me one miserable woman. Yet at the same time, I do think I have to say, John made me one happy woman, and yes, the affair was worth it.) Now, does this make sense?

~~~~~
~~~~~

CHAPTER NINE

November 15, 2002

The holidays were approaching and I couldn't get in the spirit. I hurt as bitterness set in. My appetite disappeared and my energy left me. No longer did I walk around with a smile on my face but everyone said I was grouchy and bitchy. Sometimes I didn't shower or brush my teeth and I was becoming lethargic. Dr. Louise prescribed some good vitamins and anti-depressants, and Dr. Cynthia kept assuring me that I did the right thing by letting him go, and time would take care of everything.

"He would never keep you happy on a regular basis. Of course I feel badly for you but sorrow like this is only temporary." She failed to tell me how long temporary would be.

Dr. Cynthia explained that when I was with John, whether or not I knew it, I was manic. The mood swings seem to hit me harder, being a schizotypal personality and now I was at the depressed end of the scale. When a schizotypal is manic, she is happier (up) than the average person and when she is depressed, she is more on the down side than the average person.

(There are so many mental illnesses out there, and somehow I was stuck with a very common one and one of the less common variety. I don't know why Dr. Cynthia keeps telling me I suffer from disorientation and tells me that my abstract thinking is impaired. She tells me that my organization is loose and on those days, I do feel different. In fact, I am having one today).

No turkey or dressing thoughts entered my mind, in fact, I didn't think about Thanksgiving. Carl was disappointed, but I did fix turkey sandwiches and bought a pumpkin pie. I bet John was eating a good dinner with all his children gathered around the festive table.

I kept going to Dr. Cynthia, questioning the things I did. It was not normal to just forget, and not celebrate holidays and I needed her help to understand why I was acting this way. Being a friend and doctor, she explained that the loss of a close relationship appears greater than it would to a person who grew up in a family where there was closeness. She surmised that I didn't have that closeness, and realized l couldn't talk about my problems with just anybody, so I kept them within myself. "Marsha, I am here for you and always will be. I am just a phone call away. And you have to allow yourself to enjoy life. Don't let him be the cause of your missing holidays and having fun."

In the meantime, everyone was talking about my video. People liked it and were buying it. I had no idea who was getting money from the sales, as I sure wasn't. It was in all the stores, with posters advertising it, and huge displays in book and department stores. Someone was making money from it, and I was going to find out why I wasn't getting my share. After all, it hurt me in more ways than one to make that damn video and I didn't see one red cent.

Dr. Cynthia also told me that the nurses I work with may appear to be staring at me as probably they are going out with John too, and I should just overlook it. She explained that I was insecure and believed them all to be talking about me, but that wasn't necessarily the case. She told me that I was super sensitive and everything seemed to magnify for that reason.

Next came the maybe state and it was horrible. I told Dr. Cynthia:

> "Maybe John really loved me and just couldn't express himself. Maybe I should have given him a little more time."
>
> "Maybe I should have explained my love for him and that I just couldn't live without him."
>
> "Maybe I should throw myself at him but maybe he'd catch me again and I'd have to go through all this once more."
>
> "Maybe I should have given him the benefit of the doubt and more breathing space."
>
> "Maybe he thought I was over-sexed and just couldn't keep up with me."
>
> "Maybe I should have gone for rides and to movies with him instead of just going to motels."
>
> "Maybe I should have insisted on doing other things with him besides going to a motel."
>
> "Maybe, because it was a 'special affair' I should have broken it off slowly, gradually, and not as I did."

"Maybe he figured I only wanted to get together for sex."
"Maybe I should have let him pay for things more often."
"Maybe I could have tolerated things better after he left if he would just send me an occasional e-mail or make that occasional call."

I did tell Dr. Cynthia about all these "Maybe" ideas and she told me that special affairs did have to be cut gradually, and that we didn't do it the right way. But she did say one thing I will always remember:

"Marsha, you did the right thing. I believe that anyone who has an affair, whether it is a long-term or short-term, or even a one-night-stand involving a married man or a married woman eventually will be treated the same way by someone they love. They will know the same hurt that their spouse did."

December 12, 2002

It is going to be the loneliest and most miserable Christmas I ever had, and it was. I didn't want to go shopping and told Carl I didn't want anything. The presents I bought for him were just tossed under the tree, unwrapped, without price tags even being taken off.

But I got to thinking about it after the holiday. It was my entire fault. I should have thrown myself into the task of making it a pleasant one and maybe Carl would have at least held and hugged me if the inside and outside of the house, and all the trees were decorated like when we were first married. Also, if I really plunged in and did those things, John would have temporarily been forgotten and the thought of him wouldn't have bothered me so much.

Carl's family did not come over anymore and of course it was a lonely holiday with no friends dropping in either. Christmas is not meant to be lonely. We just hadn't socialized the past year, probably because I was gone so much, therefore we had no close friends to celebrate with and I didn't even think until later that I should have asked Carl if he wanted to have an open house for his business associates.

Why, oh why did I let John spoil another holiday for me? Why oh why didn't I do things around the house to make it look better, to cheer myself and Carl up? And why did I pre-meditate and say the holiday would be the "loneliest and most miserable" one long before it even arrived?

I had to snap out of the fucking funk I was in over John. He was gone, and I had to accept it.

December 20, 2002

As you may have guessed, I started to go out again. This time, it was not on Saturdays, and not in bars near home. I stopped at the Chicago bars after work.

And as you might know, I picked the smaller ones, those that were the least popular and of the least fancy variety.

At 3:30p.m. when getting off work, the clientele was not that great, but they were men. Some were street people and some were factory workers. I met and went to Al's apartment down on Clark Street. I couldn't get used to the hustle-bustle of the city, the buses and the CTA and his apartment was just above one of the small, noisy bars. He was not clean, thanks to his factory job, nor was he the greatest lover. Although I knew his name, I didn't know exactly where he worked. When he went to the bathroom I noticed the refrigerator was almost empty. There was no food and no beers in it, and it needed cleaning.

December 22, 2002

Did you ever go to work looking like shit? I am a crier and once I start, I can't stop. I was in a "downer" state, and couldn't sleep, and looked bad. I wore sun glasses to hide my tears and puffiness, but the rest of my body needed attention. I needed to wash my hair, take a shower, polish my shoes, and just get with the program. At work, they asked what was wrong, and I told them I was up all night, which was the truth. I was one miserable bitch. I tell the nurses: "Oh the damn phone rang all night again. John won't give up on me. Now he's worried about what I want for Christmas. He keeps saying that he wants me. So needless to say, I don't get any sleep."

This shuts them up and they spread this little tidbit of gossip pretty damn fast. I wonder how the nurse he is going with now feels when she hears it.

But I couldn't ever let Carl suspect there was something on my mind. I wear a perpetual smile around him. It has been over a month now since we (John and I) had really been on good terms. And I still can't stop the fucking tears.

Oh yes, there are some good days, or should I say good hours when he's not heavy on my mind. The memories stay.

And if you haven't had an affair like ours, you wouldn't understand. You have to be involved with someone, love him completely, and give every bit of yourself and then some. You have to be on call and ready for him no matter what, 24 hours a day. You let him have his freedom six days a week but you get to see him one day out of seven for three or four hours if you are lucky and you fucking better not ask what he's been doing when he wasn't with you. But he wants to know how you spend every minute of your time when you aren't with him.

Is it fair? I ask you. Hell, no. What he does is his business, but he expects to know every little detail of my doings.

December 23, 2002

Christmas is coming. I don't give a flying fuck. Who ever saw a fuck flying?

December 24, 2002

All I can say is that I had a good day at work. We exchanged names and I happened to get Lorna's, who is a pain. I gave her a 25-cent pencil. Hey, that's not bad. It has Santa on it and writes in two colors. Saundra drew my name and got me a very beautiful spa set with soap, bubble bath, a nice brush, sponge, and a pink bathrobe with slippers to match. At that point I felt somewhat sad about what I gave Lorna, especially since everyone was looking, laughing, and saying, "I wonder what she gave John."

December 25, 2002
Christmas Day

I was lucky enough to be off that day and relaxed. Carl fixed breakfast for me and I enjoyed it. Then he brought out a stack of presents for me.

I had a new white floor-length mink that must have cost him a fortune. There were four sexy sweaters in red, orange, yellow, and white. They had plunging necklines and were decorated with semi-precious stones. I also received a diamond necklace and an ankle bracelet to match. But most of all, I received an actual hug and a passionate kiss and an "I love you."

Did he mean that? Could he mean that? I don't know, but it shocked the shit out of me.

Then he saw his gifts back behind the tree and his smile disappeared. I meant to get them out before we opened gifts but he brought breakfast to me, and everything happened so fast—

He pulled his unwrapped gifts out and opened them one by one. The first was three pairs of black stockings (he already had at least twenty-five pairs) and the next gift was two handkerchiefs which were also left in the original box with no wrapping. The final gift was a wallet, which was inexpensive and something that I knew he would never carry.

He looked at me and said, "So I hope you bought 'him' nicer things than you gave me." With that he walked away. I told him he wouldn't get his gift 'till later.' I told him these gifts were all a joke. He didn't come back downstairs after he walked to our room, but spent most of the day there while I spent it downstairs. There was no fancy dinner prepared by me, but at 4:15 p.m., I told him to get dressed because I was taking him somewhere special. He hesitated, but came out in one of his better suits, black shoes, and black stockings.

When he was in the shower, I made reservations for us to attend the Christmas Dinner Dance at the Country Club and also purchased a special gift that we could get right there. I ordered a diamond ring for him which was a 3k diamond in 18k gold. I loved my husband and would straighten up my life the following day. I know some of you will find this hard to believe as I've said it so often.

Coming home from the dance, I did sit next to him and he didn't push me away. "It is the most exquisite ring I have ever seen. I really mean that," he said to me. It felt so good to hear those words.

December 26, 2002

The year was coming to an end and hopefully my sexual addiction was, too. Sex addition is a kind of steam roller to hell. There is nothing quite like it. The double life I led and the energy it took, and everything else involved with it left me limp. I no longer had any energy. And I can't blame it all on John. It started long before that.

If only people knew and said what they wanted their lover to hear and if only your lover knew exactly how you felt about certain things, it would be so much better. They always say that if you have something to tell someone and can't say it, write it. I thought about that and decided that things between John and I weren't finished until I got something in writing to him. After you write it, they say you should burn it to put and end to it—(Finalize it.)

He hurt me, so I had to hurt him by telling my true feelings. I wrote it and made three copies. I kept one, burned one, and made one for John. My big mistake was sending it to him at work.

"Get it off your Chest, Baby
What I always wanted to say to you"

Dedicated to John

A feeling of sickness and disgust-
Oh baby, how they overpower and infuriate me,
For I once loved you so much.
But the feelings were never mutual, that I can see.
I trusted and believed in you,
and then your flirting and running around began.
It didn't take long to get the message
That our love affair was coming to an end.
I know that you'll never think of me
And know I must start anew.
But it sure as hell won't be
With a run-around guy like you.

It took a while for me to catch on to you,
My sweet long-gone lover.
We have but one life to live,
That's it-
And baby, we reap what we sow.
I must get these feelings off my chest.
I made a new goal.
So long, farewell, thanks for the fun—
Ass hole.

January 5, 2003

I started the New Year out right—I had blood work done and saw Dr. Louise. She just shook her head, and told me there was a slight problem with my kidneys and liver but not to worry about it. Also, my white blood count and red blood counts were slightly off but doctors never go into detail. So I presumed the white count was elevated and the red count was low. She gave me a prescription for Actonel for stronger bones and Ativan in a higher dosage and also something for pain. She told me to get more sleep and see her in six weeks. I marked it on my calendar.

"Dr., I also hear voices which are very unclear. I can't understand then at all. There are gurgling noises and I think I need a vacation. So much has happened to me lately. But I'm going to wade through it. When I try to think clearly I can't. "The Stripper" keeps playing loud and clear. What's happening to me?"

She said she wasn't sure, but that she would converse with Dr. Cynthia Connors and give me a call.

I left her office and went home. The voices were there. I fixed a dinner for Carl, dancing in the nude as I fried pork chops. Oh yes, I did have a scarf on. When I woke up the note was on the kitchen table:

Marsha,
I don't know how to tell you this but lately
your actions have been very bizarre.
Something is wrong.
Maybe you just need a little pill.
Please check into it.
This has been going on for a while.
Carl

He was right. But then I was working on it and I do believe Dr. Cynthia was helping me.

When I went to Dr. Cynthia, coincidentally the same day, I told her about Carl's note. I also told her that my family Dr. was going to talk to her. Once again, I refused to talk about my mother, my father, my stepfather, or my childhood. She sighed and asked if I could talk about my marriages, and I did agree to that.

"Cynthia, I am so bitter about what every man has done to me, during my lifetime. But I will try to talk about it."

"Just remember that you can tell me everything and I will listen and advise when necessary. I will not criticize you. Please, please, when you hear gossip at work, start humming or something. Ignore them. Nobody knows what you have been through."

"Dr. Cynthia, I am bitter about my marriages. I came to Chicago from Anniston, Alabama because of mental and physical abuse from both my mother and stepfather. Fifteen years I put up with it, but could take no more of the unbearable fighting, improper actions, and beatings. I packed two paper bags with my belongings and hitched a ride to my Auntie Beth's in Chicago. She didn't like my mother and I was the only family she had."

"She was a retired school teacher and since my stepfather never let me attend school, she taught me so many things, sent me to grade school, high school, and then on to a four-year college where I majored in Nursing. I graduated in three years as a R.N. Soon after, received my B.S.N."

"I met Bob Tennyson right out of nursing school when I worked in the emergency room alongside him. He was sweet, oh so sweet, and talked me into giving him money to go back to school once we were married, so he could specialize in Obstetric and Gynecology care. Of course I helped him. The school was only one hundred miles away but he said it was too far for me to drive every other weekend when I was not on the nursing schedule."

"Little did I know that my friend, also working in the emergency room as a nurse was seeing him every other weekend when she wasn't working. Nancy Nelson was her name and at the time, she was my best friend."

"When Bob graduated, I threw a big surprise party for him in our back yard. It was my aunt's house that I inherited along with $800,000.00 that she left for me."

"At the party, Bob was so drunk, and got up to make a speech: 'Hi there everybody. Please, may I have your attention? Thank you for coming to my party. It was a lot of hard work to set this up and arrange for the entertainment and flowers, and I hope you enjoy all my efforts here. (He didn't do a damn thing to arrange the party. It was all part of my surprise.) I have an announcement to make." His speech was getting to be more of a drunken slur every second.

"Do you all know the one and only, the beautiful blonde, natural of course, not like Marsha. (That really hurt.) Well, Nancy and I are getting married as soon as I get a divorce from my old lady."

"Nancy was shocked and I remembered falling backwards because I was shocked too. I had prepared for his party for days and he was doing this to me? Someone carried me into the house. That I remembered, but after that, everything was a blank. When I did wake up, everyone was gone and Bob was sitting alone in the grass."

"Oh my God, Marsha! That's how he did it? How cruel. That's horrid." Dr. Cynthia wrote it all down while shaking her long hair.

"I filed for divorce the next day and four weeks later it was finalized and he did marry Nancy, the next week. I married Tom, his best friend, a day later, to get back at him. He was also an emergency room doctor."

"Why ever did you marry again, so soon?"

"Yes, it was one of the biggest mistakes I made. Where Bob abused me mentally, Tom abused me physically. I was his punching bag, and he threw me down the stairs twice. I couldn't take any more bruises or broken arms, or blackened eyes and got tired of going to work with broken teeth and bandages. Tom bragged about what all he did to me long before I showed up at work. With Bob, Tom, Me, and Nancy all working in the emergency room, I knew I had to get out of there. It wasn't too cozy and rosy. And things wouldn't get any better. I just knew it. I received the divorce papers in two weeks and framed them."

"That was it. I couldn't take any more. I had to leave and find a new job and place to live. But I was in no hurry to work right away. I just quit. And that's when I really started running around. I went home with police men, janitors, fire fighters, business men, doctors, workers in stores, anyone I could find. I averaged four guys a night, many nights. I was free once more!

"There was no one to account to. I loved it."

"So now I know about your first two husbands and all the other men that came along after them. What happened next in your life?"

"Well every weekend I drove out west, as I found it so relaxing and this one day I passed a house, and a bell rang in my head. I went back and looked at it and fell in love immediately and had to have it. I pulled in the driveway and saw this older couple who wanted to sell the house as all the children were gone and they wanted to retire in Arizona. They took me through it, and I loved it even more."

"You bought it just like that?"

"I went through it, loved the huge five bedrooms and even though marriage was the farthest thing from my mind, I wanted to adopt children and fill the house with laughter and kids' toys and love. I gave the couple a check for price of the house, which was $350,000. and it was paid in full. They couldn't believe it. But I was dressed fine, and driving a new Lexus and I don't think they believed the check would bounce. They called their lawyer and did paperwork with the realtor and the closing date was set for two weeks later."

"I didn't tell anyone at work, sold my Auntie's house, and just disappeared one night and moved into my Crestfield Hills, Illinois, twelve-room house and I loved it. No more work at St. Gilbert's hospital for me. I got a job the very next day at North Park Rehabilitation in Chicago where I worked as a floor nurse, and I've been there ever since."

"How did I meet Carl?" One day I had a terrible tooth ache and needed attention and he was the only dentist around for miles and miles. His wife had passed away shortly before I met him and he was lonely. He asked if I wanted to go out and I told him "yes." So we started dating. I had to laugh, my first two husbands were doctors and here I was dating a dentist."

"His lease was about to expire so I made the suggestion that he come live with me. I took him to see the house. I had finally arranged furniture, bought new carpeting, and it was a showplace. I don't know what he expected but he had no idea my place was so large and I think, rather elegant. I was just as excited as Carl when I showed him around.

Leading to the back door of the colonial home was a porch with a swing. It opened to a kitchen, and to the left was a Florida room, bright and sunny and done with two colors: orange and yellow. There were ferns and plants all around. Off to the side was the indoor swimming pool with piped in music, tables, and marble surrounding the pool. There was a fully equipped wet bar."

"Like I said, it has five bedrooms, four bathrooms, a family room, a three car garage, full basement, a recreation room and a sitting room."

"Oh Marsha, that sounds beautiful."

"The entire house had huge rooms, and each bedroom has a balcony; three of them had fireplaces. White shag carpeting blanketed all the floors. The furniture upstairs was new, and the piped in music extended throughout the bedrooms."

"Outside the pine trees lining the driveway were separated with annuals, lilies, and small flowering trees. A creek flowed over rocks on the south side of the house."

"Anyhow, Carl and I continued to date and he proposed to me. He had an excellent dental practice and was so tender and polite. His parents attended the wedding along with fifty other friends. His mother did not like me from the beginning. I overheard her talking to Carl in a negative way and Carl came to my defense, and this upset Mrs. Brooke. Both of his parents left at that time, and never come to visit us, to this day."

February 5, 2003

"I walked from my gynecologist's office in tears. 'You can never have children, Mrs. Brooke. You have internal scarring, tears and damage to your uterus that's irreparable. Have you been hurt by someone?"

"Yes, I was hurt by my stepfather, and my Mother, and maybe some day I will be able to talk about it."

"Thanks to my mother and stepfather and the abuse that I endured in childhood, I was unable to ever have a single child or two as I always wanted. This hurt. Carl had finally decided to adopt, but somehow it never got past the talking stage."

"Carl was a good man and we had fun together in those days." Dr. Cynthia noted that past-tense word, and she wrote it on her pad.

"Did you begin dating right away after you married Carl?"

"No, I waited about one month. But I remember on our wedding night when he told me he neither believed in sex, birthdays, drinking, nor smoking, something in me died."

It happened again. I couldn't talk anymore. I just got up, walked out from Dr. Cynthia's office and headed home. How much more could I take?

February 6, 2003

Carl told me his wife could live without sex and he said I could too. He told me not to expect any closeness from him, and that he didn't want to sleep with me. I told him I would sleep with him and that was the cause of our first big fight. To this day, he sleeps on the far side of the bed and I sleep on the other side. If I accidentally touch him, he gives me a slight kick or a slight poke. I got that message fast.

I sat in the Florida room alone the next morning, thinking of John—after all this time. I loved that man and couldn't get him out of my mind. I don't know how John got my phone number. But he called and mentioned my name. "Marsha, Marsha, please talk to me." It took every ounce of will power that I had to bite my lips and not talk to him.

"Dear God. Dear God, please don't let me talk to him." I bit my lip I couldn't start up with him again. I was 9/10 over him, and now this? I wondered what test God was putting me through.

"Oh Marsha, you have a tough one here. Don't give in. Don't talk to him. If you start up again, you can't imagine how hard it will be to stop. Just don't start up again."

I had rehearsed little aphorisms and said them over and over and they did help but only temporarily. I said them slowly. I cried. I said them again, and still wanted to talk to John. Damn, what was it about him?

I said them out loud, and then paused to reflect after each one:

"I can live without him."
"I lived before I met him and will do fine without him."
"It's painful but God will help me."
"Please God, help me."
"I won't weaken and give into this temptation."
"I have respect for this man—but I won't have thoughts of sex."
"God will take these thoughts from me. I won't weaken."
"I don't need this addiction and that's what he is."
"An addiction is hard to break and not healthy."
"I will save money again."
"God made me to be happy."
"I will be happy."
"John should never have come into my life."
"Why did we let him enter my life?"
"They say everything has a reason."
"What the hell was the reason here?"
"I won't be used anymore."
"No more."
"I don't need him anymore."
"I don't need him anymore."
"I don't need him anymore."
"I don't need this jerk."
"I don't want him anymore."
"I won't talk to him anymore."
"I don't need to think of him."
"After what he did to me, I hate him."

John kept calling and asking for me, over and over. I bit my lip harder and said, "I'm sorry, you have the wrong number."

~~~~~
~~~~~

CHAPTER TEN

February 7, 2003

This was the day I didn't feel really happened. Once again I stopped for a beer, without thinking how I had dressed. Hell, it was the middle of winter and I was wearing white shorts, which many of the nurses wore during the summer. My stockings were bright red, and my damn shoes weren't even tied.

I had my top down on the convertible, and it wasn't all that warm out. Everyone was looking at me as I got out of my car, walked up the stairs, did a side swirl, and began singing "Mary Had A Little Lamb." Then I sat down and talked to myself and answered in a different voice.

"You're doing fine, girl."

"Thank you."

I had two beers and three shots, and thanked the bartender. After all, it was his drinks, two tranquilizers and two pain pills that gave me the buzz. That's why I left the $10.00 tip. I went to another bar, hopped up three stairs like a little girl, walked in, and said "Hello, gang." I was happy when everyone turned around to take a look at me. After all, it was a public place and I just felt like dancing and singing and since my shoes weren't tied, I took them off and threw them up and hit the ceiling. Was that cause for five patrons to leave? I popped another Valium.

I started singing, "Schizotypal, Manic Depressive, ("I need a man.")

I waltzed over to the juke box, put money in, and then danced out the front door. I felt as though everyone in the joint was nervous and jittery, wondering what I'd do next as they continued to stare at me. I needed to find that rustic bar and hummed while kicking up my heels and singing all the way to my car. Everyone stared, probably because they never saw a good dancer before. At the end of my performance, I bowed for them.

Once on highway I began talking to myself again. "I am going to stop one more time, have one or two drinks and head for home." But I always said that. It was early and I was calm, but in need of a brew, a sudsy one. I spotted a bar and knew I'd find my man in there. I just knew it.

Ten minutes later

I just couldn't get out of the car. It was too peaceful. I turned the radio on as loud as possible and sang along with Carly Simon. I loved Carly Simon. But the bar music was calling me. It was loud and clear. Then I began my mantra using the tune Carly was singing. There was a slight swing in it, because the words, "You walked into the parlor like you were walking into a yacht—" didn't quite fit my mantra, "Yes, once more. Yes once more. Yes once more. Yes once more." It had to be said four times to work.

I began walking in and singing but felt pains in my blood vessels and spiders in my ears, crawling, squeaking, and felt my arms jerk as my bones began to crumble. I knew for certain once more that the rotting process inside was continuing. I could feel it. Also, someone was following me. I made my way to the favorite bar stool, leaned up against he wall, sat down, and suddenly felt my toe nails beginning to slide off. I took off my shoes and stockings, looked at them, laid them on the bar, and saw only black spots where the toe nails had been.

Slowly, I emptied both stockings on the bar and counted ten toe nails altogether. That's when the bartender came over and wiped off the area where they had fallen. Yes, I was rotting away—slowly but surely.

I continued to sit there, and looked into the mirror and saw new wrinkles and dark circles under my eyes. I had aged fifteen years since morning. I wondered if Carl would even know me. Once I had finished my second beer I began drinking my third. I could feel eyes on me. Someone came over and asked me if I wanted to dance.

"How can we dance?"

"On the dance floor." I looked and sure enough there was one. He told me his name was Tim Benson and he promised to show me a new dance or two. Roxanne was all for that. I think he was the first man to give both his first and last names and that was a damn good start. Roxanne started to pull him away from me and I told her in no uncertain terms that I was entitled to have some fun once in a while, too. I told her to take a long walk on a short pier. She told me to fuck off and then she left. Tim was thoroughly confused hearing this argument in two different voices.

After three dances, he suggested we go to his place and it didn't take me long to say yes. It was me this time, as Roxanne had left so I can't blame things on her.

He wasn't handsome, in fact he was too short and somewhat on the too thin side. But he wore pants. He held my hand, kissed me like a gentleman, and led me to his apartment, then closed the door. Once he closed he door, things changed.

He growled like a bear, with arms swinging and his greasy hair bouncing. It was an uneven cut, and his hair was badly damaged, like it was burned. Also, his face was broken out like a teen-ager, and some of his teeth were missing, and those he had were yellow. Why hadn't I noticed this before? Man, I was getting worse with my choices.

He grabbed my purse, took my cell phone from it, and stuck it in his back farmer jeans pocket, took all my money, credit cards, keys, make up and junk that was in my purse. He also put those things in his pocket. Then things really got scary in my mind. I wasn't sure if it was a man or woman. He was too thin and short to be a man, and too rough to be a woman. He was a "freak."

My nerves made me laugh loudly and he just looked at me. The laughter upset him and he tore off my uniform. It ended up being ripped to shreds. He snapped my bra in back, hurting me, and started hopping up and down. I looked at his flat butt. He put on some lipstick and powder. That did it. Of all things, here I was being kidnapped, stripped, possibly being ready to be killed by a man who liked make-up, and enjoyed hopping and screeching, and I was studying his flat butt.

"I always wanted one of dese. Da cell phone, not da bra. Don't need no bra cause I ain't got no tits. But thanks for da cell phone. He put his hand in his pocket, and fondled my new photo phone. He was unbelievably strong for such a little shit and I tried to grab it back.

"Well, can I at least borrow your telephone to make a call?" I slurred my words. I was loaded, dizzy and confused and wondered how the hell I got the bump on my head.

"Don't got none."

"I don't believe that. Everybody has a phone."

"Not me."

"You big liar."

"No phone—No calls. Simple as dat. I don't need nobody knowing whereabouts the hell I am."

He slapped me, kicked me, and I landed on the dirty floor. Then he shoved me to his bed with sheets that looked like they hadn't been washed in four weeks—maybe five.

He stripped me, and then made awkward attempts at foreplay. He didn't know how to begin to play that game. He was another one who smelled of garlic and stale beer and when he took his shorts off, I saw he had a penis the size of my little finger. Once again I couldn't look. (I'd seen two of these lately and wondered if they were the new style.)

"Damn thing won't work. Give me a hand, will ya?"

"No way. That's not my job."

Then Roxanne chimed in: "Can't hardly see your boy toy, baby boy."

"Shut up," I told her.

"How can I give you a hand if your thing slides through my fingers?"

"Roxanne, shut up."

"Wot's da deal, talking in two voices, bitch."

He grabbed my hands, tied me with chains to the bedposts, and left. I felt like I was in another world because of the cold chains hurting my wrists and ankles. Bells rang, harps played, and I saw angels; then I neither saw or remembered a thing.

~~~~~
~~~~~

CHAPTER ELEVEN

February 8, 2003

I think I woke up, not sure if it was a dream or for real but I felt the chains and knew it was for real. But it was too quiet. The house was much too quiet. My mouth was too dry, my arms and legs felt stiff and dead. I twisted and turned quickly when I saw blood on my pillow and felt the terrible soreness in my entire body. There had to be some noise. I listened. For what—I don't know. There was no wind, no running water, no creaky floors, nothing.

I yanked my arms and the chains moved just enough for my wrists to slip through but I had to work hard at it. They were attached to the bed posts but weren't really secured. I pulled them off and quickly took the ones from my feet. I think the "man of the house" planned to be home watching me but evidently slipped out and that's why they weren't too secure.

I listened. I heard a sound. I had a premonition that something was wrong, and my premonitions were always right. I suddenly felt a breeze, and it was wonderful. Some fresh air in the smelly house would be great. What was this jerk going to do to me? When was he coming back? I heard bumping, thrashing, and whimpers that seemed to coming from the room adjacent to me. It scared the crap out of me. I listened and it grew louder. Whatever it was, it would make good background music for a Halloween movie. Suddenly another voice was heard with it, and then a chorus of voices and my curiosity was aroused so I had to walk towards the sound. It grew louder as I walked towards the door.

I pulled at the door knob and it didn't budge. I pulled harder, and the force jolted me and pushed me backwards into the wall. The door squeaked like hell. I didn't know what to do as I hit the wall with such force. That and the stench from the room almost knocked me over. Slowly, I walked into the room and couldn't believe my eyes. "Dear God, what had I gotten into this time?"

"We knew you'd be in trouble again, and this time we will tell you. It is bad trouble. But we can't stop it now. What happens will just have to happen. You made your bed, so now you have to sleep in it and you have to go with the flow."

~~~~~

Sitting against the wall in that room were six women, completely naked, covered with urine and feces from scratching various parts of their body and transferring the blood and poop, plus some probably had their period, and I saw rats and cockroaches. The women were chained to each other and there were two wooden posts at each side of the two walls where the chains were fastened. Their hair was badly in need of a good shampoo and they were all sitting with their eyes closed, with what appeared to be painful expressions on their faces as perspiration dripped down their bodies. The blood, urine, shit and perspiration was at least one inch deep on the entire floor of the room.

They were all about the same age as me and suddenly I was sicker than before. The man of the house liked older women, ones like me.

The thought of that, and the sight and smell of the women made me throw up. It was added to the collection already there. The heat was turned up to 90 degrees and the radiator was steaming in that room. It was as if he was purposely causing their discomfort as part of the abuse. I didn't want to be the seventh woman there, so I checked to see if Tim had come home or if any other sound was heard.

I grabbed some of his clothes to wear as mine were all ripped. I waited. I listened. There was just a dead silence of nothingness. I closed the door to the room after I told the girls I was going for help. Funny, but these women all looked like helpless little girls.

I then stumbled out the front door and to the road, watching and expecting Tim to pop up out of nowhere to grab me to add to his collection.

I didn't look at the driver of the truck that came past me, but just hopped into his vehicle, and I was hysterical. "Quick, quick, call the police. Six women back there are chained together and dying. Can I use your cell phone?"

"Hold on a minute, honey. Hold on. First of all, who beat the shit out of you? You're all bloody. You're going to the emergency room."

"No. Call the police for those women. I will go to the emergency room afterwards. I just want to make sure they are okay."
~~~~~

"I really don't know what happened." I was telling the truth.
"You must have some idea."
"All I know is this guy picked me up at a bar, and here I am."
"God help them. God help them." The next thing I knew, I fell asleep.

February 8, 2003
Afternoon

"I can't thank you enough for helping me. Those poor women, trapped and starving." I was crying, and he was so sympathetic. Now here was a guy I could easily call "Mr. Perfect."

"Now, don't cry honey. It's all going to work out". Why didn't I look a little better for him? I was all messy, with hair uncombed and make-up missing or smeared. The only trouble was that it was not an opportune time to meet my Mr. Perfect. I knew it.

"The man who took my cell phone also took my car keys but Saundra, my friend has a spare set. I have to call her so I can get out of the parking lot. Could I please make a second call on your phone?"

He handed me his phone but I was too nervous to dial, so he dialed the number, and then he handed the phone back to me.

"I'm on my way," were her words after I told my story. I repeated those words to him.

He squeezed my hand. We pulled into he bar parking lot and I requested that he write down his name and phone number. I handed him a piece of paper and pen. I planned to send him a generous reward for his help. Besides, I honestly wanted to see this man again.

When he finished writing his information, he handed it to me. His name was Jason. He had written on the paper and the information was tucked safely inside my bra, between my boobs.

When arriving at the bar and looking around the parking lot, I was surprised to see that the jerk hadn't taken my car. Saundra arrived thirty minutes later, and I introduced her to Jason. She took his hand and greeted him while offering him thanks for helping me out. Then she looked at me and her only words were, "Marsha. Marsha. Marsha."

"I'll tell them at work that you had a car problem and won't be coming in." Jason stood still, remaining with us and asked me, "Are you sure you're okay? Do you want a ride to the hospital to be checked out?"

He seemed genuinely concerned and wanted to ascertain that all was well and that I was able to drive. He wanted me to go to the emergency room to be checked out before he left and I told him I was fine. I bid him farewell, but hated to see him leave. Saundra thought he was cute and said, "Now that's who you should pick to go out with—someone like him." I thought she was right and wonder sometimes why I picked the losers all the time.

I could hardly stand up, but didn't want him to know that. When he left, I asked if Saundra wanted a beer and she said no, because she had to be at work by 3:00p.m.

"You wouldn't believe what all happened to me. I have to calm down. We walked into the bar the next door down the road, hiding my car in the bushes just in case the jerk "Tim" came looking for it. He of course had my keys, knew my car, and knew where it was. So we had no choice but to hide it.

The bar was set up on the left of the room, and tables were scattered throughout the room. There were three huge windows. All the table cloths were red and white checked and they had candles in wine bottles centered, with salt and pepper alongside them. "Go to the bathroom and wash up. You are all bloody," Saundra said.

I couldn't believe how terrible I looked and I scrubbed until I hurt. Then we sat down at a table, and she ordered a diet cola while I ordered a beer. I was dehydrated, and didn't want to eat, but did order another beer. It tasted so good that I ordered another and Saundra left. I ordered a shot of brandy to go with my beer.

The people at the bar were doing some serious drinking and didn't even look at the table. I was glad because when Saundra left and I was alone I didn't want to worry about any guy approaching me. Time passed.

I danced with an imaginary partner, and no one even looked my way. I had time to think and catch up with my own life.

Time seemed to go by so fast. I don't know where it went. One minute it was 2:00p.m.and Saundra left to go to work and the big old clock in the corner now told me that it was past 11:00pm, almost midnight. I had time for one more beer and that was it.

I was upset with Saundra, because she had to mention again that I should clean up my act as everyone at work was talking about me. Personally, at that point, I didn't give a damn. My only concern, to tell the truth, was what would Carl think when I didn't make it home. I didn't feel like driving, and just wanted to sit and drink. Oh well, I knew he'd divorce me sooner or later.

Saundra had seen me in bad shape so many times, but it was nothing like the present time. I was a friggin mess by this time and began doing the Tango for the patrons, and they loved it. They all clapped as I continued to dance and sway, noticing my balance wasn't that great. I remember singing some crazy song, but don't remember the words. I was loud and a few patrons left, but I kept on dancing and singing.

Many began looking at me as if I were crazy, which I already knew I was. The candles glowed in the bar, and on the tables, which just added a little atmosphere to the room. It was great. I danced faster and faster.

I ordered another beer and was still dancing when the man came in, shaking off the snow and saying, "It's horrible driving out there. I hope no one has far to go. We have an unexpected winter storm warning, and the snow and sleet are coming down like crazy now."

I honestly did not know how far I had to go, where I was, or how I got here. I knew I had to get going, and couldn't procrastinate much longer. I didn't have any gas in the car; it was on empty when I came in hours ago. So I had to gas up, put my shoes back on, and then came the biggie: I had to put my coat on.

Well, it was a biggie all right, and I proceeded to fall, as my heels made me lose my balance. It was then that I realized how bad off I was.

The bartender asked me if I wanted a sandwich or something to eat before I left and I said "no thanks, I have to go." I remember staggering towards the door, with patrons watching me. I waved to all of them. They were shaking their heads as if they were disgusted or worried about me, and I reminded them, "What I do is none of your damn business." I know I came on rather strong but I didn't care. Actually, they were being kind and concerned and I was a bitch.

When I went to pay my tab I remembered Tim had taken my purse, money, and credit cards. I explained this to the bartender and he didn't seem to understand that I **was** telling the truth. It was like inside he was thinking, "Yeah lady. Yeah sure. I believe this story. Sure. Sure."

Then I remembered the emergency $50.00 that I always kept pinned to the lining of my coat. I gave it to him and he gave me 10 cents change. Then I left.

I could barely make it to the car. To say I was unsteady was putting it mildly. I slipped in the mud, stumbled over rocks, and when I neared my car, I grabbed the door handle to keep from falling. The heavy sleet continued as I slipped again in the muddy snow.

My thoughts swirled like the wind and sleet. I thought of the poor girls back at the house, then thought of Tim. What a jerk he was. I then thought of Carl wondering where I was. Did he even care?

I thought of Jason and reached down in my bra to get his phone number. It was gone. Damn. And I had plans to look him up.

The sleet was freezing on the window. Then suddenly my windshield wipers stopped. I could see nothing at all. Visibility: zero. I had no idea what route or city I was in and there wasn't another car on the road.

Then vaguely, I saw headlights. They seemed to be around the bend, but coming closer. They blinded me and I couldn't identify the vehicle that was coming towards me, but it was rather large—like a Mack Truck.

My concentration wasn't fully on driving, I must admit, and I saw the vehicle traveling on my side of the road, at great speed. I continued to sing about the "good old time rock and roll" and suddenly I realized the huge truck was not on my side of the road, but his own. It was me that was in the wrong lane.

I couldn't see my lane, and didn't know if I should go left or right. I continued to drive, hoping he would miss me.

The "thud" I heard caused my car to spin and everything was in slow motion and the humming in my head grew louder. He hadn't avoided me after all. I know that I should never have been on the road in such an inebriated condition, but there was nothing I could do at this point now.

My air bag didn't deploy and I was sliding down to the floor, and then bouncing to the passenger seat, and the next thing I knew, I was flying through the broken windshield, upward, towards a tree. I bounced back to earth and ended up in an area of leaves, twigs, and felt myself sink deeper into the thick scum. I was now saturated with dirty, smelly, water—my very own quagmire of doom. This was it. I knew I'd never make it out alive.

I heard sirens, shrieking, and echoing and wasn't sure if it was the fire department, police, or ambulance. All I knew was that I was soaked, and there was a crowd around where I happened to land but of course no one could see me, buried in the weeds, surrounded by darkness. I could see them as my head was barely above the water, with the rest of my body hidden beneath the leaves and twigs.

Something was crawling around in the icy water, curling around my legs, and every now and then I could feel a little bite.

I heard the sweeping and shoveling of a clean-up crew and I heard them talking. "I wonder what happened to the driver of the Lexus. From what I can see, it looks like a Lexus. There's no one around. How can that be? We looked everywhere, and there's no one around. It's a good thing whoever was in the car made it out in time. But hell, we couldn't see anyone in this darkness, rain and fog, and I sure as hell hope they are indoors as the temperature has dropped down to twenty-eight degrees."

I called for help. They didn't hear me and didn't see me.

My words barely came out, so they couldn't possibly have heard them. The words just seemed to make bubbles in the sludge, allowing me to swallow the dirty slime. I was already sick from not eating and just drinking, and now swallowing the brown sewerage made me throw up. Whatever was in the water was now biting my legs harder and it felt like it was taking chunks of my skin. I moved away from the vomit and cried.

The vehicles left. I was alone. Somewhere. Cold. Alone. Hungry, knowing for sure I was dying. However, being entangled in wet leaves and vegetation above the waters saved my life. What had happened? I couldn't remember. Maybe that was better than knowing. The blowing wind was the only sound I heard, and I wondered if that had covered up my shouting sounds or maybe I was just imagining the wind and shouting. Maybe I was dreaming all of this. I just didn't know.

The stars were twinkling above, and it was a beautiful night, but I was slowly becoming paralyzed and unable to move. No voice was heard to answer me when I called for help and I figured I still hadn't made a sound.

What a feeling, not to be able to communicate with the world and on top of that, I could no longer feel my extremities. They were sore from the biting and I felt as though I was numb below my knees.

I felt a strong wind and the next thing I knew, more sirens were heard. They were coming back to look for me. "I'm over here. I'm over here." They didn't respond and soon I was alone again, still in the swampy waters.

I began to float upwards and my head was about to rise above the branches and junk on top of the water. Would anyone see me now? At least there was more hope for me above the twigs and branches than there would be below them and that meant four gold stars for Marsha. Somehow, I had done it. In fact, the twigs and branches seemed to be holding me up at this time.

The bright morning sun brought some hope, and I secretly laughed, because only two days earlier, I had told myself that it was impossible to sink any lower in life. I sure proved otherwise this time.

Yes, I had hit a dead end and finally recognized this, and only by recognizing a dead end can one make positive changes. I would change. In all ways. I would do it. But I also knew I wouldn't manage to live through this so I wouldn't have to worry about changing. I was slowly freezing and could no longer feel my body parts. I closed my eyes.

~~~~~
~~~~~

CHAPTER TWELVE

March 13, 2003

I opened my eyes, not knowing what day it was or where I was. But I closed them immediately, as I was so comfortably warm and relaxed and everything was fresh, neat and clean. However, the calendar in front of me had to be wrong, for it told me I had lost an entire month. What was wrong with me and where was I? Suddenly I was frightened.

I heard a soft clicking and looked to my left. It was rhythmic with a small sound between clicks. I looked around the room, and saw flowers, everywhere. That's when I saw the source of the clicking sounds. It was an I.V. infusing two medications along with fluids into my arm. I evidently was dehydrated on top everything else. But whatever had happened to me, I was still alive. Everything inside and outside my body hurt, and then slowly things began to come back to me.

I remembered the thud and he swampy water and vaguely remember seeing the young boy on his bicycle passing me alongside the swamp. He left and then came back with help. I was freezing to death out there and the next thing I knew was that I woke after a long nap in a clean, quiet room with a warm comfortable bed and heated blankets.

The warm blankets were heavenly. I pulled them up to my neck, rolled over on my side and noticed blood on the pillow. I felt my head and it was wrapped with bandages. I would ask the nurses when the next pain pills were due. I heard the voices outside the room: "Yes, severe hypothermia. Another few minutes in the elements and she wouldn't have been alive. Right. Somehow she got out of the water and she lay on the dirt and twigs surrounding it when the young man on his bicycle spotted her and called for help. No, we don't know how long. Snake bites all over her legs and lower body. We aren't sure what kind of snake it was, but I think it was a brown water snake. Have you ever seen those suckers? They are so damn scary, as they can grow up to ten feet long, in dark brown, with lighter squares of brown and white on the back and sides. They resemble the cotton mouth, which is venomous and would scare me to death."

"Yes, it seems like she has facial scratches, a broken leg, and cuts from the windshield glass and a severe concussion. She was out of it for one month. A whole month. Yes. That's right. Alcohol level of .18 is not too good for this young lady. Pretty bad. No. She was alone. Nobody with her at the time."

I was alive and could still hear. They were evidently talking about me.

I was still shaky from the dream, scared, as I had another nightmare, about those events happening three years ago. I will never get that friggin dream out of my mind. Over and over, the same dream, and I just had it again:

I don't remember his name, but he was a bartender and I was the waitress. We finished about the same time on the job. My car was parked further away from the building so he said he'd give me a ride to it and I accepted. His car was so old and rusty and he didn't smell too clean. Funny how I always had such a keen sense of smell.

His skin was very dark compared to my blonde complexion and he had little bumps all over his face, hands, and even his arms. He kept drinking more and more while working as he had access to the booze. He kept my glass filled too.

And when he walked with me to my car, he started laughing. He said, "No way, no way. You are coming with me to mine first I'm going to drive you to yours. You're just a little girl and I don't want you walking that far, alone in the dark. Come with Daddy."

He was staggering more and more while walking and when he walked towards his car, I was really frightened. He could hardly stand up, yet he kept drinking from a bottle in his coat pocket. I never expected he would be that kind.

He bent over and reached up my skirt and said, "Oh, you have panties on."

"Of course, what did you expect? I certainly didn't expect this."

"It would have been easier for me if you didn't have any on."

"I am going to scream if you keep up this talk. Shut up, dammit."

He didn't say anymore.

We kept walking, and finally reached his car. He completely undressed me. I was naked.

He then began feeling my body, all over. I didn't want to scream as I didn't want tons of people around to see what was going on.

He forced himself on me and did it again and again and if I acted like I was about to scream, he did it again. He had a little rubber ball at his side and squeezed it and once again, an erection came up. He could go on like this all night just by squeezing the ball to inflate his penile implant.

He smelled so bad I wanted to throw up when he kissed me. But I had to hold it. He threatened that if I told anyone, he would kill me. He did the same thing the next day and the day after. I hurried putting my clothes back on and then I cried from pain.

Afterwards, I couldn't wait to get away from him, and I ran to my car, not even taking time to put my convertible top up and it was 2:00a.m. I was scared. I just wanted to go home to Carl. From then on, I parked my car in another spot.

These events happened to me so many years ago, right after I married Carl. But somehow this dream remained in my mind and I had it over and over.

Often times the nurses would come running as I scared them and half of he patients on the floor with my screaming. I always screamed when I saw him in my dreams.

The nurse walked in my room wearing a crisp white dress and a hat. (I hadn't seen a nurse wear a hat in years.) "Hello, Marsha. I have a pain pill for you, a Mother's little helper pill, and I want to tell you about your lab work. Your gynecologist will be in to talk to you in the morning. You have a serious vaginal infection with herpes. We will have to begin treatment right away. But all in all, just be thankful to be alive, girl."

(If I heard that statement one more time I'd scream my friggin head off!)

"You're a nurse and know better than to take pain pills and tranquilizers every four hours. You don't really need them. You have two addictions already, and now you are taking pain pills like they're candy. Plus you have herpes. And of course you have no idea who you got that from. You better think about it, and tell the other guys you were with that they could expect it too."

"Get out of here. Shut up. Leave me alone."

"Pardon me," said the nurse.

"Who are you talking to, Marsha?"

"Voices in my head."

"Since when?"

They've been really bad for a few months now." It seems as if my slurring was getting worse but I continued to talk in a low-toned whisper. (I wondered who gave me the herpes and who all I gave it to).

"We might need to call someone in to see about those voices, Marsha."

I wondered when the damn relaxing and pain pills would kick in. I was a nervous wreck and hurt all over. I forgot to ask why my head was bandaged, but ten minutes later a nurse came in and informed me that I had a severe concussion. She told me I was out of it for quite a while. (She didn't say how long.)

When she left the room, I kept my ears open because I needed to know what was going on. I was next to the nursing station and they were far from quiet. I couldn't help but listen. (It seems like when you are sick, or really feel terrible, they give you a room next to a nursing station. I wondered why these nurses didn't work. It seemed as if they talked and joked all evening, and of course I couldn't sleep. I always felt like crap in the morning.)

Yes, God was punishing me for the life I had led. I truly believe he does that. He may not do it immediately, but He does get around to it. You can count on that.

They did every test imaginable. (I wondered why Carl hadn't called or visited me. I should have called him, but figured if he cared, he would call me.) People from work streamed in constantly, probably out of curiosity because I certainly can't say they were my friends.

(I missed Carl. I wished he'd call. But the sad truth was that I fucked up another marriage and deep down inside, knew he wouldn't contact me.)

March 14, 2003

A psychiatrist on call came in to visit me the next day. He was a good looking man, not much older than me. I watched him as he looked at my name, and then stared at it, as if he'd heard it before but I didn't know him. He even began talking as if he knew me.

"Good morning, Marsha. You sure have been through a lot. I noticed that he was well-built and had on black shiny shoes and black stockings. He was very handsomely dressed with a suit beneath his lab coat. His blue eyes sparkled and his smile was perfect and showed his bright white teeth.

I sat up in bed and he pulled up a chair next to me and held my hand. We talked quite a while and then got on the subject of voices. I explained that I always had sounds and voices, along with music to entertain me, and he asked me if I was seeing a doctor for this.

I told him that I was seeing Dr. Cynthia Connors and he told me that I was in good hands if she was my doctor. "I've known her for many years and she is the best in her field. I will call her tonight and inform her of your progress. I don't think we need to do any further testing here. If she thinks we do, I will let you know."

He shook my hand politely, and before leaving the room, I asked his name. "Oh, I'm sorry. I forgot to introduce myself. I'm Dr. Connors."

"Is that 'Connors' as in Cynthia?"

He smiled and said, "Yes, I was married to Dr. Cynthia not long ago. I always thought highly of her. I still do."

"It was nice meeting you, Marsha."

"Same here, Dr. Connors."

As he walked out he smiled and winked at me.

I was in a state of shock after he told me his name and now I know what Dr. Cynthia meant when she said we had a lot in common. Life was slowly but truly getting the best of me. It was too much.

Once again I thought about my life I had to change my ways. I had developed a taste for beer and sex (what a combination) and think the two go together. But I could probably do without the beer!

I remained in the state of shock for a while, after hearing the Doctor's name. I repeated over and over, "This is too much of a coincidence. I can't believe life."

March 20, 2003.

I was discharged from the hospital and Saundra drove me home, not knowing what or whom we'd see when we walked into the house. I was so happy to find it empty and put my things down and just collapsed in a chair while Saundra brewed us each a cup of tea.

"Now don't you be in a hurry to return to work. We don't expect you today or tomorrow."

"So what am I supposed to do here, just look at the four walls?" I know this place will drive me nuts and for your information, I plan to return to work in two weeks."

"That's too soon. You've been through too much. Take an extra week or two. You deserve it."

"Don't tell me what to do. In fact, you may leave now. I need to rest."

"Thanks again for the ride."

"What about a car?"

"I already arranged to get a loaner. Thanks again. Goodbye!"

"How about my tea?"

"I'll drink mine; you may take yours with you. Goodbye!"

"How about unpacking?"

"I'll do it. Goodbye!"

She got the message and left, and didn't even call that night to see how I was doing.

I went to bed, and soon heard footsteps. They were Carl's. I had been in bed and wondered what the hell he wanted—again. Hell, he had plenty of time to get his stuff out of here. He had tons of clothes, but he should have them all by now.

He didn't bother to talk to me, but knew I was home because he peeked in the bedroom. Didn't he even care that I was still alive? Didn't he read about the accident in the paper and know I had a good excuse for being gone? Didn't he even care that I totaled the car? He didn't bother to ask how I was. I cried.

I was facing the doorway and had one eye sticking out from under the blanket. There was something different about him. I took a good look, a puzzled glance at my former husband. He looked especially handsome tonight, but there was something different about him. I couldn't put my finger on it; I couldn't figure out what it could be.

Once he left, I couldn't stand the quietness of the house. No way could I ever live in that house alone. Too big. Too quiet. Too many memories. I'd get something smaller, and closer to work. I'd start over, a new life, smarter from experience, and get serious.

Carl was gone from my life. All of a sudden it dawned on me—there was something different about him. Yes! Oh how I wished he had done it sooner, when I was still with him. Too late now.

He had on jeans, white stockings and a pair of tennis shoes. He had changed! I wondered who had talked him into the change in dress.

~~~~~
~~~~~

CHAPTER THIRTEEN

April 13, 2003

I returned to work today. All the nurses "acted" like they missed me. The patients missed me and told me so, and I believed them. The nurses gossiped constantly when I wasn't around, but when I came in the room it was all "hush hush." I did hear, "Who was she with?" and "Imagine drinking like that."

My leg was still in a cast, and I had facial lacerations. Actually it was too soon for me to be working and I knew it, but hopefully at least, Delores would give me a few extra brownie points.

There were "Welcome Back" signs and decorations all over the place, and when Delores saw me coming in, she signaled me into her office. Like Saundra said, I was in trouble and now I knew it. I walked to Delores' office and was shaking;

I soon found out that all the shaking was unnecessary as it turned out to be a friendly visit.

"How are you," she asked. I told her that I was fine but it might be a little too soon for me to come back to work, and she agreed.

"Marsha, I have something to talk about. Can you keep a secret? Lorna, my Assistant Director of Nursing is leaving on May 15, and I agree I am not giving you much time to think about it, but I would like you to take her position and work alongside me."

"Do you think I could handle it?"

"I sure do or I wouldn't have asked you."

"But you have to keep it quiet as two others want this position but you happen to have the most seniority and the best personality. You would be working right here with me and I could help you. But, we have to worry on your tardiness. You are late just about every day."

"Things will be better as I am selling the house in the country and moving closer to work. There will be no excuse for tardiness, plus I am changing my ways."

I couldn't speak for a moment. I thought I would cry. Something good was happening to me. Once again, something good was arising from a bad situation.

"Will I get some training from Lorna?"

"Oh yes, you will work with her for at least a week and I'll be right by you, in the same room, should there be any questions."

"Oh, Marsha, while you were gone, Carl called. He didn't know where you were. I didn't give any information because I figured that was your place."

"Thank you."

"And also, a man dropped off some papers for you, which looked legal and I don't want to ask you about them. He left them here with me because he said he was unable to locate you at home or anywhere and none of his phone calls went through. He was desperate and to save him another trip. I agreed to hold them for you."

My heart pounded, and I was so excited, that the papers finally came, but I couldn't show it. Hell no. I had to look at those papers and begin to cry, put on an act, and that's exactly what I did. I opened the manila envelope and forced the tears to come, then I started to walk away saying, "Oh my God."

"Oh Marsha, I have one other thing to tell you. There's a new patient on your wing. He's a schizophrenic, age 37 and in a bad way. I had to give him to you as your unit is the only one with an open room and also he will fit in with the others just fine. His name is Stanley Stevens. He's friendly, just strange. He arrived last night and I don't know why, but I think he is going to give us problems."

"Okay, thanks. I'll look for him."

I walked to my station I said the words, "Oh my God." over and over. I was saying prayers of happiness, not sorrow. Everyone thought Carl dumped me, but if they only knew how happy I was. I kept a low profile.

My mind played tricks on me all day. I imagined myself drowning in a cup of coffee. I stared at my image in the cup until I was mesmerized and soon felt eyes on me, looking straight through me. Someone was not only watching me, but he was hopping on one leg and buzzing like a bee to get my attention.

I looked up, and realized I'd never seen him before. I asked who he wished to visit and he told me he was a new patient and asked for three Tylenol tablets.

"Oh, you must be Stanley Stevens, the new patient."

"Yes."

"I'm Marsha Brooke."

"Yes, I know. I asked about you and I see your name on the name tag. Happy to meet you toots."

I went over to study his chart and saw that he wasn't allergic to Tylenol so I gave him two of the extra strength variety.

"Can I have three?"

"No, these are equal to three regular ones. They will help you."

"Water please." While I was getting the water, he jumped up on my counter and began dancing for me.

"Don't worry—my special little ditty will take only two minutes." It will be called 'Marsha's ditty," in honor of you, my dear."

"But my medication pass is due now. Can't you do it later, after everyone takes their medication?"

"Nope."

Up on the counter, he said, "Ta da. Ta da." He swayed from left to right, snapped his fingers and told me he liked to dance on counters, especially in bars."

I almost said, "Just like me." But of course I couldn't do that. Then he jumped down and got his tape player and began stripping, and of all songs in the world, 'The Stripper' played.

I was helpless, not being able to tell him to get down, and here I was the charge nurse but I was enjoying his performance. I didn't even see the residents lining up for medication as they were around the corner looking at him. I saw them and I was shocked because Stanley was butt naked and there I was, watching him dance. I was as bad as the residents.

He got down from the counter, and said, "I'm sorry everybody. I guess this was bad timing," but everyone clapped. I didn't know what to do. He introduced himself, and then said, "Miss Marsha, I have this problem. Can we talk later?" He whispered in my ear and no one heard but his closeness to me made them all say: "Way to go, Miss Marsha. Way to go."

Stanley left and I couldn't help but think how much like me he was and I found myself thinking about him and his well-built-for-being-so-skinny-body. I went about my duties and about one hour after dinner, he came to talk to me.

"Miss Marsha, I went out drinking yesterday and really got loaded. I am still loaded, and please forgive me for my actions today. Let me tell you a little of my background. All of the police in this area know me as the one who showers in East Park with the statue of the Grecian Goddess, you know, the one who pours water down on you."

"Well, she pours water down on me, and I have this small bar of soap there, that I keep hidden in one of the stalls. I take my shower and run around to damp dry. The morning before, I had taken my shower as usual, and was running around to dry off. This woman and her small child saw me, completely naked, running around to get dry. The woman started screaming. The police came and hauled me away. It was the twentieth time in two months and they took me to the police station and they told me that they were going to bring me here; they had enough of my behavior, so here I am. When they brought me in, my clothes were soaked. They were in the water and as I washed, I stomped on them to clean them and therefore, had to put them on soaking wet. That's the way I always wash my clothes."

"So when I came to North Park, I was dripping, drunk, and still dancing for your Director of Nursing. The police told me that if you guys couldn't straighten me out, there was no hope for me. So let me tell you, there's a big job ahead of you."

He was tap dancing on the floor, in his tennis shoes, and one doesn't know what an effort it is to tap dance in tennis shoes. He was damn good, and what a cute butt he had.

"Yep, it was 4:00a.m.and no old lady and her daughter should be walking around in the park."

"I remember the lady saying, 'You're disgusting. Little Sarah here has never seen a man with no clothes on.' She covered Sarah's eyes and then began screaming and once again, it was down to the precinct for old Stanley. That's where they prepared the paperwork to bring here for you."

Stanley was a good looking man, about 6'2" tall, and weighing approximately 140 pounds. He was much too thin. His brown piercing eyes and dark brown hair, which was in need of a good shampoo and hair cut, and his tight jeans which showed his ass, were about to rip and he needed some shoe laces. Otherwise he was just fine. The thin jacket was all that he owned and I told him that we would see to it that he got some new clothes and I was going to order a special diet for him—a double portion with extra protein and extra desserts, in order to add a few pounds.

He stared at me and said, "One doesn't know how such a terrible hangover feels."

I shouldn't have said it, but I did. "Oh yes, I sure do."

It was non-professional and he stared at me after I said it and one would think he could see through all my clothing, the way he looked at me. I was sorry immediately for the comment I had just made, but it brought a big chuckle from him and then the comment, "Oh now I know, Miss Marsha."

"Know what?"

"Know that you and I are alike and we are going out to have a beer or two together, mighty soon."

"Yes, I'm a patient here, and a mighty crazy one. Miss Marsha, you should have seen me when I first came in. I looked like a fucking son-of-a-gun Stanley Stevens. They said we are going to put you on the I.W. Unit. What does that mean?"

"That means Intensive Watch, which is my unit. Aren't you a goof ball?"

"Yes, and I love to have a ball, and goof around. You look like you like to have fun, too."

I handed him a tissue for his runny nose.

"Such a lucky nurse you are, babes."

"Why?"

"Because you have me on your unit."

It no longer bothered me that he called me babes or tootsie, or toots. He was harmless, I decided, after just meeting him. And I was usually a good judge of character.

I began dancing and twirling for him, and he laughed. "We are alike. We're both entertainers of the same sort."

Then I heard it. I was imaginary squeaky music coming from the top drawers of my desk, adding to my own private little world of stress and sounds. But at least it kept my mind off he negative subject of my home life. I could feel myself blushing.

All of a sudden, everyone started laughing. Everyone in the med line was going crazy with something I didn't even see. Stanley was behind the counter at my desk, and I walked over and saw him. He was naked, wearing only yellow duck slippers, with a yellow feather behind each ear and he was quacking with a bottle of beer in his hand.

I pulled him aside and told him to straighten up or he'd be out of here and sent to a place where he would be locked up. Then Roxanne stepped in and said, "And I wouldn't like that, honey. I want you here."

He looked at me in a peculiar way, and once again I couldn't explain Roxanne.

I lectured him and kept a straight face, when we talked. How the hell I managed that, I'll never know. No matter how hard I tried to be firm with him, I just couldn't wipe the grin off my face. He was still dancing and hopping and guess what I did?

I stood there laughing, and walked back in the medication room and closed the door, just so I could sober up. I finally finished passing medications and it was time to leave. On the way out of the building, I took a minute to try to talk to Delores, but of course she was gone. She never worked past 4:00p.m.and soon I would be in that category.

I needed to catch her tomorrow and tell her the entire story of the problems with Carl, and eliminate the ones where I wasn't at fault. I had to tell her about Tim and why I never made it home. I left a written report for the nurse coming on, as I didn't want to take the time and give her an oral one.

Anyone who has worked with the mentally ill knows that it puts a severe mental strain on the care giver. M. I. patients have no patience, and think they are justified to require all of your attention.

Most of the patients are men, who serve as a reminder of the different wars they fought in, and returned to the states with a missing leg, arm, or a mental illness—gifts they hadn't bargained for when they went to fight for our country.

I walked out to my car. It was almost 11:00p.m., and the lights in the parking lot were on and I saw the outline of someone or something standing against my car.

~~~~~
~~~~~

CHAPTER FOURTEEN

April 13, 2003
After work

Who was it standing against my car? In a way it bothered me, but I kept walking. I was surprised to see Stanley standing there. Damn. I should have known that it would be him. When my driver side door opened, his also unlocked and he got in.

I was even more surprised when he said, "Marsha, I love you."

He put his arms around me and gave me the biggest kiss on the lips, one that almost made me faint. I blinked my eves, and felt weak all over. He was an experienced kisser, and I wondered what else he was experienced in. Fuck! Another shock for old Marsha!

I drove from the parking lot towards the driveway, forgetting all about stopping for that drink. I even forgot he was with me. He had stayed in the car, and I was so shocked from the kiss that I didn't even notice.

When I told him I had to be at work early in the morning, he kissed me passionately and slowly moved his body out of the car. I pulled away from the parking lot, shaking, perspiring and nervous. Why did he affect me this way?

Then I drove out the driveway, towards the main road and had the feeling that something wasn't quite right. "What the hell now?" I said aloud and kept driving. Glancing back, I saw the shadow of someone lurking along the side of the drive, in the bushes, alongside a tree. And that someone was watching me. I backed up a bit more to see him and he disappeared into the bushes behind him. But before he disappeared, I saw him writing something on a small tablet he took from his pocket. It didn't make sense. Who? Why?

"Find out who is watching you and why. Go back and confront him. It's the beginning of something that's not going to be good. We know. It's urgent that you go back and check it out. Now."

I kept driving.

It was a warm, summery night. I was in the loaner car, as mine was totaled in the accident and I didn't have a chance to get out and buy one yet. All they could give me was a convertible, which I accepted gladly.

I was driving around after work, enjoying the warm, breezy wind, as it danced through my hair. It was heavenly. It was warm inside the facility today, and I felt the perspiration dripping down my hair and neck.

At 2:00a.m., all was peaceful. I found myself driving about fifty miles west, past my house, before I realized it. I should have been home in bed, but Carl would understand if he saw me coming home late again. Besides, I didn't really care what he thought. I was on my own, now.

(It wasn't the newest Pontiac convertible, and seldom did they give out convertibles for loaners. I never did figure out how I ended up with it.)

I was driving through a forest preserve, and no houses, people, or buildings were to be seen. I stopped at the stop sign.

All of a sudden he jumped out at me, and tried to get in the car. Because he frightened me, I don't know what I did, maybe I took my foot off the gas pedal for a second, but it didn't start up again for me. I tried again as the stranger fumbled for my door handle. I could smell the liquor on his breath. It was disgusting, and he was so dirty. I closed my eyes. He was about ready to pull the door open and all of a sudden, after praying for a minute, saying a "Hail Mary" and an "Our Father," to my surprise, this time the car started when I stepped on the gas.

I found myself driving too fast to get back to civilization and areas I knew. My big house never looked as good when I pulled into the driveway.

Once inside I walked over to the sofa, collapsed, and pulled out the remote control. I wondered about the news of the day.

The big news was that of an escaped convict from a local prison that was on the loose. They asked us to be alert because he was dangerous. When I saw his picture on the screen, all I could say was "Oh my God." It was the same man who tried to get in my car.

I walked in the house, and upstairs, without saying a word to Carl. I didn't mention the excitement at work, my new job offer, or the divorce papers. I saw his car in the drive, and knew he was there, but didn't know how long or what he was doing.

April 14, 2003

I still didn't tell Carl about receiving the divorce papers. My day had been too hectic and there were far too many things on my mind.

Yes, Stan was leaning against the car waiting for me, and we joked for a while. "I'll give those nurses something to talk about," he said as he put his arms around me. I know they had all seen him walk out just before me, but I didn't think they could see in the dark. I wasn't worried. I thought about this all night. He had shocked me by asking to borrow $2.00. I gave him $10.00 and said it was a gift.

The next morning I was so anxious to return to work at 7:00a.m. and see him. That's the way it continued to be every day.

Carl stayed for dinner again. We ate in silence. Neither of us spoke a word.

April 20, 2003

I said to Stan, who was standing by my nursing station bright and early, "So tell me about yourself. Do you live nearby?"

He laughed. "I live here for now, maybe for a day or a week. Who knows? I am homeless and live in store fronts, or in the bushes in the park. I love the freedom. Ever since my old lady kicked me out last summer. Can you imagine that? She kicked me out, right down the friggin stairs, with no money, no extra clothes. Nothing! I landed on the sidewalk with a sore ass and back and she stood there laughing. Lucky I had a pair of jeans on, with nothing underneath, but I panhandled and bought some under shorts and tennis shoes. I also got a jacket real cheap but it has more holes than material. In the spring and summer it won't be too bad but come winter, it looks like I will be panhandling. Again."

"How about a drink?"

"No thanks. Put that back in your pocket, Stan. I'll pretend that my eyes never saw it." He did.

As he was walking away, I pulled his chart out from the shelf and noticed it had quite a few blank pages. No one bothered to do any paper work on him and I saw his physical assessment was never done or even started. I called him back.

"Stan, let's do this physical assessment now. No one ever bothered."

"That's because I only wanted you to look at my gorgeous body. I saved it for you. I want to get naked for you and only you."

"You get naked for me and I'll get naked for you," Roxanne said. I hadn't heard from her for a while and her deep voice made me laugh.

I didn't feel like doing a body check then, but at least it would be done. I directed him to the examining room and he took off every single article of clothing, as he hummed, "The Stripper." Oh no. Not that again, to bring back those horrid memories. I watched his body gyrate, and it turned me on, in a way.

I noticed that he had no bruises, scratches or marks on his body. He knew how to shake, flaunt and groove it.

"You probably think I'm skinny. I am. But if it wasn't for Bud, I'd be worse. He owns a bar and feeds me, plus gives me booze and booze money. I love his joint and can hardly wait to take you there."

He began dancing nude and I continued to examine his naked body as he danced around and just happened to rub me with his skinny ass each time he came near me. He kissed me and held his hands out for me to join him but I shook my head and laughed and then he shocked me by reaching down and rubbing my legs and continued moving upwards, then kissed me on the cheek. Why I didn't stop him, I'll never know. All that was happening much too soon for me.

"Come on. Dance with me. Don't be a chicken. Cluck. Cluck."

"No dancing, thank you. I'm working. Besides, this room is much too small and full of junk."

"Nope, I think it's just fine and cozy."

"He pulled me up from the chair, wrapped his arms around my hips, and kissed me on the cheek again. I couldn't help myself. Maybe it was Roxanne. I didn't know. But I put my arms around him, in a friendly sort of way, but I liked the feel of his body. It was firm and muscular, even if it was a bit on the thin side. We both were involved in a passionate kiss, with the music playing, and both standing amidst the mess.

He came in without knocking. I was shocked to see the facility psychiatrist come in and see us in that position. Dr. Donnell walked in to see my pale face turn a brilliant shade of crimson and he told Stanley to put his clothes on.

"I'm here to check a new patient."

"This is the new patient. Stanley Stevens." I didn't know for sure if that was who he was looking for, but I said his name mostly out of nervousness.

"I see you know him already."

"No, not really. I was just doing a body check."

"Oh, is that what you call it? Stanley get dressed and come with me and I'll give you an admittance psychiatric examination. Only with my exam, you won't have to undress, dance, or kiss me."

Stan answered, "Thank goodness."

To me, Dr. Donnell said, "Your actions are a bit unprofessional, Ms. Brooke. Do you do this to all the patients?" He glared at me when he walked away, and Stanley winked at me.

After his exam with Dr. Donnell, Stan walked over by me and talked, just as if he had never left. He began to laugh and was quite the jolly, carefree man for being mentally ill and homeless. I explained that we were going to take him shopping to buy new clothes and he was excited.

"So you won't have to panhandle after all."

He bent over and whispered in my ear, "I'm going out to get a beer tonight. But don't tell anyone." He kissed me on the cheek, and once again Dr. Donnell walked by that very second to get something he forgot, and he gave me a dirty look but didn't say a word.

Later on, however, Dr. Donnell called me and asked if there was anything going on between me and Stanley. He told me that Stanley was a sick and stubborn man, and he wouldn't want me to get mixed up with him. He also told me that he wasn't going to mention anything he saw to anyone.

Stanley left about 2:00p.m. After signing out, and I noticed the name of Connie Phelps right under his. They both signed out together and neither came back that evening.

One patient named Robbie was crawling around on the floor. He said he was an alligator, and he was knocking some of the patients in the medication line off balance and scaring some of the girls when he grabbed their legs or reached up their dresses.

Monty was a bit on the heavy-set side, and she was parading through the facility naked and the men who filled the Pepsi Machine had their thrill of the day.

Alex took $20.00 from some female's purse and bought lottery tickets from the store across the road and told me, "Damn. I almost won on eighteen of them."

Lois was walking around flashing beneath her light-weight long coat.

More alcohol was found in Nancy's toilet tank. She brought it in to keep it cold there. Then they all sat around in the recreation room and mixed it with the soda from the machine and half of them were tipsy, including Stanley. I noticed him with two girls quite a bit of the time, and wondered if he was interested in one or both of them.

One of the girls who was out of the facility quite a bit was Connie Phelps. She was about 25, small and blonde with big blue eyes. She was always smiling. I studied her record and found out that she was schizophrenic. Several times I saw Stanley walking with her, their arms entwined. Yes, I was jealous.

The other girl was Sue Ryder, who was of medium build, with dark hair, and not nearly as cute as Connie. She was about twenty-seven and Stan didn't seem as close to her as he was to Connie, and I never saw Sue and Stan embrace.

It was becoming a habit for him to wait for me after work and on days when I finished at 3:00p.m. I know the nurses saw me out there fooling around and joking. By fooling around, I meant dancing, singing, and just sitting in the car with a little bit of hugging and kissing on the cheek.

April 21, 2003

"Yeah, I heard she picks up men in bars, and now she is starting with our patients." I overheard them saying when I walked in the next morning.

I just began dancing and singing as I walked to my nursing station. I was so happy to give the bitches something to talk about. All day long it was the same thing. They gossiped constantly about who I had been out with the night of the accident and why my husband hadn't visited me in the hospital.

The drive home worried me. My thoughts were on Stan and I couldn't keep him out of my mind. Why would someone I just met be so heavy on my mind? I kept repeating his name, unable to stop. Stanley. Stan. Stanley. Stan. My hands shook and I felt weird.

I continued my drive home that beautiful day in April. It was almost May. The slight, balmy breeze delivered promises of an early summer. It was already a beautiful spring. I certainly hoped it would be a warm, sunny summer as that was my favorite season. (Something in me was trying to talk to me, in a tone of grief, as if it was bad news. Because of the wind I couldn't hear the message.)

The wind was torrential, coming out of nowhere, and it seemed like the beginning of winter once more with snow falling and ice forming from the sleet. The temperature dropped fifteen degrees in twenty minutes. I watched my car thermostat blink and click. I wondered if it was the end of the world.

There were no other cars on the road, and no people or houses around. I didn't have the foggiest idea of what was developing, and began to shiver. The silence and sudden darkness were frightening.

My eyes just couldn't believe the huge blue and white bolts of lightning that flashed across the sky and came too close to my car, and when opening my eyes, I saw a gigantic mounds of fluffy white snow piles on the hood of my new vehicle that I just got yesterday with the insurance settlement from the accident. And how this was happening?

"What the hell? How did it pile up so high and so fast?"

When I looked once again, I noticed the snow beginning to move. It was moving upwards in slow motion, until it stood up and took on the form of people. Oh my God! They were dressed in white like angels. Some snow fell as I drove so slowly, but the angels remained.

I barely had time to roll up the windows before mounds of snow started sliding from the angel bodies and blew into the car. A chill ran through me and even with the windshield wipers going full force, I couldn't see three inches in front of the hood. But the swishing movement continued. That I could see.

God help me. I was alone, in a deserted area, and scared to death. It was too quiet and too bizarre. I felt as though I was in another time zone, another world, completely isolated from civilization.

(It will take three hours to finish this day in my diary. It was a day that will have much impact on my future and I don't want to forget a single detail.)

Was I the only one left on earth? Was this in fact 'earth'?

Flashes of light, glorious shades of light, circled the entire vehicle I was driving and I blinked. I stopped driving. Lights from the angels flashed, confusing me as blue bolts of lightning played tag with white bolts and thunder roared. An extreme brightness prevailed, while everything on me shook.

My hands trembled as did my legs and arms. The sudden darkness was like midnight and made the lights on my car seem so much brighter. It was only 3:20p.m.

Now the entire hood of the car was moving, and I knew it wasn't a hallucination. Then I saw wings—angel wings—flapping? No. Of course not—that couldn't be. But that's what it looked like. There were about ten of them that came up from beneath the snow and they were beautiful, dressed in elegant garments, whiter than the freshly fallen fluff.

I scratched my head and shivered once more, as I pulled over on the shoulder of the road, locked the doors and turned up the heater. Yes, that was what I needed for my chills.

Were they angels? Were they good or bad? How could I tell?

The glowing made everything clear and bright. No this was for real. I was seeing all sorts of things. Then I saw "him." It was a look—alike of Stanley. What was he doing on the hood of my car?

I thought of him day and night and now I saw him on the hood of my car in the form of an angel?

Each angel wore a glistening halo, and all eyes were directly on me. Every one of these angel's eyes looked me over. But I only saw the one that looked like Stanley. He was saying something to me and even though my hearing was perfect, I couldn't understand him.

Maybe he was just moving his lips. I couldn't tell. I didn't hear a single sound coming from him.

The giant angels with flapping wings began going around in circles and Stanley was still there, looking in the window at me. He was crying. I blinked, not believing my eyes. Yes, he was crying.

One of the angels, with the longest, whitest, most shiny gown smiled at me as she knocked on the window. She gently pushed Stanley aside, and I understood what she had to say. She was evidently the Charge Angel, the speaker for the group.

She asked me to roll my window down and said she wanted to talk to me. I didn't know what to do. There I was, on the side of the road, in the middle of nowhere, but I decided to do as the Angel requested.

I had never seen such a glistening halo as the one she had. But then, I had never seen an angel before, wearing a halo, or an angel, period.

If only Carl could have seen me there. The angel began to speak with words that echoed throughout the dense, isolated area.

"We have delivered a man unto you. You should feel honored because out of everyone else in the world, you have been chosen to be his personal Guardian Angel, as long as you both shall live. Take care of

this special man. Protect him from his enemy. And above all, remember that it is a special honor to be chosen to be a Guardian Angel. So do you accept this honor?"

"Yes." (I don't know what made me say that word.)

"We are thankful and you will be, too."

I didn't know who she was, but her face was so familiar. The other angels slowly fluttered their wings as she talked.

Their long white gowns swished and swirled on the hood, bright and sparkling from the glow of the halos as they all slowly inched towards the windshield.

Harp music continued softly, and then it grew louder. I noticed the car radio was also playing harp music and it wasn't even turned on.

The sound was coming from a radio that was "off" and goose bumps began to form on my entire body. I couldn't move. I was frozen to the seat.

The beauty of the angels was indescribable. The Stanley look-alike was soon the closest to my face, just outside the windshield. He said, "Marsha, I love you. This was destined to be."

With that both of us began crying.

The "Charge Angel" or one in command of the group spoke to me once again in a voice that was wavering and changing pitch from high to low.

> *"Show him the light and the way, dear Marsha. Protect Stanley always. Do not let harm or "that enemy" take him from us. The enemy has been his cross to carry for too many years."*

With that comment, she fluttered away and the entire group vanished, just like that. All angels in angelic order were present. The Seraphim, Cherubim, Thrones, Dominations, Virtues, Powers, Principalities, Archangels, and Angels. I knew Stanley was an Archangel. I just knew it. My feelings were strong on this.

I was in a state of shock because as readily as they had appeared on the car hood, they disappeared. I understood the message given to me, but not the part about the enemy. Who was the enemy? How could I protect him from something when I didn't even know what it was that I was protecting him from? As fast as the angels disappeared, normal April weather returned once more.

This was too much for me to fathom. I should have heeded Saundra's advice about going back to work so soon. Or I should have heeded Delores' about taking things a little easier, and here I was trying to do my work, and I was already deeply involved with a patient, accepting a new job, (both at work and as a Guardian Angel.) I was served divorce papers, and suddenly became a superstar of porno.

I wasn't ready for all that had happened to me. I had to go in and talk to Delores tomorrow. I hoped she believed me. I had to tell her everything that happened, everything that put me in the hospital. I was finally going to let them all know that I was not guilty of the things they blamed on me. But, I had to stop for a drink right now. Too much going on. Too much to think about. I looked for that bar.

The car phone rang, and brought me back to reality. I fumbled, fished, and finally found it in my purse before the ringing stopped. Saundra was calling from work.

"Marsha, there is something going on here. I want to warn you. Stan has been asking strange questions about you and waiting for you to return to work tomorrow. He has something to tell you."

"He was talking on the phone to someone named 'Buzz' about you and it didn't sound good. All I heard was the guy's name, and 'yes, it looks good. Fine. She's the one. Let me know when."

"Marsha, he is up to something. Everyone around here thinks he's 'spooky.' I have to agree. He doesn't look or act quite normal and we are all worried about your well-being."

"Thanks for warning me Saundra, but don't worry. I'll be okay."

"By the way, Marsha, for your information, Stanley was out again last night and didn't come back. Connie was out too."

So now I had a new worry. What was Stan planning? But I continued my drive towards home as I counted "thirteen-fourteen-fifteen-sixteen-"

I spotted the bar and went in, looking for my favorite spot to sit. I ordered a tall frosty beer in a mug and asked for extra foam. I thought of Stan. Something puzzled me. I couldn't put my finger on it.

After about fifteen minutes, I felt the tapping on my shoulder. I turned around and saw the most gorgeous specimen of manhood that I had ever seen.

"Do you want another drink, honey?"

"No thanks. I have to get home." I didn't even finish my beer.

I drove home, pulled in the driveway, and Carl was sitting at the kitchen table waiting for me. He had an angry look on his face. "So tell me if you received anything at work from the lawyer. You certainly should have by now."

"Yes, I did, days ago. I wasn't going to mention it as I thought it was all a mistake. You're actually going to go through with this, aren't you? Carl, talk to me! You're going to divorce me after all these years?"

I cried. I know he expected that. The tears were so big that it took three tissues to wipe them away. (Pat me on the back for the acting.) And here Carl thought they were tears of sadness.

"Yes, I'm leaving you. I can't take any more of this. You're a real 'slut' staying out all night again, not telling me where you are."

"How could I tell you if I was involved in a bad accident? I drank too much that evening."

"You know, I even hate walking down the street with you. All the guys keep looking at you and I can't help but wonder how many you have slept with."

"Oh, I've been meaning to ask you. Tell me about all the signs on busses and billboards. When did you become an actress?"

I thought about his question but it didn't really bother me. So what if he knew. How was he NOT going to know with the friggin signs posted everywhere? Did he think "the dentist's wife" didn't have a right to be on billboards in public places? Did he think I was going to ruin his reputation?

I had a new responsibility in life and that was all that mattered. From that point on, I didn't give a damn about Carl. When love is dead, it's dead. Finished. Sad but true. Yes, I wasted all these years on him.

I was a free woman again. I breathed a sigh of relief and went to bed, just thinking about things in general. And suddenly it hit me like a ton of bricks. I had met him. I wasn't planning on it being this way, but Stanley was my "Mr. Perfect." He found me. My own "Mr. Perfect." I actually had found him and was given the extra bonus of being his Guardian Angel.

I just figured I'd meet my special man in a bar. I wasted so much time looking and here, my "Mr. Perfect" had found me.

I was up for hours tonight, writing in my diary. My Diary of Deception. I deceived Carl and myself for so long, and now those days are over for good. I am a new person. I have to write everything, even though I don't feel well.

How am I going to tell Carl, and what will Stanley say when I ask him to marry me?

I plucked two white, glowing feathers from my uniform and carefully held them while thinking of Stanley.

~~~~~
~~~~~

PART THREE

CHAPTER FIFTEEN

April 22, 2003

I continue with this Diary, not feeling well and not knowing how I will manage to finish. I have notes and pieces of paper around, in plastic bags, and I will entrust this task to someone to complete. But for now, let me just say that this Diary is for real, and my memory is going—already I have a limited vocabulary and see mistakes all over the fucking pages. Forgive me. Whoever finishes this for me will be told to leave it as it is, but just finish typing what I have not done and try to get it published. That's the most important thing. I hope readers will find the messages I am trying to pass on.

Marsha

April 22, 2003

He pulled the subject out of a hat. At first Marsha didn't know what her husband was up to. "Quite a good job he did with the signs on the bus." That was all he said.

"What sign on what bus are you talking about, dear husband?"

"Oh, come on now."

"No, I don't know what you are talking about."

"Bull shit." With that he walked away.

"That happened months ago. Forget it."

My daydream continued: Stanley entered the picture, and he was smiling, throwing me kisses, and saying, "Now you know, dear Marsha."

I began to make a plan—a plan about Stan—Stan was my man—and I was going to ask him to marry me just as soon as possible. I'd show that friggin husband of mine.

"I'm tired and going to bed." As I got up to head for the bedroom, there was a knock at the door. I didn't want to see anyone and continued to walk upstairs. Let Carl take care of it.

"Come on, answer this door. I'm sitting and you're already up."

"Well, you just get up and take care of the door. I'm tired."

It seemed like an eternity before Carl made it to the door, opened it, and when he did, in walks this dirty drunk, who pushed his way into the living room. He slurred his words, and was ready to fall over as I walked up the spiral staircase. Thank goodness I was out of their sight. But I could see everything. This man was obviously a stranger to Carl, but not to me. I had to talk to the ass hole, but now wasn't the time.

"Where's Marsha?" Hal bellowed the words that echoed throughout the house.

I thought of Carl's question. So what if people saw my advertisement all over busses and billboards. It was my life and I was Stan's future wife and his present Guardian Angel. I wonder how many fellow angels like me there are in the world, and then thought, "Maybe I am the only one."

Carl told Hal that I was upstairs in bed, and they both started up the stairs to head me off. I quickly and silently crawled into my bed and Hal remarked, "Get her up. I need her body." Carl punched him and Hal punched back.

"Get out of here. This is my house and you have a helluva lot of nerve."

"Come on Buddy. No use fighting over this. Let's go watch the video she made. It's pretty damn good. Speaking of that, it has made us quite a bit of money. I'll give you one-half of the earnings. Here, let me settle up with you." He handed Carl a wad of money, and I felt like telling him that part of it was rightfully mine but they both thought I was asleep, so I just kept my eyes closed as they watched the movie.

I thought of how I hated Hal, and went to sleep with that in mind. I spent the entire night dreaming. Making that movie was one of the worst things I ever did in my life, and here I didn't even know at the time what he was doing. He had destroyed my life—completely and entirely. The pain he caused couldn't be measured. I dedicated my new poem to him:

Night Poem

You are my problem
The reason I drink so much
Why I hurt so bad
The reason I want to cut
My wrists and die.

You are the reason for my pain
Why I can't let anyone in
My problem is you
For making me sin
Over and over again.

You are the cause
Why my heart is so dark
The cause of my depression
Your acts have left a mark
On my life.

You are my destroyer
The reason I sometimes smoke
My emotions were your playthings
To you it was all just a joke
I hurt.

You are my problem
The reason I act the way I do
I hate you for everything
And someday I'll get even
With you.

This was so true. My depression lately was because of what he caused me to do that night and I vowed that someday I would get even with him. Someday, somehow.

I reached over for the telephone, and called the lounge at work. Stan answered the phone, and I told him I had a problem and wanted to meet him for a beer. His answer was simply, "Oh does that sound good."

I could tell he was shocked, but I carefully went out the back door, silently and drove the forty miles east to meet my Guardian Angel charge.

I met him four blocks from the facility, and together we walked into Bud's, where everyone stared at me. When he went to the bathroom, Bud informed me that he hadn't brought in more than a couple of women since he left home and I was the first one with class. "That's the reason they're all staring at you."

As we sat talking, I told Stan that I was so nervous and desperately needed a foamy beer. Bud brought us both one, mine in a frosty mug, and sure enough it had foam. Stan's was in the bottle.

"Oh Stan, I don't know about you, but I think we both needed this beer. I need one for just asking to see you to see me. It made me a nervous wreck and I have to calm down."

"You think you're nervous! I never drank with a nurse before. Supposing someone we know walks in."

"The way I look at it, we're both consenting adults and I am sitting here having a drink with my patient. So what's wrong with that?"

"I'm shivering in my boots."

"Those aren't boots; they're ratty looking tennis shoes." We both cackled at that one.

"My husband was giving me a problem tonight and I had to get out of the house."

"You don't have to explain."

"So I really don't care who sees us. I just don't give a damn anymore."

He didn't comment on my language. "I don't either, toots." (Maybe it was Roxanne, and not me that was talking.)

After five beers, I suggested we leave. What if Carl walked in the bedroom and found me gone. Maybe he was still watching the movie. But just to be safe, I decided we should leave.

Bud smiled at both of us, telling us to have a good night and Stan took my hand after we left Bud's. On the way back, we passed The Republic Hotel, which Stan told me was his other favorite place. "You and I will go there together, soon. That's where I spend much of my time when I'm away from the facility."

I smiled, and said two words: "Oh yes."

And Stan was right. Once I met Bud I knew exactly what he meant about his warmth, kindness, and liking me. Even though every ass hole in the place stared at me, Bud seemed to like me.

That was when I decided that since I was Stanley's Guardian Angel, I didn't have to look for another man or stop at bars for any reason. I would drink my beers at home.

My thoughts changed channels, and I was on Stanley's home base. I thought of him and him only, and wouldn't go looking anymore. And I only hoped feelings of guilt didn't start. Once again, if anyone found out, my job and my marriage would be in danger.

Stanley was not he least bit like Carl, but one needs a change on occasion, as they get tired of having steak every night and long for a hot dog. I laughed, because I knew if I stayed with Stanley, I'd probably end up with a hot dog every night—if I was lucky.

No, this man wasn't a dentist who wore shiny black shoes, but just the opposite. He wore tennis shoes and he was homeless. Maybe that's the change I needed instead of it being from steak to hot dogs. Stan was a rough and rugged man, and looked like one who'd like to make out every chance he had. He surely didn't resemble a cold potato like Carl!

Another thing that bugged me about Carl was that he kept rubbing it in that I was only a R.N. and he was a dentist. "So what," I would tell him. But nevertheless, I felt inferior around this dentist husband, and I surely wouldn't feel inferior around a homeless man.

~~~~~
~~~~~

CHAPTER SIXTEEN

April 23, 2003
Early Morning

Driving home, I had to laugh. My promises didn't last long. I was beginning to find this out, because I had a desperate need to stop for a drink to steady my nerves.

I saw him walk into the bar as I pulled in the parking lot. I never saw such a tall man before. He sat two seats from the place where I usually park my buns at a bar. I sat, we smiled. He moved over towards me and we had two pitchers of beer. It seemed he liked the same brand as I did.

He wore a ring, had curly blonde hair, and big blue eyes, but he was different. I couldn't put my finger on it. But he was not the usual type I ran into when visiting a drinking spa. And that's exactly what this place was. There were fountains all over, and the sound of water thrilled me anyhow, and after sharing three pitchers of beer, we were both relaxed and I was ready to leave.

I was nervous. Was he going to ask me to come to his place? Would he ask to come to mine? Did he have a place away from home that his wife didn't know about? Was he really married, or was the ring just a little "safety" thingy that many men use? I didn't know.

He was not a handsome man, nor was he ugly. Somewhere in the center of the picture was where he came in. Phil was his name, and he wore a blue coat. I couldn't believe it when Roxanne grabbed his arm and he in turn, took mine. He guided me to his car and his hands began to wander immediately as he kissed me. I was frightened. He told me his tale of woe, about not having sex for ten years. Why do men always tell the same story about how they haven't had sex for years because their wife that didn't give them any, when they have so many girl friends on the side, or in Phil's case, I knew better as he had a four year old daughter. Why are these men such liars?

"I love you," Phil whispered.

"How do you know? You just met me."

His cell phone rang and I heard the woman's voice. "Yes dear, I will bring home a gallon of milk." But the woman's voice said, "It was such fun last night, Phil." He finished his lovey-dovey call and the phone rang again.

"Yes, Dear."

"Yes, Dear."

I heard the woman's voice, "Oh Phil. It was the best screw I had in a year. When can I see you again?"

His answer was simply, "Yes, Dear."

"Oh, you can't talk," she asked.

"No, Dear."

"Okay, Dear. I'll talk to you later."

"I am so happy to meet you Marsha." He looked into my eyes and asked to see me the following night. I agreed. Why? I sure as hell didn't know. He certainly didn't have a problem with self-esteem or self-confidence. It was as if he thought every woman he looked at would fall in love with him immediately. His phone rang again and another woman's voice spoke to him.

"Yes, I will bring home a loaf of bread, too."

"Thanks for the weekend and the roses, and your kisses, Phil," was her answer.

"See you soon, Dear."

"That was my wife again. Sorry, Marsha."

"Well, I have to go, anyway." I had to get away from this one.

"I'm free the rest of the week. Can we get together?"

"I'll let you know tomorrow, after I check my calendar."

Little did he know that no matter what, I didn't really want to see him again. It was a strange type of date for me, but there was just something about him that gave me a funny feeling.

He grabbed me and kissed me and I could tell by his well-practiced lips that he'd been around. He wasn't fooling me. I walked to my car, and he blew me another kiss. I did the same.

Our "affair" was to continue for another year. I was used and abused. Then he left me for another, after he had told me how happy he was with me.

He didn't call, and days turned into weeks. He told me how happy he was with his new love. But things didn't work out for them somehow, and I was dumb, stupid, idiotic, and started seeing him again. I saw him all of two times and then he phoned to say, "I have someone else and I'm serious. Let's just end our relationship—make a clean break."

Just like that—it was supposed to end? How stupid can men be? I sat in my room with tears in my eyes, followed by a smile, for another thought poem was beginning to form in my mind. I would write it, burn it, and that would be telling Phil to go to hell.

YOU LIED

Dedicated to Phil

When you looked me in the eyes and said you loved me,
I thought you were "for real."
But I was too blind to see.
You only wanted some pleasure.
You were only a fake.
Now I sit here alone
Thinking of this mistake.
All the things I gave and did for you,
I wish I could take them all back.
But it's too late now.
My heart is dead, broken, black
Maybe I will forgive you someday
For what you did to me.
You can't just end things the way you did.
You don't understand, you just don't see.

I picked up the matches and burned the fucking piece of paper.

I have learned through the years that there are all kinds of men in this world. Basically, they are all alike, but different. One can't begin to fathom the vast difference in their words and actions. I have come to the conclusion that the better they look, and the more money they have, the worse they are as far as being faithful, honest, and good.

April 24, 2003

I was late for work again, and everyone gave me dirty looks. But I was used to them by this time I saw Stanley first thing as I began to walk in the door. "I didn't stay here last night. I'm not coming back."

"Why?"

“Because this place isn’t doing me a bit of good and you are my nurse so whatever we do, whenever we see each other, whatever you can tell me to improve will do just as much good as North Park Rehab. The only person who helped me, anyhow, was you. I will never get over that psychiatrist. Dr Donnell was a trip. He asked me such stupid questions.”

“Really? Like what.”

“I’ll never forget those questions. Like asking me what it means when you hear someone say:

“A rolling stone gathers no moss.”

‘The grass is not greener on the other side of the fence.”

“People who live in glass houses shouldn’t throw stones.”

“A bird in the hand is worth two in the bush.”

Those were his favorites. It told me how any stupid psychiatrist who has to ask a patient those questions, is nuts, more so than the patient.

The next morning I asked him, “So where did you stay last night?”

“At The Republic Hotel”

I went in and found out when getting report from the previous shift nurse, that Connie had checked out for the night at 1:20 a.m. and hadn’t returned to the facility. I began to wonder about things, but told myself not to jump to conclusions.

Later, when I saw Stan, I asked him what Religion he was.”

He told me he was Catholic. He then asked my Religion and I told him the same. Then came the shocker: He asked, “Do you believe in Guardian Angels?” That was all he said, and he smiled.

~~~~~

May 1, 2003

Things continued as normal. Everything was the same at work and Stanley was not there, nor was Connie, quite a bit of the time. She would come to me when I was on duty and say, “I’m going out. My Aunt’s in town. I’ll be gone for two days.” I wondered.

That night after work, I stopped at Bud’s. Stan wasn’t there. I went to The Republic Hotel and was told that Stan was in but didn’t want to be disturbed. I sat out in my car across the street and down about three spaces, and one-half hour later, he came out of the hotel with Connie. They went to Bud’s.

I walked into Bud’s, and sat at the other end of the bar. They were kissing and holding each other, and didn’t even see me. Bud gave me a knowing, sorrowful look as I paid for my beers and left. Neither Connie nor Stan saw me.
~~~~~

I was absolutely shocked, frozen stiff with nerves, and depressed. When I got home and walked into the kitchen, I walked over to my pill stash and took two depression pills instead of one.

May 3, 2003

Stanley called me at work, and asked where I'd been. I told him I worked a lot of overtime, and didn't get a chance to call him or stop at Bud's. He said he was busy too, and so tired that he didn't get a chance to call me. But I did drive to Bud's to find him sitting alone, and he did look worn out, and his color wasn't good. Bud smiled at both of us. "You know, you two make a good looking couple." With that we sat down at the bar and ordered our beers. As expected, mine came in a frosted mug with lots of foam. Bud knew me already. Stan gently rubbed my thighs, and let his hand roam higher. I didn't care. It went under my uniform dress; I didn't care. He held me closely, and kissed me gently on the cheek, then on the lips. My heart beat faster.

The more I saw Connie, dressed so elegantly, I realized she was trying to out-do me and of course I know that no way was she paying for those clothes. Yep, Stanley was supporting her with the money he stole from me.

"More, more." I was practically begging him. I liked his hand on me, under my uniform, and liked for him to feel me.

I couldn't help but think he was special, and was glad that I was picked to be his Guardian Angel.

He began to kiss me passionately, and everyone was watching us. I didn't care. Bud came over and asked if we wanted to use the back room. All three of us just laughed.

I thought about life, and made a decision. No matter what Stanley said or did to me, I wouldn't let him go. I was his Guardian Angel and made a promise. Even though I knew he was untrue to me, I couldn't be without him. I loved my man, my "Mr. Perfect."

Yes, I went to The Republic Hotel that night with him.

On the way there, he asked if he could borrow $50.00 and I gave him a $100.00 bill. I don't know what it was about him, but I felt generous when he was near. Maybe I was one of those women that felt sorry for certain men. I know women like that. Maybe I was sad that he was a schizophrenic, homeless, and had nothing.

We drove to The Republic Hotel, simply because I didn't want to leave my car in the neighborhood of Bud's. I parked it behind the Hotel. Little did I know that the area there was just as bad, if not worse, than by Bud's. Stan guided me through the door, which was of the revolving category, and we shared a section. He stood as close as possible to me, with arms wrapped around me. I couldn't see through the dirty, scratched, plastic between the sections of the circular, revolving door.

He apologized for the dirty plastic windows in the revolving door and the dirty drunks sitting in the foyer.

The carpeting in the entry way was filthy and we went to the glassed-in window, and he greeted the cashier. She said, "Oh, you are back again—I see you have a new friend here." I almost fainted. She had no finesse'—no class whatsoever.

~~~~~
~~~~~

CHAPTER SEVENTEEN

May 3, 2003
Later

Her name was Helen and she quoted us a price of $50.00 for one night. I waited for him to hand her the money. She looked at him. I looked at him. Stan looked at me, and I handed Helen a $100.00 bill. She gave me change and said, "Stan, you can have your regular room." I looked down as we walked. "Bitch. Bitch. Bitch. I do not like you, Bitch." Stan didn't hear me whisper those words.

She buzzed us through a gate and we walked through the pull brass doors of the old elevator. They were the lattice type, designed with plenty of space in between the decorative lattice work on the sliding doors. They didn't close and latch, nor did they lock.

What a first impression I had of that place. The revolving door plastic was filthy with finger prints and dirt. Drunks were lined up along the wall in the lobby drinking their beverage of choice from bottles or cans in paper bags. I was to find out the cashier cage where Helen worked was bullet proof, and the elevator doors were not only defective, but the inside of the elevator smelled of urine and feces, and vomit as did the rest of the entrance area.

We went to the third floor, and I found out that the brown cardboard floor covering in the elevator beneath us was spongy, and then realized it was wet with urine and the floor beneath it was rotten. How the hell we made it to the third floor, I'll never know.

Stan automatically went to room 333 and once in, he grabbed me, pushed me to the dirty bed, and kissed me passionately. That room also smelled of urine and needed a good airing out, but I discovered the windows didn't open as they were painted shut, probably over a hundred years ago, when the friggin Hotel was built.

"Can I run across the street and buy us some beer?" He asked like a little boy, and even though I had enough for the night, I told him yes. He then looked at me and asked for beer money. I was shocked, but still handed him $50.00.

He returned with two twelve-packs of beer and three bottles of apple Schnapps and drank the beers, then the Schnapps while I slept. I was looped already anyhow, but when I woke up to find the liquor gone and Stan on the floor, passed out, I was pissed. So much for my thoughts of "fooling around" and having a drink.

I had asked where the washroom was, as all his room had was one twin sized bed with dirty linen, a sink, one chair, one lamp with no bulb and paint that was falling off the walls, not to mention the cockroaches in the sink and on the walls. When he told me where I could pee, I couldn't believe it. "Go down the hall, take a right, then a left, then a right, and it's three doors down." When I was told that I decided not to go at that time, and just wanted a short nap. I woke up four hours later because the urge was so strong. I called him three times with no answer, and then took my walk down the hall to find the ladies' room. There was no such thing. I found a washroom, and it was shared by everyone on the third floor.

The stalls had no doors, and men were taking showers while women were sitting on the pot across from them. I had to go so bad at that point, and really didn't care. I just peed and left.

I had such an upset stomach, that I called in sick and evidently the Hotel number came up on the caller I.D. "What number are you calling from?" the nurse that answered asked me. "It sure isn't your home phone."

I told her it was none of her business, besides she could see the work "Republic Hotel" and the number on the caller I.D. When going in to work the next day, they all said, "What a rat trap The Republic Hotel is. At least that's what I heard and you know what? You wouldn't catch me going in there for a million dollars."

And you should have seen the look on Connie's face when she walked by my station and overheard one my co-workers say, "So how did you like being at The Republic Hotel, honey?" I didn't answer.

May 5, 2003

I called Bud's and left a message for Stan to call me. Bud said he'd deliver the message and one hour later, Stan called.

"Can I meet you at Bud's about 4:00 this afternoon?" I asked.

"Sure. I'll be there."

"I walked in to Bud's, sat down next to Stan, and Bud brought us both a drink. "Stan, I can't get you off my mind. I think of you in the sunshine and dream of you at night. Will you marry me? My divorce from Carl is final. I know we haven't known each other that long, but I think we could have a little fun and a good life together. I think we have a lot in common."

I could tell Stan was shocked. He was also speechless. Finally, he said, "Are you serious?"

"I certainly am. I need you to stabilize my life. I'm going around in circles without a man. Carl is going to be gone for good now, and I need you, love you, and want you." Roxanne was laying it on pretty thick.

"I just got free from one woman and don't know if I want to be tied down again—at least right now."

"Just remember, I will never tie you down. I will love and cherish you and just think of it this way. We would have an apartment or a home together somewhere, and do things together and I know they would make us both happy."

"I just got divorced, Marsha. I like being free."

I could tell that Bud was standing nearby to hear our conversation and when I looked up at him, he walked away.

"Let me think about it. I'll give you an answer tomorrow."

I knew his answer would be "yes" and I bought drinks for everyone at the bar. Bud put on hot dogs and we all celebrated.

A few of the patrons asked, "Whose birthday is it?" Stanley chimed in, "It's not my birthday but we're celebrating because I might get hitched again."

~~~~~

May 5, 2003

The place got wild. Bells were ringing, and the drums and soft buzzing were making me crazy. The jukebox was blasting and people were shooting pool, and each person was trying to talk louder than the one next to him. I didn't want or need this. I just needed a quiet place where I could sit and cuddle with Stan, hoping he might make his decision that night.

I drank too much, and ended up at The Republic Hotel again, and it was the same old story. I paid for the room and gave him $50.00 for the booze. But this time I didn't go down to the washroom. I peed in the sink. He drank all the booze, and I begged him to come to bed with me, but his head hit the floor, and that's where he slept. In spite of everything, I realized that I still loved him and wanted to marry him. I don't know what the hell was wrong with me.
~~~~~

May 6, 2003

I got up at 6:15 and made it to work on time the next morning. I had the same clothes on. In fact, I slept in them, and three of my co-workers told me that I looked like hell. I surprised them by answering that I felt as bad as they said I looked. I explained that my boy friend was romantic and kept me up all night making love. Don't I wish!

I had a hard time working. This was to be Stanley's decision day. I had no idea, what he'd say. After work, I headed home, just to check on things. Carl had been there again. He didn't take all his clothes at once, purposely, so he could come back many times and check on me. I knew it.

Let him spy on me, for it didn't matter anymore. All I know is that since I had discovered Stan, the search for men ended, so I didn't give a damn about Carl or going out to look for a man to cheer me up. Besides, I proposed to Stan, and couldn't think of cheating on him. No more fluttering around for Marsha.

In the morning, I proceeded to get ready for work and wondered why everyone stared at me but didn't talk. When I walked by Delores, even she didn't talk to me. Fuck them all. I didn't care. I walked to my area with my head held high.

I found out that everyone's problem was that Stan called from the Republic Hotel and told Delores that he was living there now. He also told her that Connie Phelps and Sue Ryder were there with him so she didn't have to worry about where they were. But Delores was upset because no nurse had charted that information in the log book.

I can't begin to explain how I felt when hearing this. I was ready to tell someone that the Guardian Angel crap was coming to an end. Then Delores told me that she had seen Stanley out on the bench on her way home from work a few nights ago, and he was "doing something obscene with Connie." It was the night Delores had to work until 10:00p.m. and she saw them on her way out. I decided then and there to drive home that night. The hell with tracking down Stan and begging him for a decision or anything else.

May 8, 2003

Boring, miserable, disgusting. I hated my job and could hardly wait for the new one to start. Lorna began training me that afternoon, and said she might sneak out a day or two earlier than planned. Originally, she had planned on leaving May 15, but gradually began cutting days. She had to add the comment about how she liked the Christmas present I gave her. Had I known at Christmas time that she would be training me for the new job, I would have bought her something nice. It seemed like all the money I made was spent for gas but I still could have bought her something nice.

I loved my new job and was so thankful for the change. I was officially on my own on May10, a few days earlier than originally planned, and Lorna didn't teach me didly squat. It was all because of the Christmas present. I knew this.

May 10, 2003

None of the other nurses knew of the change, or that Lorna was leaving. I did my first census report and officially entered Stanley as no longer being a resident at North Park Rehab. That was the day Connie came in my office, over by my desk when no one was around, and told me that Stanley was in the hospital with Pneumonia. He was at St. Gilbert's Hospital and after work I went to visit him. He told me that he ran out of money and Helen wouldn't let him sleep at The Republic Hotel and the two nights of sleeping in the rain, on the damp ground under a clump of bushes did him in. I crawled into bed with him and was chased out by one of the nurses who worked there and darned if I didn't know her. We had been kissing and she walked in and said, "You being a nurse should certainly know better. The guy can hardly breathe and you had him in a lip lock for two minutes. That's just what he doesn't need."

"How the hell did you know it was two minutes? Did you stand there the whole time and look at your watch?" "Smart ass." With that she walked out of the room.

I felt guilty, as I was his Guardian Angel, and didn't provide him with money to at least stay in a hotel and out of the elements. But he was too fucking stubborn to ask me, and too stubborn to stay with me at my house. But I certainly would have given him some cash if he had come to me. I was more intent on finding a place for us to live after he was out of the hospital. I left him to go home, kissing him goodbye and making sure the lip lock lasted only one minute.

I was driving on Lake Shore Drive and spotted a "For Sale" sign in an upper level window of a new round condominium building. I slowed down, went to a side street, and parked in front of the building, then looked up. It was on the fourteenth floor. I couldn't leave my car there, but found a spot on one of the side streets, parked it, and walked over to the building. Once I found out the owner's name, I called him and he was there within ten minutes.

While waiting for him, I became manic, and danced in the entry way. A couple of the residents of the building walked in and saw me and stood and watched. The man asked if I lived there, and I told him, "Not yet." He whispered to his wife, "That's all we need here." Then they both walked away whispering."

"Yes. I agree." I began whispering to Roxanne and then said it out loud to them.

Mr. Jeffries, the owner asked how much money I could put down. I couldn't believe how beautiful "my new condo" was, and knew I had to have it. I knew Stanley would love it too. The front windows looked down on Lake Michigan, and it was so spacious. It had a living room, dining room, recreation room, kitchen, two bedrooms, and two bathrooms. The walls were freshly painted and the carpeting was new.

I explained that I had a house forty miles west, and that I would ask $370,000 for it. That was $20,000 more than I paid for it. I told him that I would get money from my account at the bank and give him $100,000. down and he was quite happy. I told him that as soon as my house sold, I would pay off the balance on the condo.

I expected the house to sell as fast as I bought it. I planned to do some work around it, maybe a little painting, and thought that seeing as how I bought the condo, Stanley would be happy to help me paint.

The price of the Condo was $400,000. and I withdrew $100,000. from my savings account that I had from Aunt Beth's estate. I had carefully invested $300.000. and put $200,000. in the bank savings account. After taking out the $100,000., there would still be $100,000. to fall back on.

That night when I visited Stanley in the hospital, I told him that I found a place for us to live but wouldn't tell him where. The owner told me the unit had been vacant for six months, and that the former couple just left, without any notice. He was anxious to sell it again and told me that I could take possession immediately. I was thrilled.

Stan's condition was stable, and he only remained in the hospital for a total of three days.

I went to see him the night before he came home. I told him I'd pick him up at 9:00 in the morning, as his doctor was due in at 7:00 or 8:00 o'clock to release him. Stan didn't recognize me and asked who I was. He called me "June," and this hurt. I wasn't sure who June was, but he didn't mention Connie and this made me feel better. Maybe June was his wife's name, and I planned to ask him that when he was released.

I left the hospital and headed for my home in the country, figuring that two days of work would get it ready to put on the market.

May 11, 2003

I had worked until 3:00 a.m. scrubbing and cleaning. I did get some rest and then headed in to Chicago to pick Stan up and either take him home with me or drop him off at The Republic Hotel or even the condo which would let him sleep on soft carpeting in a warm place, a good choice compared to sleeping on the damp ground outdoors.

Thank goodness it was a day off for me. I didn't have to worry about coming in for the 3-11p.m. shift and just wouldn't answer my cell or home phone unless I knew who it was.

I asked Stan if he wanted to go to the house with me, and he said, "No, June. I have work to do in the market." I didn't know what he meant. I asked him where the market was and he said he'd direct me. He directed me all right. I dropped him off at Bud's.

"Can I come in and have a drink with you?" I asked.

"They don't serve liquor here. This is the market."

I asked if I could come in with him, and he told me, "No, because the train was due any minute. "Just go home, June, and I will see you tomorrow."

I wasn't sure of what he meant. He was thoroughly confused and had me as confused as he was. I almost cried, but I did go back to the house to do some more work. Then I went shopping for furnishings for our new home. I bought a sofa, two chairs, a television, white shag carpeting throw rugs for heavy traffic areas in all rooms to cover the shag carpeting that was already down, a king size bed, two dressers, and two lamps and end tables, a kitchen table, and chairs to match. I bought furniture for our recreation room, towels for the bathroom, new sterling silver, every-day silver and two sets of dishes. I bought two sets of pots and pans so I had plenty to choose from when cooking, place mats for the dining room table, a new hutch, and tons of candles. I loved candles, in all colors, for all the rooms. The furniture was to be delivered the following day.

Then I went to buy groceries. I bought all kinds of food, and had enough to feed an army. Stan would be happy about that. And I bought five twelve packs of beer, vodka, schnapps, and a variety of mixes if we were in the mood. I put them in the condo refrigerator. I was extremely happy and wrote all this down for Dr. Cynthia. Man, did I spend a fortune!

I had cleaned the condo thoroughly and was told that someone would steam clean the carpeting but it was not really necessary. When I wrote in my little book, Dr. Cynthia would be almost as happy as I am just to see me in better spirits.

May 11, 2003
Later that afternoon

I stopped to have a hamburger and a beer at a local bar, and then headed home. I didn't look or talk to any strangers, and was very relieved to walk in my back door and lock it. I did not sleep worth shit.

I had been seeing Dr. Cynthia on a regular basis, and knew I was due again. I had much to talk over with her and was glad that I did have the appointment tomorrow. That way I could see her in the morning, be with Stan in the afternoon and be there for the furniture delivery, and supervise North Park Rehab on the 11-7a.m. shift. This was one of the reasons Delores hired me for the job, and asked me if I'd be willing to pull night shifts on occasion and check on the staff. I agreed. The CNAs weren't too happy about that.

May 12, 2003
Afternoon

"Dr. Cynthia, I think I'm having a Schizotypal Personality Disorder attack. I was fine yesterday, woke up feeling great, and ever since noon, everything seems to bother me. I see things that aren't there. Or maybe they are, but it's all so strange. For example, last night I woke up and there were angel feathers all over the bedroom. I even tripped on a halo. This happened once before. And the wind was talking to me last night. But most of the time the voices in my head were so loud, I didn't know what the wind was saying. I feel so mixed up and unsure of things. For example, I asked my boy friend to marry me, and he never answered. Of course he was in the hospital and I haven't had a chance to sit and talk to him since he's out. He's acting strange, too. I don't know what's wrong with me, because I don't feel like myself. Something is really wrong with me, too."

"Like what. Tell me."

"Like-I think Stanley is cheating on me. I can't put up with him sometimes, and here we aren't even engaged. I feel him staring at me when we are together. The other day he asked me what was wrong because I hadn't been combing my hair or wearing clean clothing like I used to do. This is true. But Dr. Cynthia, some days I wake up so tired, and don't even care. I don't even know who I am, as I have different moods. And the funny thing is I can't make my mind up for hours sometimes, but I saw the Condo I liked and bought it just like that. What do you think is going on with me?"

"I wonder about my mother. It's funny, because I haven't seen her in over twenty years, and the past few weeks, that's all I've been thinking about when I haven't been thinking of Stanley. Remember, I told you all about him last time I was here? Well, he's procrastinating about giving me an answer about marriage, but maybe that's good because it's giving us both a chance to think about marrying me."

"I finally broke down and went to The Republic Hotel with him a. few times. What a place. There were cockroaches in my slippers, and rats in the hall. If I ever see that friggin place again, it will be too soon. You know, I still want to be with Stan even though he has done some rotten things to me, but I still feel love for Carl. And John is with me always. I just feel suicidal at times because I have so much on my mind."

"Marsha, are you suicidal now?"

"No, not now. But I never know."

"Promise when you are, you will call me immediately. I can help you."

"Marsha, think about this. You mentioned three men. Which one do you really want? I'm going to leave the room to let you think. I expect an answer when I return."

I thought and thought and finally arrived at an answer, and when she returned, I told her, "I want to be with Stanley. He's my Mr. Perfect and I want him and nobody else. No matter what he does to me, I want him."

She sat down with her yellow legal pad that she had been writing on and said, "Marsha, if that's what you want, go for it."

"Marsha, are you sure that you want a homeless schizophrenic for a husband?"

I didn't want to get on that subject, so I changed it.

"Dr. Cynthia, do you think I am a nymphomaniac?"

"Wow, what a change-of-subject question. Why would you think that?"

"Because I want sex all of the time and Stan hasn't wanted it once when we are together. Maybe he thinks it's too early in our relationship, but what the hell, we are going to be married. So what's the big deal? Maybe I should give it just a little more time. I guess I am overly anxious and over-sexed."

"Marsha, almost any woman who enjoys sex could be diagnosed as a nymphomaniac by some medical specialist, especially if she has a sex drive stronger than that of her male companion. It was actually a diagnosis given to women who liked sex more than what they thought was the normal amount. But what is the normal amount? Don't worry about it. Things will work out. He is a man, and all men want sex, sooner or later, usually sooner!"

"If I am in a bar and have a few drinks, I want it badly. All the guys look at me and I guess they all figure this and I end up going home with them. They probably think I am waiting there to be picked up by one of them. A man can sit at a bar alone and drink, but if a woman does that, right away people think she is looking for someone."

"I know, and it really isn't fair."

"Marsha, did you know that at least 50% of all married woman are living with a husband who has been or will be unfaithful—although some experts and surveys claim this number could be higher. But what makes the world of infidelity so different today from a generation ago is the number of women who are playing the same game. Women are catching up to men with these statistics. The times in marriage that are most vulnerable for cheating are at four years, fifteen years, and thirty years for some reasons. Women cheat because they are looking for something they don't get from their husbands. So when you see a man sitting at a bar alone, or a woman sitting alone, think of these things. It may not be so innocent after all."

"And you know, sex addicts aren't over-sexed, and they're not people making excuses for deliciously bad behavior. They're people without any real intimacy in life and they keep searching. Sex is a powerful addictive, substitute for loneliness because for a few minutes it fills the emptiness. And that fleeting comfort keeps you coming back for more."

"So you don't think I am a nymphomaniac? I beg to differ, but if you say I'm not, I'll let it go at that."

"Now getting back to my subject, why would you want a homeless schizophrenic when you could have a wealthy man?"

I didn't answer.

"Marsha, it all goes back to self-esteem. Let me give you an example. This is not you I'm talking about, by the way: There is a woman with very low self-esteem. Perhaps her parents didn't allow her to feel good about herself, and she grew up feeling that she was no good or inadequate. So what does she do? She marries the first man who comes along, thinking no other man will want her. Because her self-esteem is low, she figures that she couldn't do any better in finding a man, so she better grab this one fast. After a few weeks, she realizes that a terrible mistake has been made. Two years later she wants out of the marriage. We get ourselves into predicaments because of how we feel or don't feel about ourselves. I want you to always remember this: Before you can love anyone else in this world, you must love yourself. And you must carry your head high, and know you are just as good as the guy walking down the hallway behind you."

Later, Same Day

I was on time for the furniture delivery, and it was placed exactly where I wanted it. It only took forty-five minutes. Then I went to Bud's, and Stanley was there alone. I sat next to him, and he was deep in thought. He didn't look so good, and I asked him if he had made a decision yet.

"I just want you to know that I am allergic to work. So don't expect me to support you. I need an allowance, besides you buying the groceries and paying the rent and utilities."

"How much allowance did you have in mind, hon?"

"I thought $200 per week would be fair. What do you think?"

"That seems a little high, with me buying the groceries and paying the bills, including doctors, hospital, and medicine."

"It's either $200.00 or no marriage."

I wanted him so badly that I really didn't have a choice. I told him, "Okay, I can arrange for you to have that extra money. We can work it out."

"Will you spend the night with me? And regarding marriage, the answer is yes."

"Oh Stan. I am the happiest woman in the world. How about coming to see the place I picked out for us after we eat?"

"I don't know about that. I'm not in the mood."

"I insist. I have been looking for weeks and weeks and finally found this place and you have to at least come look at it—that's an order."

"And then we go back to The Republic Hotel. Right?"

"If that's what you want, okay."

"That's what I want."

"I was thinking we could sleep in the new place, on the carpeting, with the windows open if you don't like the bed and want to sleep on it. I know you like to sleep in the fresh air and this would be just like sleeping outdoors. You could even hear Lake Michigan hitting the shore."

"Hell no. We're going to The Republic Hotel."

"Will you make a quick trip home with me and let me check on things and I'll be back, and yes, we'll see the new place and I will spend the night with you here at The Republic Hotel."

"I don't want to go but will wait for you here."

I drove home. Millions of thoughts crossed my mind. I prayed, meditated, and talked to God. I needed some answers. I needed some answers. Did I really want to marry Stan? Had I really seen those angel feathers and the halo? Did angels really talk to me? Was I cracking up?

When I arrived home, I went to get a change of clothes, and found out that all of my clothes were gone. Everything. All my dresser drawers were also cleaned out. I went to the safe and all my jewelry was gone, except for a few things. What was I going to do? I no longer had that house, and now had no clothes. In the kitchen I found the note:

Okay, Marsha.
You found someone else.
I am happy for you.
I took care of you and did a super job.
You wanted for nothing but still had to fool around.
Let your new man buy your clothes this time.
I gave your things to the Salvation Army.
Maybe someone will appreciate them. You sure didn't. You didn't appreciate me, either.
Carl

~~~~~
~~~~~

CHAPTER EIGHTEEN

May 18, 2003

I double checked, and sure enough, there was nothing of mine left except a few pieces of jewelry, and for some reason, I left them. I headed back to Stan and told him about my clothes being gone. He didn't seem worried and told me that if I had nice stuff once, I'd have it again. "After all, you make good money. You can buy more just like you did the time before. Don't worry about it."

"I planned on bringing my things from the house with me to start anew with you. My things were new, and the best quality. I could never go out now and replace things because my money now will go for you and me and our home."

"Oh, I feel so sorry for you, Miss-Hoity-Toity. You'll just have to panhandle for it like I do if you don't have enough money to buy it from your pay check." Damn, I didn't like his attitude. It was disgusting, lazy, and made me want to kick him in the balls. He took it much too lightly. I had all designer clothes, boots, coats, hats, sweaters, and everything was gone. With Stanley, I knew I'd never have a life such as I had with Carl. I had everything and I was so sick about what I could be missing that I almost threw up. But I loved Stan. I was his Guardian Angel. We headed back to Bud's, with ears ringing like I've never heard before.

I couldn't stand the noise in Bud's. I was a wreck thinking of what all I lost. Once more, my ears were vibrating. I wouldn't even mind going to The Republic at that time, just to rest my ears, head and tired brain. But Stan told Bud, "Hey Bud. It's dinner time. How about fixing us something?" Stan knew that I hadn't eaten and I suggested going to a nice restaurant and getting something special.

"No, Bud can cook just as well as them." And the next thing you know, we had hot dogs in front of us, with chips. The buns had green around the edges and the hot dogs didn't resemble meat of any kind that I know. Even the potato chips were stale. But I told myself that I'd better get used to it if I was going to stay with Stan. And there was nothing that I wanted more, nothing in the whole wide world.

Then, he shocked me. "Let's go to see our new place now." But he had to add: "Might as well get it over with." I couldn't believe his lack of enthusiasm. I guess I was just in a bad mood, but if I was, it was because he had dragged me down.

"Okay, we can go see it if you want. You wouldn't go with me to help pick it out, so I sure as hell hope you like it. And that also goes for the furniture I ordered."

"I'm sure I will like whatever you pick out. Let's celebrate." We toasted our new place and I bought drinks for everyone. After a few drinks, I had to coax Stan again to go with me to look at the condo, and reluctantly we left to head in that direction. We looked it over from the outside, and then I gave him one of the keys.

"What's this for?"

"It's a key for our new place."

"But, we don't need fucking keys. Everyone will know it's our territory."

He was actually angry, but he did go with me. "Oh shit. An elevator? Do you mean I have to take this damn thing every time I want to go to my fucking own territory?"

I didn't quite understand the "territory" bit, but told him, "Yes," When we arrived inside the foyer, I led him to the windowed elevator and said, "Look what a beautiful view we will have while riding up to our place everyday." I began dancing and singing; with my skirt flying, and since we were the only two on the elevator, I had plenty of room to do my ballerina act.

"Maybe you will have fun, but not me. Hell, I hate heights and also how fast this baby rises to the roof." During the entire ride, he sat on the floor, by the window with his eyes closed with his tongue sticking out at the people below.

"And you say it's on the 14th floor? Holy shit! I knew I should have come with you when you picked out a place for us."

"Yep, this high-rise place wouldn't be my choice. It's a little too fancy for me. Hey, I'm used to sleeping in woods and cardboard boxes. This is too much of a change. I don't know if I can handle a change like this."

"Hey, cut it out. Give it a chance. I looked for a place like this for a long time, finally found and bought it, and plan on finishing payments for it soon, without any help from you. Now, all *you* do is criticize."

"Any guy would be happy to live in a place like this, completely bought and paid for by his girl friend. And all you do is moan and groan." I started to cry.

He did take his key, and put it in his back pocked. "Damn," he said.

I showed him around the condo, and all he did was complain and find fault with that, too. I told him how sunny the living room was and that all day the sun would shine in directly on him. "I don't like the sun shining in my eyes all day."

I told him how the bathroom had a whirlpool tub. "Whirlpools make me nervous. They make me feel like I am drowning, being pulled under by a green monster."

I told him how big the bedroom was and that it even had a hot tub on the balcony. "Hot tubs are a waste of time and money. Look at the expense to keep the water clean and hot without being too hot." I reminded him that I was paying the bills and I happened to like hot tubs.

I finally gave up on it, and said, "Let's go." On the way down, he asked what we would do if there was a fire in the building. I told him we would take the stairs. "I don't like stairs. They bother my legs. My legs and feet are sensitive." I told him that if that were the case, he'd have to stay on the fourteenth floor and burn.

"You know, a condominium isn't something new to me, Miss Hoity-toity. I sleep in them many a night. I sneak in behind people who live in them and sleep under the stairway or by the mailboxes or hide behind a plant. So what's the big deal for you?"

"Let's go eat. At least let me take you out for a fancy, special dinner before we go back and start drinking at Bud's. We went to the "Prime Rib" and that's what I ordered. He had a hamburger deluxe. This time he grabbed the ketchup and poured it all over his arm and began screaming. "I cut myself. I'm bleeding to death. Help. Call an ambulance."

Somebody did call an ambulance, and when it arrived, he promptly wiped off the ketchup and laughed his friggin head off. I told him it wasn't funny and the ambulance company gave him the bill which he handed to me. I paid the $250.00 cost (the charge for taking him to a hospital) Needless to say, I couldn't finish my dinner I was so pissed on. (Not off, but *on.)*

Then he began to sing. He stood up on our table, right in the middle, and began stripping. He was down to his Jockey shorts and the manager came over and told Stan to sit down and act like a dignified patron, which was the wrong thing for him to say because Stan began shouting and blubbering then squirted mustard at the manager's shirt, and we were both chased out.

On the way out, I began singing and dancing to divert the attention from Stan to me.

"Have you been taking your medication, Stanley?"

"No."

"How about you?"

"No."

I cried and screamed hysterically while Stan began to laugh and then I laughed and Stan screamed, and we both began skipping down the street."1-2-3-, look at me -4-5-6-, we do tricks." We are not taking our medication.

We headed for Bud's, and had 2 beers and I went to pay but noticed my wallet was empty. I was shocked. I had $200.00 in it just one hour before and didn't spend any more since then, so Bud paid. I was silent as we went to The Republic Hotel because I know who took the money. That, plus the fact that he still refused to officially move into the condo upset me.

May 26, 2003

It was a beautiful wedding day. I had on an off-white wedding gown, with a long train, a special order dress from France. Little did I know that Stan was going to refuse a church wedding at the last minute and insist that we get married in City Hall. "Church weddings don't last any longer than those performed by a justice of the peace." My dress was far too elegant for a city hall wedding. It was purchased believing we'd have a church wedding.

When Stan came out of the room he wasn't dressed in the tuxedo I ordered but was wearing jeans, full of holes, and a tee shirt, along with the ratty looking tennis shoes. His black formal shoes and tie, pants, jacket, and tie clasps remained in the bag. And on top of it he adjusted his baseball cap as he said, "I'm ready. Let's go." At least he had taken off the tee shirt that advertised beer.

I had sent special invitations to approximately 125 people and only 22 were present. The room was decorated with flowers everywhere, even on the chairs. But it hurt to see only 22 people there. Afterwards, I had a dinner planned at a nearby Hotel, and arrangements were made for Stan and me to stay at the hotel bridal suite. I lost my $500.00 deposit.

Stan informed me that my plans were too "hoity-toity" for him and he wanted to go to Bud's and have pretzels and beer instead. He told me that was what all normal people had. So all the food at the hotel went to waste, the people left and went home, and I lost my deposit on the banquet table as well as the honeymoon suite. At least on the way out, and walking around, I found a few people who were hungry and told them to enjoy the buffet.

Needless to say, no one wanted to go to Bud's with us, and when we walked in, everyone looked at me, and considered Stan to be dressed just fine. Bud made a comment that helped me: "Marsha, you look beautiful."

"Yes, she looks like Miss-Goody-Two-Shoes," was San's reply. Stan played pool while I cried but Bud comforted me. (Bud understood my disappointment about wanting to be married in Church, and then ending up in City Hall.)

Later when Stan lighted on the barstool by me, I told him that at least we could go to the condo for our wedding night. His reply was, "What's so damn different about a wedding night?"

"If you don't know, I won't tell you."

"You go wherever you want; I'm sleeping on the beach. It's a nice night."

~~~~~
~~~~~

CHAPTER NINETEEN

May 26, 2003

We spent our wedding night with Stan on the beach, and me in the condo. He told me that if I slept with him on the beach I would live to a ripe old age and be beautiful forever. He told me it was an old English Proverb: "She who spends her wedding night in her gown, on the sands of Lake Michigan will live to be old, wealthy and wise, and forever beautiful." He then proceeded to do a sexy little dance for me, and I didn't even want to watch.

I told him, that I was going to sleep in comfort, in my own condo, and if he felt like it, he could come visit me later. I went to the condo, took a shower, and put on my white wedding night negligee and slippers with fur, and was ready and waiting for him. He came in at 3:00a.m. and ripped a blanked off the bed and left. "Its cold by the Lake," he said. "By the way, you look like a two-bit floozy in your gown." He left.

You can't imagine how cheap I felt. I felt like a dirty slut. No man had ever talked like that to me before. He was absolutely disgusting, and even though I may have loved him, I did *not* like him. After all, it was our wedding night, and I was disgusted when he barged in and talked that way he did to me, grabbed my blanket, and left. I knew he didn't go back to the lake, so I drove and went into Bud's, and sure enough, Stanley was there alone—on our wedding night, taking a beer break alone, leaving his "floozy" at the condo.

I was nervous but said, "I counted on being with you on our wedding night. What a way to start a marriage. All the plans were made and to get married at St. Bart's Church. I can't believe you did this to me—and now we aren't even sleeping together on our first night?" I had to say it in one breath for fear I would chicken out and begin to stammer and stutter. I wanted to cry, but didn't want to make a scene.

"And the owner of the condo said we could take immediate possession. But you wanted to sleep on the beach on our wedding night? I can't believe it." I did make a scene, and walked out in tears.

May 28, 2003

Delores told me she heard that Stan was in the hospital again with pneumonia. I called the hospital and sure enough, he was a patient. I found out that he had slept on the wet ground again, three nights during the past week. This time, he will be hospitalized for five days. I was informed that he could not sleep outside, and being his wife, I should keep better tabs on him, but they had no idea how difficult that was. I couldn't even keep tabs on him when he and I were both at home. And how the hell did they think I could manage and be at work the same time?

Once we were married, I thought I would be able to keep a much better eye on my husband but it just didn't work out that way.

He continued to take money. The house in the country sold today for $370,000. I put $300,000 in the bank and kept $70,000 in my wallet, thinking of buying a new Lexus and going shopping for myself. If Stan could spend money, so could I. But in the morning all the money but $10.00 was gone. There was only one person who could have taken it, and I checked his wallet and found race track tickets, liquor store tickets, and only $50,000 in cash. He was supporting someone, making house payments, or buying things I did not know about. He had to be doing that as it was impossible for him to spend that much otherwise.

I began drinking heavily because of depression when I found out about this missing money and the next morning I was two hours late for work because of the terrible buzz I had. I no longer had "a long distance drive" excuse to use, and my entire body hurt. I received my second verbal warning at work. My thoughts were serious about calling it quits with Stan before it even began. He had it made. We stayed in his favorite Hotel; he had his liquor and an allowance, plus anything he could steal from me. He didn't want me to work and was doing everything possible to have me lose my job. And he surely wouldn't get a job of any kind for himself.

He constantly said, "Miss-Goody-Two-Shoes" prefers her condo on Lake Shore Drive over my Hotel."

"Yes, as a mater of fact, I do."

"And why don't you like it?"

"Why bother worrying or being concerned, Ms. Angel. Get out now. You still have time to get out. So what if you bought that expensive condo for happiness, it's in your name and you can sell it and get your money back."

On Sunday, I mentioned that we should get away for a few days, just to take a little honeymoon. Stan said we would stay at home and he'd show me how the homeless lived. It sounded novel, like fun, and once again, I agreed.

We walked down an alley in our worst clothes, looking for something to eat or a restaurant or something that was thrown away and still good enough to eat, or other food, sandwiches or chicken that was half-way fresh. Nothing looked good. We went inside, after the restaurant owner saw us out back, and evidently felt sorry for us because he brought us coffee and sandwiches. This was to be our breakfast and lunch, which enabled us to save a little money and to help pay me back for the money he had taken from me.

It was rather warm outside, so we decided to find a cool spot and take a refreshing short nap. There was a construction site nearby, and the workers were putting in new sewers and culverts. "Let's pretend we are homeless with no place to sleep. See that culvert over there? Let's crawl in it and take a nap."

I hesitated. Just the thought scared me and my claustrophobia. I could feel myself suffocating with insects, snakes, and slimy rodents crawling all over me. I visualized a mad dog coming in and tearing us apart. I thought of how the voices in my head would echo so loudly that Stan would be able to hear them. I thought of my weak stomach. But he dragged me in despite my fears.

The culvert was about five feet in diameter, and we managed to crawl inside and since it was cool and quiet, we both slept a while. There was no activity on the site, so we didn't worry about being buried alive somewhere.

I thought back to how I had nothing as a child, then everything I could want in my last three marriages, and here I was, sleeping in a culvert after just being married to my fourth husband. I had gone from nothing in childhood to nothing now. My life had made a complete circle.

We got up and walked to the Harbor, and watched the boats, first in a safe sheltered area, and then they ventured out into the rough current and unknown waters.

That night, I decided to sleep with Stan on the sandy shores of Lake Michigan, but it hurt to think of our elegant condo so close. I could see it from where we were. We stopped for beer and wine, and Stan drank himself into oblivion. There was no television, but I read with a flashlight—totally bored.

In the morning I had to waken him. Delores Norton had given me days off for our honeymoon and I said, "Let's pack a suitcase and get away for at least two days. That's all I'm asking. Let's get into a new environment for a couple of days."

"Why do you have to talk like a big shot? Can't you just say, can't we go away on a vacation?"

"Sorry." Everything I said or did was criticized, and I was far too sensitive. We would both have to give a little and meet in the middle.

He surprised me and agreed. "I'm so tired and weak, but let's go. You're right."

We had fun packing for the trip, in the suitcases we panhandled to buy. Of course we had ice and liquor in the cooler, and we planned to stay in the Wisconsin Dells that Wednesday, Thursday, and Friday.

It was an active area and we planned to eat and drink in a fancy restaurant just adjacent to our hotel I looked forward to it. Maybe Roxanne would go and help me get a passionate kiss and something more, as Stanley had yet to make any advances towards me.

We found our Hotel and made it to the outdoor pool and then the hot tub and once we finished with the hot tub, we stopped at the bar across the street for a beer, even though we had plenty of booze in the cooler. We had planned to save that for tonight. I called Stan, who sat on the floor by the cooler, and he didn't answer. I called him again, and he still didn't answer, but his loud snoring continued. He was asleep for the night already.

We slept in the next morning. And then it started. Stan's cough was slight at first and proceeded to get deeper and deeper. It was his pneumonia, and we had no choice but to make it back to St. Gilbert's Hospital in Chicago as they had all his records. He was admitted to Intensive Care with a severe case of pneumonia, and his temperature remained at 103.2. I spent the night with him. He started on antibiotics, I.V. and was given fluid and oxygen. "This is the worst case he's ever had. What took you so long to get him here?" The nurse asked me as if it were my fault.

I explained that we were on vacation and as soon as the symptoms were noticed, I rushed him to the hospital. She had a bitchy, typical nurse attitude.

He has a fair chance of surviving, if we can just get the temperature down and get him hydrated once more." Extra fluids were given and by Friday morning, his temperature was down to normal but he was so weak, they had to keep him in bed. I know things were bad because he didn't fight their orders.

But on Saturday, I drove him home from the hospital as he more or less ordered me. "I insist on getting out of "this dump."

He promised to take it easy, but once home, things changed. It was back to drinking and smoking pot and regular cigarettes, plus not eating the correct foods. At that point I gave up and said "fuck it." He was a grown man and a wife gets tired of being called "Mother." So he continued doing "his thing" and I thought "the hell with it." But I didn't say a single word.

Saturday night he informed me that he wanted to go to Bud's and I drove there and had a few beers with him, wishing sometimes he could drive, but he no longer could because of three 'driving under the influence' arrests. (Bud took one look at him, and then walked away—he looked bad.)

He continued to smoke against the doctor's orders, and told me he didn't ever want to go to a hospital again. He also informed me that he would sleep in the condo, either in our bed or on the sofa but summers would be spent on the beach and I could either stay with him there or return to the "hoity-toity condo." Why I continued to take the verbal abuse, I'll never know. I guess it was because I was his Guardian Angel.

I argued with him about sleeping outside. He then informed me that he was staying on the beach that night and I could join him but I went home alone. Needless to say, I worried as he certainly shouldn't have slept outside so soon—especially with the temperature drop to52 degrees and there was a heavy rain falling.

July 14, 2003

On Monday morning, I returned to work and was quite upset as he hadn't returned from sleeping on the beach on Saturday night. I had no idea where he was.

How I made it through work, I'll never know. About two o'clock that afternoon, at work, I had a mysterious call from a woman telling me that she was with my husband since Sunday, and that he loved her. She sounded like an older woman. After she hung up, that call left me shaking the rest of the day and evening. What really upset me was finding one of Carl's rings on the condo bathroom counter top. How did it get there? It was the same one I bought for him five years ago.

~~~~~
~~~~~

CHAPTER TWENTY

July 14, 2003
That Evening

Stanley came home about 7:00p.m. and was solemn and extremely mysterious. I kept thinking of the jewelry and in my heart I knew, but didn't want to admit it. Stanley was involved with Buzz in activities that weren't on the up-and-up. I knew that he was involved in the robbery with him.

"So what'cha doing tonight?" Stan asked me, and I detected a little guilt in his voice, and don't think it was my imagination.

"I haven't thought about it. For one thing, I'm going to bed early. I have to give a presentation on charting and have to review my notes tonight."

"How about spending the night with me at The Republic Hotel?"

I had spent enough nights with him to know the routine: I bought liquor, he drank it, and crashed, and I was left alone. At least in the condo I could be alone in comfort. No way would I go to The Republic that night to end up spending it alone.

Before I left him to go to the condo, I asked Stan about Connie and Susie. He admitted spending the mornings with Connie and the afternoons and most nights with Susie. He admitted that he had sex with both women because all women were different and he liked variety. I was deeply hurt, seeing as we never had a sexual relationship. We argued, and I didn't sleep a wink that night. I think it was Roxanne that said, "If you like variety so much, why don't you try me on for size. You just might like it."

I can't explain the look on his face. He told me, "I like you because you give me other things I need. I think of you as a friend. They are lovers. There is a difference." I was hurt, truly hurt. Sure I was his friend, and wife, and Guardian Angel. And he called them his lovers? Give me a break, man.

My money kept disappearing and I was down to just hundreds of dollars, no more thousands in my accounts. I knew I'd have to get another job to keep up expenses for Stanley and myself, and that day Dr. Cynthia told me about Sexual Compulsive Anonymous. I planned to attend my first meeting the day after tomorrow and thought of what I'd wear, and knew it would be none of Stan's business where I was going. Hell, he didn't tell me where he went, so why did I have to tell him. He was drinking more, and seemed to have something on his mind. I knew his health was deteriorating, but there was something else. He mentioned seeing his ex-wife in town, and said he thought they could get back together, but I hoped this wasn't true. And then I worried about the two young girls from North Park Rehab, the two "schizophrenics." Was he serious about one or both of them?

~~~~~
~~~~~

CHAPTER TWENTY-ONE

July 18, 2003

I never had such a busy, tiring day at work as I did today. There were salesmen from duplicating machine companies, bands that wanted to play for residents, answering the phone because the receptionists weren't here, and on top of that I had another presentation.

I was tired after work, but made it to the Sexual Compulsive Meeting that evening. I followed driving directions and once there, hesitated walking in because everyone was so young. Finally, a group of older women arrived and I slipped into their group and walked in with them.

The Moderator spoke first, and it was enlightening. I remember his words. "You eventually get caught and have to pay the consequences." He asked us if we thought people wanted to get caught. Then he told us, "It's partly deliberate, partly a numbers game, because you need to cheat more and more to get that certain 'high,' soon the odds increase that you will be discovered."

"There is a parallel between cocaine and sex withdrawal: dizziness, body aches, headaches, sleeplessness, and extreme restlessness. Those who have recovered from drug addiction and also had a sex addiction stated that it was by far harder on the individual to recover from sex addiction. Probably, it was less severe initially, but more prolonged and more painful in the end stages."

"Often people cry uncontrollably, grieving for everything they've suppressed." He talked for a while longer, and then the six of us who were first-timers had to go in front of the group, on the stage, and 'tell our story.'

It was my turn, and I was so shy in front of formal groups, believe it or not, and of course Roxanne wasn't there when I needed her. If only she had been there to talk, but she was the "bar girl" not one to attend a "Compulsive Sexual Meeting." I felt my face redden and my legs were wobbly but I looked at the group and stammered: "I—I—I—I—don't know where to begin."

There was complete silence, then one young woman stood and said, "We're all friends, honey, so go ahead. We don't judge. Just begin anywhere you like." The next thing I knew, about twenty people stood up and clapped for me in agreement of what the woman had said. Believe it or not, this did give me confidence.

I told them about my marriage that just broke up, how Carl wasn't a warm person and that I unrealistically blamed him for starting my habit of cheating—going out just about every night, looking for someone new. I explained how I felt I had a void from the lack of sex in my marriage.

In the audience, some people shook their heads in agreement, as if they were or had been in a similar situation. Then I mentioned that our divorce was finalized and that I had remarried, and my fourth husband was actually my patient in a psychiatric facility where I was his nurse. I told them that we had been married for two months and had yet to have sex, but he was going out with two younger women and having relations with them. I told the group everything. I told them about John and how I had been in love with him and how it hurt to break up.

Butterflies filled my stomach and rabbits ran across the stage. I wondered what the hell I was doing up there.

"It all started out so innocently. He was a married man but we became friends and then things became serious and he was going to leave his wife for me. I planned to leave my husband and then thought of what a good husband I had and how he gave me everything. I began to cry and it took me about three minutes to regain my composure. Once again people stood up and clapped for me. It was then so quiet one could hear a pin drop. I saw tears in several women's eyes and that made me start crying again. I told them how an affair like ours will graduate from something innocent to something dangerous, that will almost break up marriages.

How I managed to relay such an intimate subject to this strange group without difficulty amazed me. Just looking at them would show how understanding and compassionate they were, and it seemed that they had done a lot of negative things in their lives too. I hadn't heard anyone tell such an intense story that night as I had. I brought up stories of Fearless Fred, Hal, the small penis guys, and about my Saturday afternoon shopping. They just shook their heads, and then stood up and applauded me for about five minutes.

The tears I cried were tears of relief. Just sharing and getting it off my shoulders had done wonders.

We had a coffee break, and when I came out of the washroom, I felt a tap on my shoulder. All I could think was, "Oh no. Not here, too."

He said to me: "Good job, Marsha. I know how you feel. I went through the exact same thing a few months ago. It hurts so much and hits you right in the gut. It lingers, won't go away, and when you think it does go away, you dream of it. It returns. I still can't stop thinking of her. She was married too, and if only people would stop and think before getting involved with someone when you or they aren't free, things would be different."

I didn't comment. He had said it all. But we continued talking into the next part of the session. I knew that if things had been different, we probably would have gone out together, and knowing me, I would have gone to his bed. I kept reminding myself as he did, that we were at a SCA meeting and trying to heal and mend our broken hearts and fences, plus re-establish good relationships with our inner selves and our spouses.

His name was Dan Evans; he was an engineer, involved in a very depressing marriage. We became good friends, and began using each other as a support system and we talked about anything and everything. We even exchanged e-mail addresses and I looked for those messages the minute I walked into the house. There was always one waiting for me and I answered it promptly.

"You know, my wife refuses to have sex and told me I've had my lifetime quota as I'm almost sixty years old. She told me to "get over it and think of doing things around the house. Can you believe that? Then one night she walked in when I was having Cyber Sex with Diane, my girl friend, and that did it. We haven't talked since. Neither my wife nor Diane will talk to me anymore."

He told me how he belonged to three dating sites, even though he was married and explained the ACE Model of Cyber sexual addiction to me.

"Cyber sex and Internet Addiction have made so many marriages end in separation and divorce. Sex Addiction is rapidly growing too. It's scary, but I just want to get back to having a normal life once more. Darn. And now I meet you." (Then he explained that he was just kidding.)

We looked forward to seeing each other again and again. We shared drinks, danced, went to movies, and yes, if it had been in earlier months, he would have ended up being my Mr. Perfect.

That night for the first time, I went on an internet dating site, and within two days, I had letters from fifteen different men, all telling me how they needed sex. I didn't bother to answer, but found myself signing up and even paying for four other sites, and enjoyed reading the replies I received. I got to thinking that it might not be a bad idea to make a date with one of the men, but I never did—yet.

Dan and I met at the meetings every week and sat together causing many people to wonder about us. Our kisses grew more passionate and he asked me to run away with him. I just thought, "Oh no, not that again." We continued to date, and our love for each other grew. I didn't know what the hell I would do.

It seemed like whenever I was pissed with Stan, I called and met Dan. I began to long for his body and knew I must do the right thing and let him go. So I told him. "Dan, we both went to the Sexual Anonymous meetings for a reason and I have to let your marriage have a chance. Mine doesn't have much hope but I have to say goodbye to you. Please call me once in a while because I can't say that word: 'goodbye,' plus I want to know how you are doing. I gave him a peck on the cheek and left before I changed my mind.

While driving to work the next day, I realized that I couldn't stop "cold turkey" with Dan and called him and to meet for coffee and pie, agreeing to continue our meetings as frequently as possible on a 'friendship only' basis.

We sill enjoy good movies now and then, and just smile when our hands accidentally are placed on each other's thighs. It is wonderful to have a mature, male friend and not have to go to bed when you see him.

If I was a bad influence on him, I didn't care. I enjoyed his company and wasn't doing any harm that I could see. I still love Carl—but was married to Stan—and in love with Dan—and think of John. "Yes, Marsha, you are one crazy bitch."

After another few days, I drove around to look for Stanley, stopping first at Bud's and then the hotel, realizing he would be with Connie, Sue, or both and I couldn't take that. So many times I wondered what would happen if I walked in on him and he was having sex with both girls at once. I went back to Bud's and ordered a drink and was deep in thought, thinking about how I had the same regrets leaving Dan as I did when leaving John. It hurt. I learned that breaking up is the hardest part of any union. I hurt badly in the region of my heart and thought I'd have an attack. I felt as though I'd been stabbed.

A few minutes later, Stan came in. "How about it if we go for a hamburger?" I asked. He agreed. Then he did a strange thing. He asked Bud for some mustard and squeezed it in his hand from the squeeze bottle, and then proceeded to smear it on his face. Then with a yellow face, we both went out for a hamburger. First it was ketchup for a bleeding arm and now it was mustard. He laughed at those who laughed at him, and I found myself looking the other way, but I was laughing too. His behavior was becoming more strange and I found out he still hadn't been taking his medication.

July 23, 2003

Once again, the next week when I saw Dr. Connors she asked what I wanted to talk about. I told her I kept thinking of John, and how he made me so happy until he gradually lost interest. Along with this, I told her about my guilt feelings toward Carl and my new interest in sex videos.

"Marsha, I feel that it is absolutely necessary that you visit your mother and the sooner, the better. How do you feel about this? Do you think she still harbors ill feelings towards you?"

"Yes, I'm sure she does. And tonight I'm going to find out where she is, how she is, and make plans to visit her to ask a few questions. I have to help you get to the bottom of my problem. Then I will drive to wherever she is and talk to her I have to get a map and make plans to leave as soon as possible."

"Yes, Dr. Cynthia, I have a terrible confession to make. I went to the SCA Meeting as you suggested and met someone that I like very much."

"Marsha, you can't get serious again. You can't take any more mentally or physically."

"We're just good friends. I won't let myself get hurt again."

"Well, there is such a thing as a man and woman being just friends, but not in your case, I hate to say."

"It was just as you said. Everyone there had things in common. Everyone was considerate, caring, and friendly. They listened to and respected me and I made several new friends. We understand each other so well that I found myself telling them about my new problems, and found out we had similar backgrounds and situations."

"Cynthia, I read all those books on self-esteem and learned a lot. Self-esteem has to be learned along the way. You have to practice and learn it. Many experts agree that low self-esteem is an epidemic among women whose lives and happiness have been constricted because they grew up feeling inadequate."

"We get the wrong messages in life, and since we don't like or respect ourselves we marry men unworthy of us, choose jobs which we're over-skilled for, based on what we *think* we deserve. We are over skilled and make other unfortunate choices in life. I saw myself upon many of the pages in these books and learned that the greatest victory one can achieve is to be able to live with herself or himself. We must learn to accept our shortcomings and those of others. Even though one is a long way from the desirable human as she thinks she should be, she must realize that she isn't so bad after all."

"So Marsha, what else is new?"

"Did I tell you our house was robbed?"

"I saw the guy running away with two sacks of stuff he took from our house and I think I recognized him."

"Who do you think it could be?"

"I think it was someone with the same body build as Stan, but this guy had on a coat and it made him seem a little chubbier. But he walked and ran like Stan. I think he was Stan's buddy."

"Marsha, don't trust Stan fully."

"I have to. I **am** his Guardian Angel and have to stick close by and protect him."

"Marsha, make sure about him. That's all I can say. I guess now is as good a time as any to tell you this. No time is really good but here goes: I talked to Delores Norton and she told me in confidence that Stanley is a schizophrenic and that he's not the one for you."

"His category is 'unclassified,' but he has other mental problems too And you have a couple yourself, therefore you don't want to get mixed up in a marriage like this. You see, Schizotypals and Schizophrenics do have some of the same symptoms. I think that's why you related to Stan so well in the beginning and feel a strange, strong attachment to him now. But I don't think it would be a good combination. I hate to tell you this."

I didn't hear a word she said. I didn't want to hear. I began talking about something else. "I had to make a police report, fill out tons of paper work, and it was horrid." I said this to divert her attention somewhat.

"Marsha, did you know that sexual addicts promise themselves and others that it won't happen again. They say all sorts of things, like 'I know I've been wrong, and this time I did learn a lesson. You'll never have to worry about me again. I won't repeat my actions.' All kinds of precautions will be taken. But unfortunately, it's a hard habit to break."

"Like dating another when you're married. That happens again and again and each time the promises we make are broken. You get away with it time after time and can't seem to help yourself because it's in you and we have to find out why. Personally, I think it is an inherited trait."

"How are you doing with the medication?"

"Just fine. I don't take them unless I'm desperate."

"Okay, go ahead now, and have a good week."

That afternoon
July 23, 2003

I left her office, but the footsteps behind me continued. Who was following me and why?

Later that afternoon
July 23, 2003

"Marsha, come here." He knew me but I didn't recognize or know him. He dragged me into his car, and took all my clothes off and fondled my body, began kissing me all over, and took me to his apartment after putting my clothes back on. "Marsha, I know all about you. You are my favorite movie star. Just remember this—one month from today will be your big day. And don't forget it."

I am only letting you in on this because I really enjoyed your movie, Baby." You have a nice little "cookie."

Later that Night
July 23, 2003

After he finished with me, I stopped at the first restaurant I saw. I had to have a cup of coffee. It looked like I was the only one there who wasn't a trucker. A man came over to talk to me and we walked out to his truck together. I didn't know his name but I found out what it was like to do it in a sleeper. I drove to North Park to do some work and be alone. Thank goodness no one came to see the tears flowing like a river, down my cheeks.

July 24, 2003

It was a good day, but three times I hung up the phone after dialing Dan's number. I couldn't start up my habit again with a man who was trying to come clean as I was.

I passed Dr. Cynthia on the street and told her, "I'm going to stop for an ice cream cone on the way home. Isn't that the silliest thing you ever heard of?"

"No, not really. You know what they say about ice cream, don't you?"

"No."

"They say it's a substitute for sex. You know how all the fat ladies sit around eating ice cream? They say that if they had sex, they'd leave it alone and lose weight. You know what? I'm going to join you. I really miss my man, especially today."

We both laughed.

"Why is it supposed to be a substitute for sex?"

"Because it's so soothing, refreshing, and relaxing."

"Don't give me any ideas." With that, I walked out the door and decided to drive to Bud's instead. I was anxious to hear what Stan had to say about his day and also anxious to watch my new XXX movie but Stan wasn't at Bud's, or at the hotel, or at home.

I hurried home to call Dan, and against my better judgment, asked him if he'd take me out for a drink. What the heck. If Stan did see me, tough shit. I know he was seeing others, so why should he mind if he saw me with someone else? Chances are that he wouldn't, (if he followed his regular routine) as he'd been gone for three days again.

I met Dan and couldn't get over how comfortable I felt with him. We could talk freely about anything and we always did. I just didn't know what to do about men. They had me thoroughly confused.

Stan didn't come home for a week. He never told me where he went and I never questioned him. I was his Guardian Angel, and yet I never knew where he was or with whom. This meant I was not a good Guardian Angel, and I vowed to do better.

I felt horrid, terrible, miserable, and hate to admit it but sometimes I wished death would just claim my body. Since my days were limited anyhow, what did it matter when it happened? I can't describe how I ached all over, with stiff bones that rubbed each other, and blood that pounded in my arteries, head, heart and veins. Even my toe nails hurt. My teeth felt as though they were all cracked and broken and the nausea on top of it was the crowning glory. The snakes in my legs kept crawling, and every time I bent over, I felt like my last meal was coming up.

I was totally out of those little white relaxation pills and had to watch my money, since there was only necessity cash left. Stan saw to that. The rest of the money was put aside for emergencies happening at the condo. No way could I pay for my little white pills unless I was really desperate.

Stress kills. I know my pills acted as a bandage, and didn't solve the deep down problem. But I was addicted to them and would have to save for my co-pay of $20.00. What the hell. A dollar here and a dollar there, fifty cents here and ten cents there, and eventually I would get them.

I could feel the round core of my "slight" mental abnormality growing, and desperately needed to talk to someone. That night I drove west and found a little bar, and went off with a guy on a Harley. We stopped in a cornfield and made love, without exchanging names. After all, he had a suggestion for solving my problem, and I helped him with his. What difference did knowing his name make?

I asked myself again if I really waned to start that habit over again. What did I want? I do know for sure I wasn't going to call Dan again. Then I decided to let him call me. I would let his marriage have a chance.

I was stressed and couldn't make up my mind. I wavered from 'yes' to 'no' and then back from 'no' to 'yes.' One can take so much in life, and it seemed as though I had reached my quota. I began to laugh, and then I prayed silently:

"Please God, don't hand me any more complications." I already have concerns over Dan, Stan, Carl, my health, my disappearing money. I have memories of John, not knowing of my future financial situation, hallucinations and delusions that are happening more frequently. And my eye sight is so bad, that I don't know how much longer I will be able to see. And help me not to see Dan. I seldom had a cigarette, but always carried a pack. I inhaled deeply and smiled.

I actually became so disgusted with my behavior that I thought seriously of taking an overdose of something to end it all. (That's another thing: I was thinking of suicide more these days.) Instead of doing that, I gave in and called Dan. I think that was the better choice of the two, don't you? I put out my cigarette.

~~~~~
~~~~~

CHAPTER TWENTY-TWO

July 24, 2003

I waited for him to answer and when he did, I broke down and said, "Dan, oh Dan. Can we meet for a drink?" I figured if his wife was nearby or if he didn't want to, he would tell me "no."

"Oh Honey, I'm so glad you called. I've been thinking of you day and night." I didn't tell him the feeling was mutual, but it was. It was so good to hear his voice.

I waited in the parking lot for him to meet me. I could feel the round core of my "slight" mental abnormality growing and only Dan could comfort me. Stanley could either be gone for hours, or days, and I never knew, plus as I said before, he didn't care to listen to my complaints anyhow, and if he could do it, so could I.

I began to laugh hysterically at that one, for no reason at all, as I made up my mind to sit and wait for Dan, rather than go and meet him. He pulled in the parking lot, and I followed him to "The Cork" and we each had two beers and held hands, and he kissed me passionately. After that, I told him of my marital doubts and how I cared for him and wanted to see him and then said, "Let's fuck."

~~~~~

I shocked the crap out of him. But we left and went to a motel and "we did it." It was the most tender, sweetest, and loving act that I ever had. He kissed me the entire time, and we both felt so gratified afterwards. We left with the mutual understanding of definitely meeting again.

I longed to go to bed with Dan every day, but was happy just holding him closely and kissing most of the days. I knew that I would eventually sleep with him again,
~~~~~

but I was so happy being with him that I didn't have the same desperation as I had with other men. He was different. I know now that he was my Mr. Perfect, but it was a little too late.

I then went to Bud's to meet my Guardian Angel charge, and Stan was there waiting for me. He drank more than me and of course I paid the tab, my way of seeking approval from others, according to Dr. Cynthia. She explained that as a child, my parents probably didn't approve of a thing I did, never praised me, and now I found the only way to gain approval was to treat people (men) in a special way. Besides, I was Stan's Guardian Angel, and any friend of his was a friend of mine, so I picked up the tab for everyone as I had been doing lately. That's one of the things that confused me. Why did I pay for everyone's booze and yet not buy my own friggin pills? I didn't mention Connie to Stan at this time, although I certainly wanted to. Something was going on with them. I could feel it.

Stan suggested that we go to the Republic and I told him "yes" without hesitation, because maybe, just maybe tonight would be that long-awaited night where he took me to bed.

We were given the same room and when I entered the room, I could tell he had been there earlier in the day. Since I was there unexpectedly, and he didn't count on me visiting, he didn't have time to hide Carl's black onyx ring but left it in a conspicuous spot on the dresser. It was among the things taken the night of the robbery. He saw me looking at it, and quickly asked, "Do you like that? That's quite a whopper of a stone in it. I just bought it from a friend for $5.00."

"Does your fiend have any more jewelry to sell? I'm always looking for rings and things. Could you check with him for me?"

"Sure, I'll talk to him tomorrow. He acted innocent when answering. That ring should have been the subject of my concentration But Roxanne stepped in. Still I should have asked more about it. Her question was," well, did you decide when we are going to have sex?" That seemed to still concern her more than it did me.

I turned a brilliant shade of crimson, and Stan ignored the question. once more.

We stopped and got the liquor, but once more, he drank it all and passed out on the floor. I didn't have a taste of the booze he bought with my money once more, and there were ever-so-slight tears in my eyes when I opened them. It pissed me to have this same thing happen over and over and over again.

I couldn't figure out why with Stan, I didn't feel the urgency for sex as I did with other men. Maybe I had given up on it with him. Probably the desire was gone. It was as if we were celibate and I accepted this with no problem.

We spent the night there but when I left, Stan was still asleep. I went back to throw a glass of cold water on him on my way to work, as I surely didn't want to pay for an extra day at that flea trap. I started to leave but turned back to him. "Come on, that bitch is going to make me pay for another day." He still didn't budge and I left. He ended up staying there, snoring away and I knew he was going to have company soon and have a little fun on my money. Marriage didn't mean a thing to him. I just knew he'd have someone there. I could feel it in my bones. I remember the night we talked about marriage, and he told me he could never be true to one woman. Now I knew what he meant.

I drove to do some errands and stopped first to talk to Delores and asked her what consequences there would be, seeing as how I was married to Stan and we were living together. What will happen to his Public Aid?

She told me it was such a dumb question to ask.

"Excuse me?" I said to her.

"Once you two were married, his benefits stopped. Stanley is now your full responsibility and open enrollment of insurance won't be for another six months. At that time, if you want, you can put him on your plan."

"Remember, I discouraged you from getting married in the first place, but you told me that you were both old enough, and were two consenting adults, and it was your own business."

I knew that in my heart, Stan was the man for me, but had no idea of all the expenses it would incur. I didn't know the reason why I picked him, but surely there must have been a good reason. It certainly wasn't just the angels on the hood of my car that day that made the announcement to me. Did I do so much for others that I was willing to give up my own life and desires to take care of him and protect him from evil? And what exactly was the evil? I never did find out. I remain confused on many issues.

It was evident that Delores doesn't approve of Stan, nor do any of the nurses. But I don't give a damn. He is my man. And they also have to comment on that damn movie I made, every time they see me. "How did Stan like those close ups of your twat?" Stan never even mentioned the movie to me.

I do think it would be fun to watch it with him, but seeing as how we never had sex, I suddenly changed my mind. Those who saw it didn't know a thing about Roxanne and that she was the one who made it, not Marsha. Who could possibly understand that? All I needed was for more skeletons to be uncovered in my closet of blackness and unanswered questions.

"Marsha, I don't know how to tell you this, but I was talking to Cynthia Connors today and she told me about one of her clients that worked here at North Park that has married or will be marrying a real winner! Seems like he has been married and divorced three times, which the client doesn't know. Marsha, has Stanley been married before?"

"I don't really think so."

I tried to change the subject but she came back with, "I checked his records out of curiosity, and discovered that in actuality, he had been married three times before you. So it's true. I called his brother in Iowa and found out that he can't be true to one woman and I just wanted to warn you about this, although I know it's too late. I don't want to see you hurt."

At that point I did change the subject. "Delores, did you know that I sold my house and found a condo near work? I forgot if I told you." I couldn't stand hearing about Stanley being married before. Just the thought hurt me.

I knew that she loved saying negative things about Stanley, but I didn't believe a word she said about his marriages. Hell, if he'd been married before, wouldn't he have told me?

"Well now, you won't have an excuse for tardiness, living so close to work, will you? Now that you are so close, what will you use for an excuse?" I just walked away from her at that point.

"I have to go now Delores. I have work to do." Sometimes I didn't like working in the same office with her because she talked too much and I couldn't get my work finished in a timely manner.

I walked out to my car, singing and humming. It was a new tune that just popped into my head. I loved it and began dancing and singing as I drove. Then came he vibrations and echoes—new sounds always began when I was nervous, and that I was—nervous and anxious. Why the hell did the future keep popping into my mind? I had to worry about the friggin present for now.

First of all I'd have to decide if I wanted to stay with Stan. He held some magical power over me, and whatever it was, served to frighten me. Maybe it was the fact that I was his Guardian Angel that gave me a certain feeling of obligation. But what if he had been married three times before? Would I still want him? I thought about that and decided that I would. When I arrived home, there was a note on the table. "See ya," That was all Stanley wrote.

I didn't know why, I put up with his being gone more than he was with me as I was a woman of above average intelligence. He was my husband and I am not a jealous woman, but enough is enough and it was beyond me why I didn't say something to him. But I couldn't. I loved him too much. No matter what he did, the love wouldn't die and I was afraid to talk to him about anything he did.

Evidently he had been home and left again. Quickly I checked my top drawer where I keep my spare cash and found over $1,000.00 gone.

~~~~~
~~~~~

CHAPTER TWENTY-THREE

August 8, 2003.

Stan was gone for three days now, but he decided to come home late Friday, explaining that he was in a fight. "Someone was in my territory and I had to punch him out." Of course Stan was weak from being ill and had a bad cold plus the flu. No wonder he managed to get mangled. I had to leave for work on Saturday, but Stan kept telling me to do this and do that for him.

Sure, he could go away any time he wanted, but when he came home, I was supposed to wait on him hand and foot. I wondered who did it for him when I wasn't there.

"Don't believe all he tells you. There's more to his story than he is telling you at this time. Oh Marsha, we hate to see you being hurt again, Prepare yourself."

Stan wanted me to bring him ice water, a heating pad, blanket, extra pillow, and a peanut butter and jelly sandwich. I arrived at work about forty minutes late, and they started whispering, but surprisingly had no comments directed specifically to me.

"Marsha, you look like hell," and rather than tell them the truth, I just smiled. "You know how it is with newly weds. One of these nights I'll get some sleep." Then I just smiled and walked away and I think this bothered them more than anything.

August 9, 2003

The next night after work, I stopped for a drink in a different bar. I ended up having six brews and went home with someone that I didn't even know. I blamed my actions on Stanley. When I did get home, he smelled the beer and asked where I had been and I told him that I stopped off with the girls and had a few joints of marijuana and a few beers. I didn't feel the least bit guilty.

Then two days later, I did feel guilty. It hit me like a bomb. I had lied to my sweet husband. The Guardian Angel who lies is really a bummer. I was a bummer bitch.

"Stan, I think I am going to increase your allowance to $250.00 per week, even though I know you take money from me. I wish you would tell me first before taking it. But I also see race tickets where you play the ponies and lose and you don't even tell me about that. And the liquor store tabs. Maybe this increase in allowance will help you a little." It might help him, but it was putting me back on the poor farm. He was an expensive charge to take care of.

August 9, 2003

I began stopping in at Bud's after work looking for Stan, and he was never there. Nor was he at home. I stayed and sure enough, after a beer or two, Bud gave me that same knowing look, and didn't have to say a word. He knew Stan was playing around at The Republic Hotel or under a tree somewhere or in a cardboard box with a little Tootsie Poo.

August 22, 2003.

The days dragged and it was the same every friggin day. I went home and found Stan passed out with a bottle in his hand and new cigarette burns in my carpeting. I couldn't take any more. I left the condo and walked down the hall, then ventured to the first floor bar of the condo and decided "What the hell. I'll have just one drink."

The bar was beautiful, with walls carpeted in red, a shiny black bar, red bar stools, and black tables with glass tops and glowing candles. Each table had a fresh rose and the bar had baskets of snacks, and glowing candles were even on the bar.

I sat and thought for a while. I would go in and talk to Dr. Cynthia tomorrow. I had come to depend on her so much and thank the Lord that I had met her that fateful night.

I felt the tap on my shoulder. He had been sitting two barstools down and came over to tap my shoulder and sit by me.

I whispered "Thanks a lot" to Roxanne as I had already made up my mind that I'd be true to Stan. No more fooling around and I meant it this time. I was almost positive, anyhow.

I looked at him, not meaning to complain, but when he asked what I was doing there alone, I told him. "I've been married about three months and would you believe that my husband has passed out again from drinking? Every night it's the same old thing. I just think a little change of scenery would do me good. So here I am."

"I'd say you have a good reason. Do you live in this building?"

"Yes, on the fourteenth floor."

"Hey! Me too! We're neighbors. I live alone, as my wife left me last week."

"Are you a lady of leisure or do you work?"

"I'm a nurse, and far from being a lady of leisure."

"Oh, how interesting. A nurse. Where do you work? It seems that I've seen you around. I'm the Administrator at St. Gilbert's Hospital and we surely need nurses. Are you looking for a change?"

I almost forgot for a moment that I was right in the heart of Chicago, about two miles from St. Gilbert's Hospital. So it wasn't strange that I should run into someone who worked in the first hospital where I was employed right after graduation, and the one where Stanley always ended up when he had a problem.

Oh how the name of that hospital brought back memories. My first two husbands were probably still there, so I didn't dare mention any names.

"No thanks, I like my job. I'm Assistant Director of Nursing at North Park Rehabilitation. But thanks just the same."

"You know, there are two doctors at my hospital who knew a nurse that once worked with them at St. Gilbert but then changed to North Park about fifteen years ago. They were both married to her, at different times, of course."

My face must have turned a bright red as he spoke, for I knew he was talking about me. I bet that he and also knew how easily I blushed.

"So what's your name?"

"My name is Marsha Stevens." I hoped he would let it drop there, but of course he didn't.

"Oh my God! They were both married to someone named Marsha. It has to be you. This is too much for me to fathom! If you were married to both Robert and Tom, and then divorced them and married someone else, and are on your honeymoon now with a new husband, it has to be you."

"Yes, my name is Marsha Stevens now that I just married Stanley and we moved here on our wedding day." I didn't tell him about Stan and the Republic Hotel and that he never really 'moved' here.

"Did you say Stanley? You're married to Stanley Stevens?"

"Yes, why? Do you know him?" I knew damn well he did, but had to ask.

"Yes, I know him well and so does everyone else at St. Gilbert's. Say, he's due to get pneumonia again. He gets it about three times each year, mostly in the spring and summer, and ends up at St. Gilbert's."

"Do you know that you're his fourth wife?"

I hesitated answering that one in the affirmative, but finally did. After about thirty minutes, I told him, "I think it's time to go back upstairs and see what's going on. One more drink and I'll be going."

"Marsha, I won't say a thing to Robert or Tom, I promise. Seeing you here is between you and me. But let me tell you something. Robert has been married five times and Tom is on his sixth wife. So I know you weren't the problem. Those guys are crazy. Robert is one of the top doctors in OB-GYN and Tom is Department Chairman of Internal Medicine. They're both excellent in their fields. I have to say that. But as genuine people, they suck. Yet the one thing they have in common is respect for you and I can't help but feel they are both still in love with you to this very day. They always bring up your name in a positive way."

"By the way, my name is John Raymond. I'm so glad that I finally got to meet the woman that two of my doctors are still in love with." He signaled the bartender and ordered and expensive bottle of champagne, saying, "We're going to polish this off." And we did. He held my hand as we entered the elevator, both of us smiling and slightly tipsy. He was so tall and handsome and I felt comfortable with him.

When I heard his name, I almost fainted. He looked just like John Reynolds and their names were so much alike. Lately the events in my life were just too much to handle in every way. I felt as though I was breaking in the middle and the circuits in my mind were over-loaded. I couldn't take any more. When the elevator stopped I told John good night and I went towards the left as he turned right. We waved to one another before entering our respective dwellings. (What a difference in elevators, between The Republic Hotel and the condo!)

August 23, 2003

I hurried to see Dr. Cynthia after work. I knew immediately that something was wrong. When I walked into her office, she looked as though she was crying.

"Dr. Cynthia, what's wrong?"

"Oh Marsha, oh Marsha."

"What."

"Why don't we play a little game today? You be the Doctor, and I'll be the patient on the sofa. Listen to me tell you a story, Use my yellow pad and write notes and a diagnosis."

I was confused, but agreed.

She lay on the sofa

I sat at her desk.

"Marsha, would you be my bridesmaid? I'm getting married."

"I'm shocked. I thought you were never going to marry again."

"I can't help it. I love him so damn much."

"I never stopped loving him. He never stopped loving me. What's wrong with me? He divorced me, but said it was the biggest mistake he ever made."

"Do I know him?"

"Yes. And it's because of you that I am marrying him."

"What do you mean by that? Is it good or bad? You have me worried now. Do I dare ask who it is?"

"Dr. Connors, my former husband, the one I am still in love with and the one who gave you the consult when you were in the hospital. He contacted me and things started up again. I always loved him. So much. Oh Marsha."

We both cried. I was so happy for her, and now all of a sudden I was not only a Guardian Angel, but a soon-to-be-bridesmaid. We cried together—tears of happiness.

"We're getting married around the holidays."

"Dr., your diagnoses are: 1) Love. 2) You go girl!"

~~~~~

I didn't sleep a wink that night, between Cynthia's news and meeting John. I was happy and hyper and manic and went for a walk.

I wondered if the "surprise, something special" that the stranger had told me would happen on August 23 had happened, and was it John's news or Cynthia's news. No wonder I couldn't sleep. The more I thought about it, the more I wondered. Was the world getting smaller? Why is it that no matter where I went, someone recognized me, or knew me from someplace? Why the coincidence of meeting John who worked with Robert and Tom on the first night I went to a new bar? And of course they all knew Stanley. We were bound to meet, living on the same floor of he same building.

A few minutes later, there was a knock at my door. I couldn't imagine who it was. "Yes, who's there?" I called.

I was alone in the condo at the time and not sure where Stan had gone. I figured he had passed out on the floor or the sofa and would spend the night there. Evidently not.

"Who's there?" I asked again.

"It's John, your neighbor down the hall. Can I come in a minute?"

"Well, I don't know. Oh I guess so. Why not? Stanley has friends over, so why can't I?"
~~~~~

John Raymond entered the living room and sat on the sofa. "Nice place you have here." He spotted the rug with cigarette burns and the empty beer cans strewn all over the floor, but didn't say anything.

"Marsha, I think you should know something. Are you sure you are alone here? I've had just enough to drink that I'm brave enough to tell you a couple of secrets. I don't want to hurt you. I just don't want you to be the last to know."

I didn't like his tone of voice. It was bad news. I could tell. I could always tell.

"Check to make sure no one else is here."

I did, and then I came back, and told him. "Yes, I'm alone. Tell me. Tell me. What is it?"

"I am hesitating here. Be patient. Maybe I'm not as brave as I thought I was. Maybe you already know."

"Well?"

"Marsha, Stan was in prison."

"What?"

"You heard me, Stanley has a prison record."

"For murder?" That was my first thought.

"No, for grand larceny. He steals from unsuspecting women, rich women. Watch you rings and things and money. Especially your money. Don't trust him. If you want me to tell you more about this, I will."

"I—I—I—"

"He has taken so much money from me, you wouldn't believe it. And I am broke. I had money. Lots of it. Now I am living from pay check to pay check. And he has helped rob my house in the country. I know that now. Oh. I wish I had known this sooner."

"Also, I don't know how to tell you this, but the results just came out today. The testing was done at our hospital, by Robert, your ex-husband of all people. He is her doctor. Marsha, Connie is going to have Stanley's baby next April, around the twentieth of the month."

~~~~~
~~~~~

PART FOUR

CHAPTER TWENTY-FOUR

August 23, 2003

John sat for a while after telling me the news. I suppose I was happy to know what he had to say. We planned to catch Stan in the act of stealing or sleeping with Connie and take action. But do you see what a spot this would put me in? I'm Stan's Guardian Angel.

Needless to say, I didn't sleep a wink the rest of the night. I could hardly wait until Bud's opened for the day, so I could begin looking for my husband. Hard telling where I'd find him, but I'd start at Bud's.

Walking into Bud's, he said, "Come on, have a drink. Sit down and relax a while. He's due in any minute now. He comes in every morning." So he brought me a cup of coffee with two shots in it. I waited. Finally, Stan came staggering in about 9:30 and I wondered if he had been drinking all night. He had grass on his coat and evidently had been sleeping outside.

He was noticeable moody, and kicked the bar as he sat down. "Don't talk to me," was all he said to me.

Well, I talked to Bud. I hoped Stan would get over his mood soon. I wondered why Bud kept watching the door, and then Stanley started watching too.

And sure enough, Connie came in and sat down next to Stan. She was dressed like a model and had her hair and nails done and that's when I knew she was being supported in style by my money. I studied her clothes compared to mine. She sat by Stan and they talked about this and that, nothing important, and after a few minutes, she left. I didn't understand what was going on but do believe they were talking in code.

Stan and I went back to the Condo. I didn't mention Connie and neither did he. Once in the Condo, he spit on the floor. "I hate this carpeting and furniture."

"So why didn't you go shopping with me?"

"Everything is so blah."

"No baby, you are looking at first class stuff here. I had an interior decorator help me pick out things."

"Hoity-Toity Bull Shit."

"And you don't fix peanut butter and jelly sandwiches with fries for dinner."

"So what does that have to do with the carpeting and furniture? I am a nurse, remember? And peanut butter and jelly sandwiches with fries are not that good for you. That's not a balanced meal and therefore I won't serve them as a regular diet."

"Hoity-Toity Bull Shit."

I did fix him what he wanted for dinner that night but told him it wouldn't be an every-day thing.

When we got ready for bed, after watching television a while, I put on my short, white gown. I didn't care about Connie. I loved Stan. No matter what he did to me or against me, I loved my man. I put on the gown and combed my hair and even put on make-up. The only thing Connie had on me was youth. I felt good and tonight would be the night. I just knew it.

He walked in on me in the bedroom and once again told me I looked like a floozy. I tried so hard and everything I tried with him failed. Can I help it if I wanted to sleep with my man, with his arms wrapped around me, sniffing his body and feeling his hairy legs (and they were hairy).

I decided then and there that I would resume my old style of life, before I married him, and if I found someone else, I would have a Mr. Perfect Number Two. Imagine that. After leaving Mr. Perfect Number One, I go with Mr. Perfect Number Two who came after Husbands One, Two, and Three. Oh Marsha!

I placed $200.00 in my top dresser drawer to see if it would still be there in the morning. Since Stan didn't buy me a wedding ring, I bought myself one and it wasn't too expensive, but did cost $3000.00 and I had many compliments on it. He knew how much it was worth, and also how much he could sell it for. I planned to check my drawer in the morning and see what was missing.

He was asleep within one hour, on the couch, out cold from the alcohol. I pretended I was asleep too, and waited. No way could I go to sleep if I wanted, even as tired as I was. I was watching and waiting.

I woke about three hours later with Stan running through the condo with no clothes on, screaming: "Where do you keep the peanut butter and jelly in this fucking place? I haven't had any in weeks."

"It's the middle of the night. Go back to sleep. You just had some a few hours ago."

He didn't go to sleep, but kept running around and once again he was looking for Buda.

I finally did get up to fix him two peanut butter and jelly sandwiches, plus a glass of milk, and he fell asleep. For a while! I heard him creeping around about an hour later. He finally made himself another sandwich and dropped crumbs all over the floor and between the cushions. He had now burned five holes in the carpeting and it was such an expensive sofa, now out of shape, greasy, and smelly from perspiration and body odor. He didn't take showers, except in the park. He refused to take them in the condo. There was spilled beer and popcorn, plus about ten new burns, and it broke my heart.

In all my other marriages, the husband was neat and organized. Never did they make the messes as Stan did. I wasn't used to this. Even my stepfather didn't leave messes like this and did shower more often than Stan.

Why don't we see things more clearly when we're in love? Was I in love? Hell, I didn't know anymore. (I know, I keep repeating this.)

I was off from work that day and we barely talked. The voices in my head were loud and clear and that night, while looking at the ceiling, Stan remained in the living room drinking, with the money I had given him earlier. So far, he had not touched anything in my drawer.

"Marsha, Marsha, Marsha, don't stay with him. We told you this over and over. He's a bum and he's dragging you down there with him. Get the hell away from him. You can get an annulment very easily. Can't you see your marriage was never consummated? You have grounds. He is just using you and don't make the mistake of staying with him. We foresee terrible things happening soon. We can't say what they are, but get out now. Don't wait another week, but go for the guy who rescued you after your accident. He drives a green Ford, with an Illinois License Number 3530471. Look for him."

There was no way I could even find he driver of that car even if I wanted, even if I looked for months. But I do remember him. I thought of Stan and how he didn't sleep with me, but preferred the floor, or the ground, or the beach, and there still hadn't been any real show of affection. I didn't dare say a word to him about the ashes on the floor or the spilled beer, so I just kept quiet and cleaned up after him as I wanted and needed him so desperately. Yet, I wondered whether I should seek that annulment and go look for someone else, or stick it out being married and lonely because that's what I was. Maybe I didn't need him so desperately after all. He didn't satisfy one single need that I had. But, I think that I was stuck, as I was his Guardian Angel.

What if I kissed him on the neck, or started playing with him? What if I ran my fingers through his hair, or put my hand in his jeans and started to play with his dick? Maybe he was the kind that needed the female to initiate lovemaking.

I did kiss him on the cheek, and that's when he slapped me and started snoring again.

The following night, I slept alone once more, after the gurgling and pounding in my head worked its way up to a higher volume and stopped. But that's when Stan began running through the rooms because "Buda" was chasing him again, which was becoming a nightly habit. He scurried around the table, on the chairs, on the stove, on a lower shelf, over the couch, and chanting all the while, "Cast all devils into the sea of fire." Naked as a jay bird, with hair flying, this was truly a sight to behold.

Needless to say, I wasn't ready to get up when the alarm went off. Stanley took my bathroom time and went to the park to air dry. I was four hours late for work. Once again Stan had kept me awake in hopes that I would lose my job and that day I almost did. Delores informed me that if I was late once more, I would be terminated. She kept giving me one more chance, and I loved her for that.

I came to the realization that I was broke, and now knew Stan took everything from my wallet, plus my ring and money from the drawer. But I didn't say anything to him and instead I went to the bank and took out the very last of my trust fund. I had been saving to buy "something special" whether it is a summer cottage or a boat. Funds were gone now and I'd have to start using money from the house sale (what was left of it) as something to fall back on. I kept the money hidden under my mattress and slept with one eye open every night watching it. What a way to live, but I had promised to be his Guardian Angel.

Because of Stan, I knew I'd have to take a part-time job besides my nursing job. Between what he spent, and what he took, I had nothing left and lived from pay check to pay check, with only a dime or quarter in the change section of my coin purse on payday.

I remember Dr. Cynthia telling me one day, "Didn't you figure out by now that Stan is an alcoholic? You know Marsha, diabetics and epileptics are the victims of their diseases, ones they didn't choose. Alcoholism is a disease too but in this case, Stan doesn't choose to stop his drinking and he *does* have a choice."

"Alcoholism can be stopped but he desires to continue this habit. Then of course, the drinking escalates and Stan, being a schizophrenic should be on medication and not drinking. You can't deny that he has this illness, like he denies it. No way is he going to act normal without taking his medication as directed and stopping that darn drinking. He is going to do these things plus others you can't even begin to imagine."

"You know, once you were certain that you were schizophrenic, but I assured you that your thoughts were way off. But now you are married to one who is. He is not living in the real world, Marsha, but he thinks of himself as being some king or prince who doesn't have a thing in life to worry about."

"There is still time to get out of this marriage. Somewhere out there, you will find the man who is right for you. It sure as hell isn't the one you have as a husband now. And don't worry. I won't lecture you on this again."

"I'm his Guardian Angel, appointed to take care of him and I have that certain feeling and love for him and it will all work out. He's just new to the idea of marriage because his first one didn't work out but this one will. I'll check on him and make sure he eats right and takes his medication."

"Yes and this man is going to make you lose your sanity."

I started to leave and she pulled me back into the office.

"Marsha, you will lose your sanity if you stay with him. We are friends. Listen to me. About 989% of schizophrenics do have auditory and visual hallucinations. And I was told by his psychiatrist at North Park that he's suspicious and delusional, sometimes speaks his thoughts out loud, and his behavior in general is bizarre and will only get worse."

I turned and walked away from her, my tolerance level was zero. I'd prove everyone wrong. I loved this man. They all hated him. I know it. I went home, fixed a nice dinner, and he was actually there and enjoyed it. Afterwards, however, he disappeared again. I could just see him out sleeping on the damp ground and smoking pot, but he was a grown man and I had enough to worry about. For one thing, I thought that I was pregnant, and didn't know who the father might be. I hadn't been feeling too well lately, and it would be a miracle for me to get pregnant, but then miracles happen every day.

August 26, 2003

I was overwhelmed with worries. No doubt about it, with the way my money was disappearing and Stanley's hospital bills which I had to pay, I would have to sell my Lexus for sure and get that second job. But then, they wouldn't insure Stanley once open enrollment did come around, because he had a pre-existing condition of chronic pneumonia. Once they checked his medical records, there would be no chance in hell for him to get insurance.

It took all the money I had from the sale of the country house, supplying us with very little spending money, and of course Stanley had helped himself to more of that money. The Lexus brought in enough for more hospital and doctor bills and two months living expenses.

September 2, 2003

I loved my job as a waitress at Gert's Grill, which was just around the corner and two blocks west. It was to become a new place for Stanley to visit, and wait for me to meet him after work plus they gave us food to take home, which saved on the grocery bill. Stan was as happy as I was when I told him about this job. I really didn't need a job as I could easily walk three blocks to either job.

After a dinner of hamburgers, fries, a lettuce and tomato salad, and a vegetable, I thought I would die when Stanley came home, looking so rough, tired and beat. I told him to go have his dinner.

There were tears in his eyes. He walked over to me, kissed me so passionately and hungrily that I couldn't believe it. This was the first passionate kiss ever from him. Yes it will be a day that goes down in history. Three good things happened to me on that day.

He had no explanation of where he'd been for the past week, but it didn't matter to me. He was my husband, and I was his Guardian Angel and I loved him with all my heart.

I told him that I had to sell my car and get a second job at "Gert's Grill." and the tears just flowed down from his cheeks. I always did hate to see a grown man cry. "It's entirely my fault. It's entirely my fault." He kept repeating those words.

"I'm sorry, I'm sorry." He also repeated those words.

Evidently he was sorry for something, but I didn't know what he was talking about and figured it had something to do with Connie's baby.

He pushed me to the sofa while kissing me, while lying on top of me, and you know the rest!

I was both shocked and happy. I felt like a new person. That was the day our marriage really began. It was over three months since our marriage, but today it actually began and at the same time, it marked the beginning of a new life for me.

~~~~~
~~~~~

CHAPTER TWENTY-FIVE

September 3, 2003

I called in sick that next morning, saying that Stanley just got home from being out of town and needed me. That was the truth. We stayed in bed all day. I fixed our meals and we even ate in bed. We made love throughout the day and night.

Ah, the beginning of true happiness and good things to come. I knew this. I could feel it. We went from a horrid marriage to a super good one. We held each other closely, fondling, and hugging and making up for lost time. We held hands constantly, in the grocery store, on the streets, but sometimes we stopped to kiss.

September 4, 2003

We played like kids. The games included tag, checkers, window shopping and we even had gifts for each other now and then from panhandling. We went to parades and one day Stan bought two bicycles home and we went riding. We took the train and bus rides with our free passes, and went out to eat cheap meals sometimes, and more expensive ones at other times. Gone were the days of steaks. We sat side by side at Gert's with Stan holding my hand and both of us smiling. When I worked in the restaurant, and wasn't busy, I stayed in his booth and when he had nothing to do, he came and met me. When he'd hold my hand and let his hands wander all over my legs, it bought back memories of other guys doing this. The only difference was, this was my husband and this felt so right.

September 5, 2003

We walked and walked until we could walk no farther and then stopped for a cup of coffee and walked home. Along the way we just sat in store fronts and must have looked pitiful because we came home with seven $1.00 bills.

September 6, 2003

We found a bike trail and rode until we could pedal no more. The path came to an end and there was a park, where we both stretched out and slept until dark and headed home. Bud and everyone else noticed our newly found happiness.

September 7, 2003

We took bubble baths together and washed each other's backs in the shower. On occasion, we went to the park when it was still warm and bathed with the Goddess but brought big bars of soap and plush towels that I bought months ago to dry off. Stanley admitted that it was better than air drying.

I don't know what possessed him to return home but I really didn't care and never questioned him. A whole new world had been born for us and it was too damn good, unbelievably good. It had taken months for me to find out about this new world, and I thank God that it happened. He was so excellent at making me feel like a woman, that I found the wait made it all worthwhile. For being a schizophrenic, and drinking, he had unusual stamina. I loved this man with all my heart. I just can't help repeating this.

September 8, 2003

We made love outside, beneath the trees and imagined the clouds were all sorts of animals and objects flying and floating around above us. We laughed at each other's description of the clouds and tickled each other as we rolled in the grass.

Each day was a new day to experiment and discover things about each other, our thoughts and suggestions as to what our plans were for the future. When it was warm out, we stretched out in a play field or empty lot and let the fall sun warm our bodies. I was always an overly emotional person and found myself shedding happy tears all the time.

September 9, 2003

We went to a restaurant at 2:00 a.m. in our pajamas. It was a two-mile walk to get there, but an unusually warm night. We ordered breakfast. I had on a frilly night cap to match my pajamas and Stanley had on pajama bottoms, duck slippers, and a baseball hat. I was in my stocking feet.

They almost didn't want to serve us and everyone was looking at us, not believing what they saw. We explained: "We are homeless and didn't have clothes, so we panhandled all day for money to buy what we are wearing. Please, will you give us something to eat?"

They brought our breakfast, but didn't take any money. Then they gave each of us a sandwich for lunch. We laughed all the way back to the condo.

September 10, 2003

It was unbelievable how we didn't need a car to get around. We even walked ten blocks to Bud's in our pajamas and bedroom slippers, Stanley in his Donald Duck slippers and me in my Barbie Doll specials. We drank beers, ate hot dogs, and after about eight beers each, we left quacking and Bud was shocked when we told him how far we walked and had to go. I think he believed that we were still homeless.

September 12, 2003

It was starting to look like winter. Stan told me he would educate me to live in the streets as we both knew we'd be there soon. We met many other homeless people and made friends, and when the weather turned rainy or cold we had inside games, like checkers, dominoes, and went to their "territory" or brought them to our "temporary condo" to have parties.

We all went to Navy Pier and enjoyed just sitting outside eating hot dogs with fries or drinking milk shakes. We enjoyed the giant Ferris wheel and seeing Chicago areas from such a height. It was always busy on that pier. Sometimes we even managed to take a sight-seeing tour where they served free drinks.

September 14, 2003

Dr. Cynthia was just as happy as I was when I told her of my wonderful, changed life. She admitted that maybe she had been wrong about Stan and told me that she was sorry.

I thought of Connie now and then, but pushed her to the back burner. Stan had forgotten about her. He loved me. He never left my side, didn't go out anymore, and I knew she was out of his life. I knew it. I knew it. I knew it.

September 15, 2003

I was always a saver, one who stashed money, and our friends and Bud were surprised when we told them we were going to the Bahamas. It was money left over from the sale of the car, and we did get an excellent price for the trip. We flew from Chicago to Miami, and took a Cruise with Carnival Cruise Lines to Nassau, and our room was on the seventh level with a window looking out at the ocean.

The ship was beautiful. Talk about food! There were ice carvings, fruits, vegetables, and full meals. We had our own spot at a table with eight others, and there was live entertainment and a pool on the top deck. We jogged in the morning, ate at mid-morning, had lunch, snacks in the afternoon, dinner, and then snacks later. Neither of us lost or gained a pound.

There was dancing around the pool area at night, and then a midnight dinner like you have never seen.

Nassau was an experience, and we managed to bring home some little items as souvenirs, a memory of the trip. There was a hand carved elephant, and when we visited St. John's Bay, neither of us could believe how white the sand was. It was not at all like Lake Michigan. And the water was such an unreal shade of turquoise blue, that we bottled some to take home. One could see the tropical fish floating beneath the surface. The bus driver was on the wild side, taking the turns somewhat too fast, but then I guess he did it on a daily basis so I closed my eyes and hummed. Stan laughed at me.

The bus wasn't crowded and we managed to make love behind the back seat of the bus, and giggled when he took fast corners or when it bounced over rough roads. When it stopped, we received a questionable look from the driver as we finished dressing and walked down the aisle, with messy hair and silly grins. It was back to the ship and then to Puerto Rico.

We went to a dinner theater presentation and enjoyed it tremendously. We loved the city and the view as you were pulling in to Puerto Rico. I will never forget the memories of that trip.

I only had two weeks off from work, and was shocked when the time came to return and Stanley told me he had a surprise for me. I couldn't guess what it was.

He told me he also had a part-time job in a liquor store. I didn't like the idea of him working in a liquor store, but it was better than nothing and we certainly could use the money.

October 13, 2003

Believe it or not, the weather remained warm some days and we enjoyed the colors of the trees which continued to change throughout the month. We both loved Illinois and its change of seasons; one never knew when they woke up if it would be fall or winter.

Stan told me, "I was born and raised in Chicago, but this year for some reason, is the most beautiful I've ever seen. I think it's because I'm with you." He didn't care who was around. He grabbed me, pulled me to the grass, and we all but took our clothes off making love, kissing, holding, and fondling. Several watched us and grinned (jealous)!

Things were going well at work and I decided it was time to visit my mother. I had just seen Dr. Cynthia two days earlier and she agreed. "It's about time!

The day before I left, coincidentally, Stanley ended up in the hospital again with a more serious pneumonia. Each time it seemed to be a little more serious.

Delores knew of the problems I'd had at home, and encouraged me to take this trip. She was very understanding and I would check on Stan everyday so it wasn't like I was just leaving him.

October 15, 2003

As I drove to Anniston, memories of childhood came back, as if it had been just yesterday. I remember Bonnie Sue, the only friend I had those growing-up years. She lived at the bottom of the mountain in a cute little house and we lived at the top, in a one-room shack. That's what I call it, because that's what it was. (My mother will never read this so it's okay to write.)

When you walked into our place, there was the bed, a sink, and a dresser. To the left, in the same little room, there was a little table, a pantry, and an ice box. There was no electricity, just a box that kept our food cold, and a person called "the ice man" delivered two huge chunks of ice every four days.

There was an outhouse, and a well that had horrible tasting water and a tub nearby that I used to wash clothes. There were clothes lines for me to hang up clothing and a huge garden where we grew all our own food. It kept us from starving during the long, cold winters. We had an old pot-bellied stove that kept us warm during winter. I did all the work because my mother was perpetually sick. She was pregnant fourteen times but I was the only child that lived (from my real father, her first husband) and I often wished that I had died too. From the beginning, life was much too hard. My real father loved me. Ben loved me in a different way—the wrong way—one I am not ready to talk about.

My birth father died in an accident, but I did not know the details, as mother never told me. He was only thirty-eight.

Then she married Ben, whom I did not like at all, and my mother hated me because Ben loved me more than he did her, but not in the right way. I pushed him to the recesses of my mind, the dark caverns of my back burner!

I remember when I was growing up, if it wasn't for Bonnie Sue, things would have been hopeless. She taught me to read and write, as Ben wouldn't let me go to school. Ben thought a woman's place was at home, having babies. Bonnie Sue would bring me books from the school library and together we read them. I began writing to my Aunt Beth in Chicago, and she would send the letters back to Bonnie Sue's house. Auntie Beth told me that if things ever got too bad for me in Anniston, she would like me to come and live with her in Chicago, and she would welcome me with open arms.

Deep in thoughts, I was nearing Anniston, and felt butterflies in my stomach. I was anxious to locate my mother and see Bonnie Sue again, yet it was scary, not knowing what to expect. I didn't know if Bonnie Sue was married, or had the same name, or where she lived. So I contacted her mother. I went to visit her after finding out that she lived in the same house.

"Hello Nilda, remember me? I'm Marsha Lou. It has been a long time."

She embraced me and cried, for what reason, I didn't know.

"How is my mother, and where is she living now?"

(The old shack at the top of the mountain had burned down and I knew she didn't live there.)

"Oh well, she is well."

I knew something was wrong—I could tell by her answer.

"How are you Marsha Lou?"

"I'm fine, but just looking for my mother."

"Oh well, oh well, she's pretty well."

Why oh why didn't I keep in touch over the years? But I knew the reason. No one else would understand, and I didn't fully comprehend it myself, but wouldn't talk it over with anyone. The bruises and wounds mother gave me when I was young never healed in my mind and heart. I couldn't dream of talking to her before the healing process took place, and finally that process was taking place, or at least beginning to.

Those bruises and wounds appeared and the conditions around their origination had been sent to the back of my mind, which was really overloaded with negative childhood memories. There they remained all these years but on occasion, they moved temporarily to a front burner. Now I was obligated to remember things. They were now on the front burner. The time had come.

~~~~~
~~~~~

CHAPTER TWENTY-SIX

October 16, 2003

My Mother was in a Nursing Home. Bonnie Sue didn't want to tell me at first. I could see the pain in her eyes as she spoke. "Marsha, you deserve to know. She is your Mother and was put in a mental hospital about five years ago. It seems that and she has Alzheimer's. One night she forgot and left the stove on and started a fire which almost burned the house down. The moonshine out back that her boy friends were constantly making caused an explosion."

"On another occasion, she had a party. There were about twenty men over and they were all nude, running around the yard, then down the driveway, and onto the street which just happened to be a main highway. They were all stopping traffic, and right in the middle of the group was your naked Mother dancing the Charleston. All of them had been drinking moonshine, and all were jailed. Somehow, the men were allowed to leave after a few hours, but your Mother was sent to HAPPY VALLEY NURSING HOME for a psychological evaluation and they admitted her with Alzheimer's. She may have forgotten many things, but she sure remembered how to dance!" (So now I knew why I was a wild woman, and all this time I was blaming it on Roxanne!)

Bonnie Sue didn't want to go with me to visit Mother, so I went alone. I don't think I'll ever forget my first glimpse of Mother when the nurses brought her out into the family room. She was once a big woman, but now she was thin, just a bone, weighing seventy-two pounds, and small like a little girl. She was only seventy-eight years old but looked at least ninety-eight.

Mother had two pointed brown teeth on the bottom and none on top. Her hair was hanging, in greasy, stringy strips, and she smelled of urine and feces. I was ashamed to be standing next to her dressed in a $3.00 dress. I didn't look the greatest in my cheap dress, but next to her it was like night and day.

I was looking at her shoes, the simple, black men's type that laced, but they had no laces. Her toes didn't have any room, and the shoes had holes in the front and later I checked the bottoms to find out they had more holes than leather-substitute material.

Mother's faded dress was fastened with safety pins and all she had on underneath was a diaper. I put my head down and fought the tears by biting my bottom lip, an old trick of Carl's. One could see her little sagging boobs hanging out in two places where safety pins were missing.

My little Mother was expressionless, showing no recognition of me whatsoever when I greeted her and this was too painful. I told her repeatedly what my name was, and wrapped my arms around her, but she failed to have any indication of my identity.

It was hard for her to eat and follow directions. I don't know if it was from a hearing problem, or a mental disability. She was stubborn, that I know, but found another psychiatrist had evaluated her and found she was also schizophrenic and *did* have Alzheimer's.

I couldn't talk to her any longer, and couldn't bear to see the nurses, so I left Mother and said I'd be back in about one hour. I wanted to buy some things for her even though I didn't have much money. Now, if I was still married to Carl, it would have been a different story.

I bought her some shoes, and some bedroom slippers and three house dresses. I put her name on everything.

October 17, 2003

I called Stanley every day when I was gone, and we talked about an hour. He wasn't doing too well. I needed little breaks when visiting my Mother, as we both cried too easily and I didn't like her to see me with reddened eyes.

I then stopped at Bonnie Sue's house and asked her if she'd like to go shopping with me and stop for a cup of coffee and see my Mother on the way back. She agreed and it was a wonderful break for me. We bought her some stockings, powder, lipstick and perfume. Then we talked over a cup of coffee.

"She had plenty of men since Ben died, because she couldn't be without one, and each one she picked made moonshine, just as Ben did. She began drinking more than the men, and ran around singing, dancing, humming, and doing bizarre things. Plus, she loved getting naked. She had no lady friends, but sure liked the men and her booze." (I didn't like hearing this.)

At first they had labeled her as having a schizotypal personality, but it was changed to schizophrenia, and the nurses explained how both were similar." (I didn't like hearing this.)

"Once at HAPPY VALLEY NURSING HOME, she really missed her drinks as she had become an alcoholic but now and then a man friend would smuggle her in something to drink, somehow, without being caught."

I sat and listened in disbelief. The words I heard were about my own Mother, whom I didn't know anymore and I'm sure that after all these years, she wouldn't know me, especially since she had Alzheimer's disease. It amazed me how much alike we were, just from hearing the few things that were said.

Bonnie Sue and I both agreed that HAPPY VALLEY NURSING HOME was anything but happy, and there was no valley to be seen.

Patients were sitting around in wheelchairs, with soaked pads beneath them. (I, being a nurse, checked these things) and their diapers had been on for hours.

Nobody pushed them around the halls, and the patients didn't know who they were, where they were, or what they were doing there. Orientation to time and place was zilch. They just stared into space, humming or mumbling things you couldn't understand. The staff didn't give a damn and didn't change their diapers or reposition patients when in wheel chairs or beds, as they should have done.

The Nurses and Aides offered no conversation, whatsoever to these patients. They didn't feed them unless a supervisor or family member was around and then, when visitors were around, sometimes they even played games with them.

They sat for a while in the family room, with the television on, but none of the patients were watching it, just the staff. In the background one could hear rap music coming from a boom box and four aides were dancing, if you want to call it that. The records that families brought remained unopened and never played.

(The nurses were outnumbered by the CNAs and if they crossed one of their helpers, they would find their tires slashed or money missing from their wallet. So they joined forces, did what the CNAs did, in order to have peace at work. Work was hard enough without fighting between staff members. One could figure this out immediately when walking into the family room.)

I went to call Stanley and checked back into the hotel down the street where I was staying. I didn't want to impose on Bonnie Sue or Nilda.

October 18, 2003

I walked in about lunch time, and had an alarming visit. The staff were talking about their own personal things, so I began unloading trays from the cart so patients could eat while their food was **still hot.** Nurses and aides continued to talk. The programs on the television (soap operas) didn't interest the patients in the least. They each had their lunch before them, and not many of them could feed themselves so they didn't eat because the staff was still busy talking. I fed a few, but couldn't stop the others from messing in the food, grabbing, or throwing food across the table.

Nobody got coffee or dessert because all of a sudden the staff did show up and took back all the dishes that the residents had and put them on the cart to send back to the kitchen. Almost none of the food was touched. But the coffee pot and chocolate cake stayed for the staff afternoon break.

The staff continued to work only when a chair alarm went off so they wouldn't have "fucking paper work to do."

After lunch, residents were seated around the television again, before taking a nap, and since many of them didn't eat their lunch, they were tired and the nursing assistants let hem pee in their diapers a while and then put them to bed. No, diapers were not changed before their naps. I peeked!

I went into my Mother's room with her, hoping some recognition to the fact that she needed help and attention, would be shown by the staff. I noticed her bathroom was piled high with wet and poopy diapers and I walked into several rooms and noticed the same thing. No rooms had windows open to bring in fresh air as this place really needed it.

"Hello Mother, I tried again. "Lori Lee, it's me. Your daughter, Marsha Lou." She didn't recognize me. I sat with her, talked to her, held her hand, and did bring the remainder of lunch to feed her in her room. All of the residents were so thin, and probably didn't know what food was or even how to open their mouths anymore. Besides, most of them had puree diets in varying shades of gray, brown, dark green, and who would like to eat that?

Mother just did not recognize me, no matter how hard I tried to talk about the olden days and she just sat and looked at her pureed spinach and carrots and swirled her small finger around in the vegetables without eating a bite but smiled at the orange and green fingers.

I cleaned her up and changed her, then put her to bed and went to call Stan. His condition was the same. He didn't feel good and I was worried about him too, and missed him so.

October 19, 2003

I was determined that my Mother would find out my name before the day was over. She had a picture of Ben and me on her night table. I took the picture and pointed to the girl and then to myself and said "Marsha Lou."

That had been my southern name, but as soon as I moved to Chicago with my Aunt, I dropped the 'Lou.' Mother stared and studied that picture, but still there was no recognition made on her part. She ran her finger over the picture with a blank stare.

October 20, 2003

Finally, on the next day, just as I was about to give up hope, she looked at me, then looked at the picture and pointed with her long thin finger, then said two soft, barely audible words: "Marsha Lou."

I couldn't believe it and my mouth remained open in shock. The tears flowed from her eyes and instantly I took the picture, and when pointing to myself said, "Marsha Lou. Yes. Me. Marsha Lou."

It was as if those tears we both shed repaired all the fences broken in almost twenty-five years since we had seen each other.

I ran over and put my arms around her but she didn't say anything else. I had left the picture with her and she just rubbed her hands over it. She looked at me, without speaking a single word, just crying, and I couldn't take it any longer. Tears continued to flow down her cheeks and she wanted to talk to me. I could tell. But the words just wouldn't come out. Instead of saying something like "Marsha Lou, I missed you," she would say "Green plates on he table floor." This is known as a 'word salad' and makes no sense whatsoever. Oh how she tried to make sense.

She wasn't getting her medication on time, sometimes it was forgotten altogether and she was almost totally ignored as she lived in her little room alone, and no call light was ever placed near her bed or table. She was helpless.

All of a sudden, I heard, "Prick." She rubbed Ben's picture.

"Dick always hanging out and ready to fuck. Always ready."

"Prick."

"Mother fucker."

What did she know that couldn't be put in words for me? What did she want to say?

"Mother fucker."

"Damn dick head. Prick."

She sounded like a wind up "Chatty Cathy" doll or a cussing parrot.

When I tried to feed her, she continued to stare at me, and I know she wanted to talk but just cried. I felt so damn helpless. My Mother. My poor little Mother. No matter what she did or didn't do, she was still my Mother.

Of all the diseases, Alzheimer's has to be the saddest for both patients and their families. One can't imagine how hard it is to see their loved ones, once active, now in this state. Try as they might, with words ready to flow, they were never spoken by those afflicted with Alzheimer's but sounds, word salads, rocking, jerking, twitching, and simply staring into space was enough to make one want to leave the room. That's why not many visited. They wanted to remember their loved one as they were before, not as they were now.

(Now don't get me wrong. Not all nursing homes or Alzheimer's Homes are like this one. This one just happened to be exceptionally negligent in the "care" area and my innocent Mother just happened to be placed here. Please forgive me for telling it like it is at HAPPY VALLEY. Nursing homes are inspected regularly and monitored closely, but I don't know what happened here).

October 21, 2003

I decided to leave that day and spend time with Stanley back in Chicago. I wasn't making much headway, anyhow. Mother hadn't said much, but I was able to put some pieces together.

All of a sudden she started talking and didn't stop. "Wrong. It was wrong. I let it happen. I didn't stop him." She cried hysterically.

I sat by her and when the shock of what she said actually hit me, I left for a minute or two. I didn't want her to sense my hatred for Ben.

"Marsha Lou. Marsha Lou. I love you so much."

"Prick. Prick. Prick."

She repeated those words over and over and even with all the negative feelings floating around that room, we managed to enjoy the ice cream the kitchen girls brought up for us.

I did stay the night, and after calling Stan and talking, I spent it in the hard chair next to her bed, in case she wanted to talk to me during the night.

October 22, 2003

Once more, I was ready to leave, told her goodbye, and was saddened at the thought of my leaving. She stood up and wrapped her thin arms around me and the story finally unfolded.

It was as though I was a little girl again. She motioned for me to her lap and I let her hold me and I felt her soaking wet diaper through my dress and changed her. Her wet things must have been on for at least six hours as they were so full of piss that they weighed ten pounds. Her buttocks area was bright red as if they washed her with some harsh kitchen cleanser. Damn. I knew it hurt her and I planned to buy some good lotion and put her name on it so it wouldn't walk away.

"Do any of you out there know what it's like to change your own Mother's diaper and see a bright reddened butt?" I couldn't begin to tell you the feelings that went through me.

She spoke to me in an almost normal way. "Marsha Lou—Please don't hate—me—I watched as—he did things to you—and I didn't try to stop him—He did terrible things and made me watch—If I didn't watch, he slapped me around—later and threw—me against the wall—He hurt both of us so many times—Afterwards, I went—crazy, and beat you—Oh how I beat you—I broke your leg twice and—it wasn't even you fault—. I hit you with anything I could find, and he—was the—guilty one. Not you—Oh—honey, please forgive me—I should have beat him—not you—I loved you but he wouldn't let me show it—He wanted you—all to himself. You worked so hard—doing things—I should have done, and later in the day, once—again, I—was made—to sit and watch—him fondle you. It made me—sick to watch all—he did to you. I know it hurt you but I was jealous because—he did it to you and not me—. I know—why you left home. It hurt to—see you limping down the driveway and then—he ran trying to stop you from—leaving that night, calling out your name—in a drunken slur that one—could hardly understand. He loved you—he staggered onto—the main highway and of course Ben—never even saw the car that—hit him and threw—him across the—narrow road and into a tree—They said—he died instantly."

"I had said—terrible things—about you, called—you terrible names, and said—it was all—your fault that he ran—after you, but—it wasn't. You didn't do—anything wrong. He started things—and I blamed—you. Oh baby, baby, baby. Oh—I forgot to tell—you that—Ben—was—a—borderline schizophrenic, undiagnosed—with—a manic depressive—side sickness. I had—lost the two—only people—I had left in—the whole world that—night. Your—birth father—was a schizophrenic—and ended up—in a nursing home—when you were—so little."

(She paused to take a bottle of liquor from her drawer and took four manly swigs, then blinked her eyes and continued.) "I never—had a chance to tell you this—before, so I'm telling you now. I am a—schizophrenic with Alzheimer's disease. Talk about luck"

She was perfectly lucid and made a helluva lot of sense.

"He was—in a—nursing home and—jumped out a window to—his death because—he couldn't deal with—his problems. And I'm also psychotic. It—runs in the—family, you—know. Everyone in the family is schizophrenic."

(And that's when I found out what I wanted to know, along with many other things.)

All of a sudden she changed. She was a different person, someone crazy, and I listened in disbelief as she talked in a deep man's voice that gave me the heebie-jeebies.

"AT FIRST I DIDN'T WANT TO WATCH AND THEN I ENJOYED WATCHING AND LISTENING TO HIS VULGAR LANGUAGE WITH EVERY OTHER WORD BEING "FUCK. I WAS MARRIED TO HIM BUT YOU GOT ALL THE ATTENTION. HE REALLY LOVED YOU. BUT I ALLOWED IT AND LOVED IT. I GUESS IT WAS PART OF MY DISEASE AND PARTLY IT WAS TO SHOW YOU THAT I JUST WANTED AN EXCUSE TO BEAT YOU. I LET HIM DO THINGS TO YOU SO I COULD BEAT YOU LATER."

Then she was going back to her female voice. And she carried the words evenly, without pausing.

"I loved you. I always did. You were my only child that lived. Please forgive me. Please, I beg of you, forgive me." She reached for me and embraced me so tenderly, like a Mother should embrace a child, and no matter how old I was, I was still her child.

"Oh Mother, please forgive me. I think of you every day and love you. What I wouldn't do now to go back to those years."

I left her room and stopped in to see the Administrator. I wanted my Mother with me. I told the Administrator that I was a nurse and quite able to take care of Mother. Things sounded positive. She said, "I'll be in touch within the week, Mrs. Brooke."

Then on the way back to my mother's room, I stopped to call Stan once more, and we each told the other how much we loved our life together and I told Stanley it was not an easy visit in Anniston and that I would tell him all about it when I got home.

I went to say goodbye to Mother, and told her I'd be back soon to take her "home. (I didn't like the nursing home, the administration, personalities working there, care, and also wanted my Mother with me. That was the main thing I wanted and it was as simple as that).

Together Mother and I cried, and then laughed, and we both danced down the hall singing. The staff almost choked on their cake! We woke up sleeping residents, and the next thing you knew, several joined us in singing and quite a few did the Charleston, but Mother was in the middle of the group.

I told her once more how much I loved her and promised to keep in touch. We embraced for the last time

~~~~~

I began driving home and knew I had to lay all my problems on somebody's shoulders. I stopped at a bar alongside the road, slightly back from the highway, and pulled in. There was a handsome hunk sitting there, and first we talked about weather and sports and then our Mothers. He asked me to come outside with him, and I did. We sat in the grass.

They brought us three beers, and he said to me, "You know, I just saw my Mother. She is getting old, and I was not the best child. I can't make it up to her. God help me, I can't make it up to her now."

"She has Cancer and only months to live, and I love her so much" He walked away. I caught up to him and embraced him as we both cried and then I got in my car and began the long drive back home.

I called Dr. Connors on the way home, told her I had lots to tell her, and made an appointment for October 25, my first day back to work.

October 25, 2003

The work day was fine. My desk was clear, not cluttered, meaning I really didn't have much to do that day. After work I went to see Dr. Cynthia.

"Dr. Cynthia, I just got back from Anniston and think I have all the puzzle pieces now."

After telling my story, she told me, "Marsha, I don't know if you know this or not, but I want to tell you the long-term effects of what happened to you as a child according to psychology books. I'll just mention a few of these to you and let you think about them. We already know that because of Ben you can't have
~~~~~

children. In addition to that, his abuse caused: Obsessive-compulsive disorders, like counting, It also caused depression, anxiety and panic attacks, promiscuity, lack of self-esteem, sexual problems, drug and alcohol abuse, alienation and aloneness, and never being able to trust anyone. These are all results of having an abusive childhood, either mentally or physically."

"Oh my goodness! There is a chance I'm pregnant now. I told Cynthia. I just don't know how, but will talk to you about it at a later date. "Either I'm pregnant or starting with an early menopause."

"And the fact that you were so young at the time of abuse, according to my studies on this subject, both of your parents are guilty of causing physical injuries, nightmares, flashbacks, hallucinations and delusions, things you tend to push out of your mind, fear, guilt, shame, anger, anxiety, despair, terror, rage, numbness, confusion, loss of control, sleeplessness, and self-blame. Marsha, the list goes on and on and my heart goes out to abused children, whether it is mental or physical." She then came to me and held me, gave met the biggest hug and told me I was special to her and that I could always depend on her.

"Obviously some of these things have persisted for a very long time. Some can actually develop into longer term effects on behavioral and emotional well being. This is what happened to you".

"I knew there was a problem in your early years, because you never wanted to talk about them. But nothing like this. No wonder you have so much going on now. I don't know how you do it. I want to talk about this again at our next session."

"I just don't know who the father is, but I know for sure it isn't Carl." I started to leave.

"Oh, I have a note for you. I don't know who it's from, who sent it or how it got here. It was just under my door with your name on it in care of me."

Carefully, I opened it.

It was from the Administrator at HAPPY VALLEY and she wrote to inform me that at the present time, I couldn't take my Mother because I was "unfit." She said she would call me and explain.

October 28, 2003

I returned to work on October 28, and it worked out just fine, because Stanley came home on the 29th.

October 29, 2003

The doctor had discharged Stan on the 29th, and when I saw him, I wrapped my arms around him and it was as if we hadn't seen each other for a year. He was thinner but looked good. We kissed some more and it is impossible to describe how wonderful it felt just to have his arms around me again.

~~~~~
~~~~~

CHAPTER TWENTY-SEVEN

November 5, 2003

Stan and I had a delicious Swiss steak dinner that I prepared, along with fresh rolls, green beans, fresh fruit, and apple pie for dessert. He fell asleep, and I decided to walk downstairs to have a drink at the bar.

I enjoyed the drink, and was able to sit and relax without being bothered. I had another drink and John came in and sat by me. I greeted him pleasantly and told him about my trip to see my Mother.

"Can I see you sometime, Marsha? I mean like for dinner, dancing and have a little fun, like going to a play or something?"

"I don't think so. Everything is fine with Stan and me lately, and I really don't want to start anything." We just chatted and shared another drink, and decided to leave. Yes, I did like him, but I was in love with my husband. While traveling to my condo, my mind wandered back and I found myself singing in the quiet elevator:

As night time falls, his voice it calls
He's waiting for me I can't wait to see
I check the bars, look inside all cars
If he wears a ring, I'll dance on bars.

I wondered why, now of all times, my life was reverting to earlier years. Had I forgotten to take my medication? Was this a warning of some sort? What the hell was going on now?

"We warn you Marsha. Be prepared. It won't be long and you will know. We can't tell you what it is, but it will really be the beginning of the end."

I didn't know what beginning of what end the voices were talking about, but it didn't sound good.

Stan was asleep on the sofa and I lay alongside him, our arms entwined and we woke up in the morning, noticing that neither of us had moved all night.

It snowed a bit early just enough to cover the grass, and we went for a walk in the newly fallen stuff.

Then we decided we would have to panhandle to get some boots and winter coats. We stood at a busy corner by an office complex where doctors and dentists worked and together we collected $140.00 in only four hours. We shivered with no mittens or hats, and shoes with holes in the bottoms and sides. Evidently the people who passed by felt sorry for us as we stood there, holding each other to keep warm which did help a little.

At the thrift shop, we bought boots, gloves, winter coats, scarves, and shoes. The sunshine helped to warm us in the frigid weather. I had my first lesson in "winter survival" that day.

Stan told me that when the weather changed and you didn't have proper clothing to protect your body just wear what you have on, preferably dirty, and people will see and feel sorry for you. If you pick a good area, it won't take long to collect the money you need. "If you need mittens, for example, stand there blowing hot air on your hands and people will take the hint and maybe give you a dollar or fifty cents and every little bit helps."

"In case something happens to me, I want you to know how to make it through the cold Illinois months," he told me. He taught me how to make a shelter beneath trees, alongside a building surrounded by tall weeds, how to find shelter at churches that had outside stairways to the basement with twists and turns until you finally make it to the bottom level. The twists and turns serve as wind blockers and keep you warmer. "Of course you have to make sure you have your blankets and wine with you so you don't have to make so many trips back upstairs."

I told Stan that nothing could or would happen to him because that would surely do me in. I meant it. I wouldn't want to live without him. I couldn't live without him.

We made love every chance we had, and at Bud's, he would fix us hot toddies and let us sleep in a bed behind a curtain in the back of the bar on cold nights. It was always clean and fresh as if it were waiting for us. Nobody walked in on us, and we were quiet and it felt so good to sleep inside on a bed. The linens were always clean and there was plenty of heat and blankets and all the comforts of home. Actually, there was a kitchen and bathroom back there, and the refrigerator was always well-stocked with food and beverages.

"Remember, whenever you want, you are welcome to spend the night here."

November 6, 2003

(I had to panhandle to buy another book in which to write my daily diary. I found another green one and will get caught up tonight. I have about seven more months to tell you about. Perhaps there won't be enough room to write it all here. I certainly hope it will work out.)

Today, Stan taught me how to make a shelter behind a soda machine in store fronts and how to position my body up against the building so the wind wouldn't hit it. It was depressing in a way to have him show me these things "in case he wasn't here with me."

We then walked to the lake and played. We walked out about ten feet in the frigid waters and found two huge rocks and sat on them. The water was beginning to freeze, and we were just trying to prove that we were brave and could walk out in it.

Then after splashing around awhile, and becoming soaking wet, and freezing, cold, we decided that it would be more fun to play this game in the spring or summer. (I don't know what I was thinking about when I allowed Stanley to walk out in that cold water. My mind just hasn't been with me.)

We had to live in the streets by now, as there was no money to pay our utilities and we couldn't live without water and electricity. (I could have asked someone for help, but I didn't.)

One morning, bright and early, we packed our bags and left. Just like that. There was money for food for three days and that was it. I was so tired of spending the days outdoors and not sleeping well, plus still working at North Park Rehab. I didn't know how much longer I could handle it.

All these hard days when I was off, plus the nights, I had to spend outside caused a horrid chill to go through my body. For a break we would go to Bud's. I really didn't sleep well outside, because people sometime harm the homeless, and I think I slept with one eye open whereas Stan slept like a baby. Of course he was used to it.

November 8, 2003

We went back to the condo that night, even though it had no heat or electricity. We used candles. During the night Stan said, "It's so damp and cold up here, we might as well go outside." And we did, with no clothes on, and ran around the yard, looped and screaming at 3:00a.m. Some neighbor called the police, and North Park also found out about Stanley's behavior in the restaurant a couple of months ago, and my attendance/tardiness record wasn't the greatest. So I got my pink slip. I lost my job.

"Marsha, you had a good job and didn't appreciate it. Even though you have a new place to live, and are close to work, you come in late every morning, and we know a few things about Stan and don't approve of his behavior either. It's been great having you here with us, Marsha, and we wish you the best of luck." With that they handed me my last pay check. That was one of the biggest slaps in the face I ever had. That and not being allowed to have my own Mother because I was 'unfit.'

November 10, 2003

We had to concentrate on setting up a sheltered area for ourselves now and it wasn't easy. We placed a "FOR SALE" sign in the window of the condo and only hoped someone would drive by and love it as I did. The money from it would certainly help us get a fresh start, and this time I told Stanley that he could pick out the place to live.

We visited Union Station, both the main one and the Communications Center nearby. We became lounge lizards, at the high tables and upstairs where we wandered around and went out to see the trains at the end of the line. At Union Station we kept changing seats on the brown benches, pretending we were waiting for "our connection" to arrive. We took turns between the two stations, and did manage to get money here and there so we had enough food.

Sometimes we took the train to one of the northern communities and ate and slept on mats at PADS. The ones in the northern suburbs had more food and bedding and they even gave you breakfast in the morning and packed a lunch for you. They surely are appreciated for the work, efforts and personal attention they give the homeless.

November 12, 2003

Today we spent the day in the library, walking around and pretending we were looking for a book. At the end of the day, we walked upstairs, and hid behind the book rack, and when it was time to close for the day, we took the draperies off the hooks, spread them on the floor, slept on them and used them for blankets. We spent the night entwined, and later I walked downstairs and washed my hair in the washroom, (using hand soap.) I dried it as best I could with paper towels and it felt so good.

November 13, 2003

Ben allowed us to sleep on his front porch. It had a swing, and we were both able to sleep side by side. He brought us blankets and food, and asked that we be gone by 9:00a.m., when his wife usually came out to get the paper. We made love on the creaky old swing, and hoped it didn't wake her up early, and just in case it did, we left at 7:30a.m. just to play it safe if she was awakened.

November 14, 2003

We slept under Phil's porch. It wasn't warm, but he brought out blankets and hot soup for us, and at least we were sheltered from the snow storm that night.

November 20, 2003

We continued to exist; each day was just another day. We decided to panhandle and go to a movie, then sleep in the theater in the balcony that night. The entire theater was empty, and we found two seats, and darned if two men didn't come in and sit right in front of us. I couldn't see over the one in front of me and I kicked his seat and told him politely to scoot down a little. We should have just moved but we didn't think that should be necessary since we were the first ones there.

The guy turned around, and said "Sorry," and scooted down. He looked just like Carl, my former husband.

I realized it was Carl, with a man, and they were holding hands. That surely explained a lot of things to me!

"Hey, that's my wife. Don't talk to her," Stan said.

"She was my wife before she was yours, buddy."

Stan was a fighter. The punches started and the manager appeared and told Carl and his friend to sit somewhere else.

Later on, when I had to go to the bathroom, I found Carl, and told him I was going to call him.

"I'll call you."

"No that will be impossible because we don't have a phone."

"Okay, please call me. My office phone is listed in the book. So is my home phone, under my name."

Stan happened to see me talking to him and came over and dragged me out of the theater. I think Carl was happy to see me, but unhappy that I saw him with another man, and Stan was just pissed because I had gone over to find Carl.

When we left, Stan was quiet for the longest time, and then said, "If you love him so much, why don't you go back to him? He can give you more than I can. I know you still love him."

"Don't be silly, hon. I love only you." I then had to explain to Stan that he was the first man that ever made me completely happy but he remained quiet and we went home to our territory beneath the bushes, and had a few drinks from bottles we had stashed. Then Stan did his usual thing. After drinking everything in sight, he was out of it, but this time it lasted only minutes. Then he got up and left, telling me he'd be back in two or three days.

I thought, "Oh here we go again," and wondered what I had done wrong. I had talked to Carl and that upset my jealous husband. Besides, he didn't need an excuse once he decided to leave.

~~~~~
~~~~~

CHAPTER TWENTY-EIGHT

November 23, 2003

Stan came back and found me under the bushes and we went to Bud's. After having a few drinks, Stanley announced that he was leaving and would be back in two or three days, (the exact thing he already told me three days ago.) It was such a terrible feeling knowing that I was a failure and once again I wondered what was wrong with me. Could I blame it on my parents? I just didn't know.

Five minutes after Stan left, I called Carl and asked if I could borrow some money.

"No problem honey. How much do you need?"

"Could you spare $700.00?"

"No problem."

I told him that I'd meet him on a nearby corner, and within fifteen minutes, we met. I told him thank you over and over.

"Hop in," he said.

"Okay."

We drove to a nearby motel and held each other closely and made love, then fell asleep for four hours. He surprised the hell out of me. He didn't make love to me when we were married, but now—and WOW!

"I just want you to know that I can do it, and love sex now as much as you did when you were with me. Why and where did we go wrong? I want to try again with you."

I didn't say a thing.

I didn't care whether or not Stan returned or where he was. I thought it was so bizarre that Carl told me he married again on the rebound, but found his new wife didn't like sex.

He went to therapy after we parted and this changed his idea about sex. Then he married her and she didn't like it. I almost LMAO! (Laughed my ass off) See, I do repeat things!

Poor Carl, he now couldn't get enough sex. He asked me to marry him again and again.

He also told me he had been dating a guy for six months and had discovered himself to be bi-sexual. Then he actually begged me to come back to him and he would tell his friend to leave. He made a joke about my video making us both rich so I wouldn't have to sleep under bushes.

He told me he was going to split the money with me.

I told him that I planned to use the money he gave me that evening to get a small apartment, a new dress, and then go job hunting. I thanked him again for his help and especially for seeing me again.

"I'll keep in touch with you, if you don't mind. I enjoyed our time in bed and also your company in general."

"Promise you will keep in touch?"

"Yes."

"Oh Marsha, here is your share of the movie proceeds thus far. He handed me $20,000.00 and I was speechless. I planned to hide it under the blanket under the tree and planned to put it in the bank the following morning and go apartment hunting with Stan. I did just that. I didn't want that money stolen like all the rest was.

Stan was gone for four days, without a cell phone or anything. I was worried sick. All I could think of was that he would be exposed to outdoor elements and he would have pneumonia once again His job at the liquor store actually started that night, and he went to work, but he came home coughing and looking pale.

December 10, 2003

Stan and I spent the day at the Museum of Science and Industry and the Aquarium. There were so many unusual sights to see but all the walking we did was unbelievable. I never knew how gloomy a coal mine could be until I saw the one at the Museum and I felt like a little child discovering the world. We walked around all day, and then walked home after a seeing the parade. I literally fell into our cold damp bed under the bushes.

I didn't believe how little energy we had left. (Just enough to make slow, passionate love!)

Decembe12, 2003

It was so beautiful outside that Stan asked, "Where should we go today?" The liquor store where Stanley worked were cutting down on his hours so we decided to visit Lincoln Park Zoo. (I just wanted to be with him. Crazy. I know. The apartment hunting could wait. He was my outdoors guy with the skinny butt and we had money in the bank now.)

We hitched a ride to Stockton Drive, where it runs into the North Beach and first walked to the Lincoln Park Conservatory and then the Lincoln Park Zoo. We walked around, sat in the sun, and after being in the sun, the cold weather didn't seem so bad. We sat in the shade and drank hot cocoa. We also had cold beers which were disguised beneath the advertising mugs that kept them cold. The cooler only carried four mugs, and they fit perfectly. That was enough for a cold wintry day as we planned to visit Bud's later. I was learning to rough it in the cold weather, too.

We left after eating our hot dogs, thumbed a ride and spent the night in Bud's back room. He was happy to see us.

One doesn't need tons of money to have fun in life. All you need is a compatible partner and that's what I discovered I had with Stan. At first, I had my doubts, but we both had moods and knew each other so well, it was fun enjoying life with him.

We slept close to each other on the bed; once again it reminded me of what a honeymoon should be.

All in all, it was a wonderful day. I looked in the mirror and it was the first time in a long time that I saw "her." She had gray hair, with just a touch of black left, tons of wrinkles, and looked so old.

I screamed and started hitting myself in the head. "I hate myself. I hate myself." By then, she was gone.

Work was a disappointment for both of us. They told me at the restaurant that I came to work too often smelling of booze, said they were sorry but they would have to let me go. I didn't know what to do at first, and it hurt to think that neither of us had a part-time job.

I had used every cent that I had and didn't quite want to go apartment hunting yet. Something told me it wasn't the time. Why I didn't just take the money and pay the utilities I didn't know. My brain was no longer functioning. We panhandled. We had to stand out with our tin cups and get money for the train fare to go to a PADS shelter. We couldn't bother Bud every night.

Being homeless could happen to anyone so one shouldn't point a finger. It doesn't have to be a downhill trip with alcohol and sex that puts you in this predicament. It could be gambling and smoking. But addictions will break you mentally, physically, and monetarily.

Addictions start out ever so slowly, then escalate and become full-blown—and when that time comes, there is no turning back.

Our gas and electric bills were temporarily unpaid, and we were glad the bill collectors couldn't find us, as we changed locations so often. Yes, I was a Miss Hoity-Toity, and unlike Stan, couldn't get used to bill collectors.

~~~~~
~~~~~

CHAPTER TWENTY-NINE

There was a promise of spring in the air that February. Things just started to feel better mentally and physically for both of us. I enjoyed my time alone when Stan was away or busy by just walking in the park downtown. I always enjoyed sitting on that bench and watching people.

It's exciting and different to "rough it" at first, as any new experience is, But after weeks and months of sleeping in store fronts with other homeless people, smelling the garbage in alleys, and sleeping in the same alleys at times, plus sleeping between buildings, it becomes old hat and even PADS felt degrading to me, but it kept us going.

The days drag on and on for the homeless as there are no goals, nothing specific to do, no birthday cards, gifts, or Christmas to plan for—it begins to bug me and things like this leave me antsy with a desire to "do something productive."

Sleeping in construction sites by the heavy equipment or in vacant lots or vacant cars and seeing animals running wild was not my cup of tea (or bottle of beer.)

I remember sleeping in a dump truck, with half a load of gravel, and I had to mound it around me for warmth. Believe it or not, we were desperate, and when you are that bad off, one thinks of all sorts of things to survive. Survival is the name of the game.

In the wooded areas or vacant lots and parks, people would sleep up along the side of trees with blankets wrapped around them, or in sleeping bags on the ground or on picnic benches or tables. There were so many cardboard boxes that housed these people—more than one could begin to fathom.

Thanks to Mother Nature and her tall grass and weeds that not only served as a substitute blanket, but also hid us from people who would just as soon club us to death as look at us.

We slept beneath overpass roads, under the road above. We would set up a slab of wood, heavier than plywood, and fasten it to the road above, and five of us would sleep side-by-side to keep warm. But the only problem there was that if the guy in the middle had to pee in early hours of the morning before we wanted to wake up, we had no choice but to begin our day early or tell him to 'hold it.' Otherwise, we kept each other warm staying there. (It bothered me at first to sleep with all men, but then I belonged to Stan and nobody bothered me, plus I was in the same boat as them.) That twenty-four inches of space above us and the overpass allowed twenty-four inches less on the road beneath us.

It's not hard to find an empty, unlocked car parked conveniently along a curb, or better yet, in someone's garage. We quickly learned where to look for them. The only problem here was the possibility of the owner deciding to take his car to work or someplace earlier than usual, before we had vacated his source of transportation. Some of these cars were in heated garages, and those were the ones that we looked for first and we made ourselves at home in the back seat or in the hatchback area.

Stan preferred the park, beneath his clump of bushes, over all other areas. That's what he called his territory. (I finally learned the meaning of that word.)

He was well-liked and respected as he was one of the senior members of the homeless clan. Now, they also accepted me, since I was his "woman." The fights over territories were noisy and lasted a while, and even when San ordered them to "stop," the fighting prevailed, making it difficult to sleep at times.

We continued to take showers with the Goddess, and were not caught even though we still run around to air dry in the early morning air. Maybe the police did know, and did see us, but gave up on telling us to stop air drying. Or maybe it was the big joke of the precinct, as not everyone had nudies running around in parks at 4:00a.m. drying off after showering with the Goddess.

We were bound and determined not to miss those showers when in the area of the park, and continued this habit day after day. We treasured the small piece of soap that was hidden in the fifth stall, wrapped in toilet tissue, just beneath the top of the toilet tank cover where we placed it.

I missed work tremendously. When working, you are able to see other human beings and interact with them. But when you don't have a job, you are bored. Don't tell Stanley this, but a woman needs to work at something, in order not to succumb to temptation and go to bars flirting, or go shopping and spending money which they don't have. Of course there are exceptions—some are content staying put where their husband is.

The sign "No Bathing or Showering Allowed" was written by the Goddess' pool. But people like us continued to shower there. Stan told me that there was no sign saying: "No Laundry to Be Done Here," so he continued to wash his clothes there. I washed my two dresses and slacks in the laundry down the street with panhandling money.

Yes, the blankets we used were kept beneath the trees, but were often damp so we first covered the damp ground with a board, then papers, and put blankets on top of our "base." That along with a bottle or two of cheap wine plus a few beers and the cold and dampness didn't bother us one bit. Once we warmed up, we were able to cuddle and have a little fun together. That is something that never grows old with us.

The branches that hung down to the ground covered us and it was actually private enough to allow us to fool around every night if we wanted. And we both "wanted." Also, we would enjoy fooling around in the morning and that really made the cold shower feel invigorating and kept us that way the entire day. I marvel at the way my life style had changed during the past twenty months. I couldn't believe that in two years, I had gone from a woman who had everything to a homeless waif, sleeping in the park and showering outdoors.

One day I found a surprise and knew that it was two police officers that just left the area. I found the three very expensive blankets under the bushes and ran to the park entrance to shout, "Thank you," but they kept driving. I love the smell of a new blanket, the softness, and the way they felt next to you body. We put them to good use.

We took every advantage of every chance we had to get beneath them and cuddle and screw! We held hands and wrapped our arms around each other at night, and were completely happy.

Buzz visited our territory now and then just to say "hello" and asked if he could take us out to breakfast. He would invite us over to his huge house for the night, but that ended when I caught him peeking through a hole in the wall and watching us make love. I didn't like him, I guess because something about him reminded me of my stepfather. Maybe it was the way he looked at me with his huge, brown, angry eyes.

Stan walked to the bathroom and Buzz was full of all kinds of questions to ask me. "So you have a house in the country, Marsha?"

"Not anymore."

"You sold it?"

"Yes."

"How much did you get for it?"

"I forgot."

There was no way I would answer that question.

"I just loved those green shutters that decorated your house and the pool just as you come in. I bet you are going to miss that home."

"When did you see it?"

"I was over one night with Stan and Connie. Did you know she is going to have Stanley's baby in April?"

I pretended I didn't hear him, remained neutral to his question and said, "No way, he's my husband."

But suddenly, I knew it must be true. Stan spent so much time away from me and so much of my money was missing. She evidently became pregnant not too long after we were married, if it was true. I'd wait for Stanley to tell me before I believed Buzz, even though I believed John when he told me. In other words, I already knew.

Stan returned and Buzz completely changed the subject.

"Yes, that is right. Anytime you guys need help or money or a place to sleep think of me. I've known Stan for a long time and he is my best friend so you both are always welcome at my place—anytime—remember that.

~~~~~

I pushed it all to the back burner once more. The hell with what Buzz told me. I wanted to hear it from Stan.

Stan and I didn't feel like going back to the park that night. In fact we didn't talk. I didn't know who I was, where we were, or who I was with. I was out of it, completely out of it, probably because of what Buzz had told me.

We took the elevator in an apartment building to the fifteenth floor and walked out the unlocked door, to the roof. Stanley showed me where there were vents that delivered heat and we took off our coats and used them for blankets, sleeping on the gravel that covered the roof. The warm air sometimes actually turned hot as it blew on us, but then, the temperature outdoors was below zero. The winds blew and the snow fell, but at least we were together, side by side, embracing each other and still managing to kiss, hug and screw our brains out.

Stanley began an occasional cough and it worried me. It always worried me when he coughed. We didn't realize how cold it was outside until we climbed down from the roof and walked with people on the sidewalk. We met Buzz. "Come on guys. Go with me to Union Station." He didn't look at me when he spoke.

We all hitched a ride and went inside to warm up. While sitting on one of the long wooden benches, Buzz spotted a wallet that an older man had dropped. I had a chance to witness Buzz in action. He took the wallet, put it in his pocket with such smooth, practiced moves that I know he'd done it many times before. The older man returned from buying his ticket, looked in his pockets first, then on the bench.

"Is everything okay?" suddenly very concerned Buzz asked.
~~~~~

"No, it's not. All the money I have for this month is gone. I just lost my wallet somewhere."

"Here, I'll help you look for it."

Buzz looked under and on the bench, and of course he didn't find it.

"Here, let me give you some money, just a little bit. I'm sorry, so sorry that you lost your wallet, Sir. I don't see it. You probably had valuable papers in it, too."

"Yes, it had about $1,500.00 which was my Social Security check that I just cashed and car keys and title. I just bought the car."

Good-hearted Buzz searched in his own wallet and handed the man $50.00. I would have laughed so hard if he accidentally reached in his pocket and pulled out the man's wallet instead of his.

"Thank you again. Thank you." (He made Buzz look like a hero when he was really a thief.) "But how can I repay you?"

"That's fine. Consider it a gift." Sure it was a gift! Now Buzz had the money, car, title, and keys to the car. He isn't any hero in my book. He made a damn good haul in that one action.

Stan whispered. "He has this history of taking things. I think he sells what he steals, but if there is anything it a wallet that he can't use, he takes it out before tossing the wallet. Just watch and see what I mean."

It hurt to see that as he was so smooth in his actions with everything pre-planned, anyone would know he was doing this for ages and ages. Buzz bought dinner for everyone, but there was no way I could eat. I couldn't even watch the rest of them, and begged Stan to take me to our little clump of bushes.

His cold was worse and he was wheezing.

Buzz glared at me with hatred. Pure hatred. He had been talking to Stan about selling the newly acquired car to a friend in Texas, and I had interrupted their conversation.

April 5, 2004

We left and I knew that I had to see Dr. Cynthia soon. Before I did see her, I had to panhandle to get something decent to wear and needed money to pay for the visit. I couldn't go to the hairdresser and have a blonde rinse applied to my hair since it was beyond the point of looking half-way good with just a rinse. I couldn't do it myself because I had no place to do it. But I could manage to buy a new dress.

I panhandled and collected $42.00. I could afford to buy some shampoo at least, but I couldn't walk in a wash room of a restaurant or in a service station and come out with a towel wrapped around my head and I knew the pool by the Goddess wasn't appropriate for this, either.

It is so hard for a homeless female. (I never thought of asking Dr. Cynthia, either.) She finds herself among men and is the "odd ball" and I couldn't help but wonder what the hell had happened in my life to put me out there with "them." I just pissed away all my money, with someone else's help, of course. With the money I did get from panhandling, I bought a cheap dress which cost $2.75 and he remaining $39.25 I put in my old purse which I kept beneath my pillow.

I told Stan I was going to see about getting my job back, and he gave his blessings and told me to meet him at Bud's when I was finished.

I'll never forget the look on Dr. Cynthia's face when she saw me walk in her office. To say she was surprised, was putting it mildly. She knew I was coming because my appointment was in her book so she shouldn't have looked so damn surprised.

She stared at my long, mousy gray, misshaped hair cut, no longer a perfect style in a glamorous blonde shade. It was greasy and smelly from not washing it in over two weeks. My skin was broken out and rough, and in various blotchy shades. My teeth hadn't been brushed and several were broken or missing and my hands resembled those of a construction worker who didn't know the meaning of the words, 'hand lotion.'

My two-dollar dress suddenly looked faded and cheap and I was now in the same category as Stan as I stood there in my dirty tennis shoes with no laces. Why did I think at one time that it was so cute for Stanley to be dressed this way yet for me it was downright pitiful?

I hadn't taken a shower in four days because I finally did get my period and didn't want the Goddess' icy cold water on me, and I was sure I didn't smell so good. I didn't have money to buy sanitary napkins, so I took one of Stan's old white stockings, filled it with toilet tissue from a roll on a gas station's bathroom floor and I turned down the loose end of the stocking. Later during my visit to Dr. Cynthia, some of the bloody toilet tissue fell on her office room carpeting, as the stocking had a hole in it. I didn't know this at first and didn't know what to do, but Dr. Cynthia gave me some pads from her drawer and told me, "Don't worry about it honey."

Needless to say, I thought of the good old days when I had everything I needed. But in life, one can't go back. Like the saying goes, "We make our own bed and we have to sleep in it."

Cynthia's facial expressions told me that I didn't smell too clean and suddenly I felt like an orphan in my cheap dress. It really was faded and not worth the cheap price that I paid for it, but it was too late to do anything about that now.

Cynthia stared at me and didn't say a word at first, but then said, "Oh Marsha, come and sit down. Let me give you a cup of hot coffee and a Danish pastry. I was never one for Danish, but I was starving, and ate it so fast that I hardly tasted it. I realized that I really was hungry.

"Marsha, what happened to you so soon? I can't believe it. It has only been a few months and I hardly recognize you."

"Dr. Cynthia, all my money is gone. Everything is gone. Stanley drained me already and I'm not used to living like this. Between you and me, Dr. Connors, the honeymoon was a disaster. How could anyone spend their entire day drinking and looking at the lake and smoking pot? That's what we both do now. Yes, I do it too."

"Then he comes home at night and drinks some more. I do too. By the way, we have no home. Our home is beneath a clump of bushes in the park and the ground is cold and damp. He practically lived on hot dogs at first, and they didn't always agree with me. I bought some good food and just had to throw it out. All he wanted was a hot dog or a peanut butter and jelly sandwich."

"Then guess what. We finally had sex almost four months after our marriage."

"Oh my Good Lord, Golly, Gee Whiz, Fuck! How was it?"

"For the first time in my life, a man satisfied me, 100% and knowing it's my husband I'm with helps too. I am relaxed and don't have to worry about getting home."

"My one-night-stands made me feel dirty and cheap but since I love my husband more than anything in the world, there won't be any more of that. Thank God. Now Stan enjoys the finer things for lunch and dinner as I do, but we just can't afford them without panhandling."

"Neither of us works but Bud helps us out much of the time. He fixes food for us and even gets us free beers and lets us sleep behind the pool table in his bar when it is so cold outside."

"Marsha, let me rephrase a question: Is good sex really worth all you went through to get it?"

"Yes. Hell yes. Gee Whiz, Fuck!"

"Then I think you better get him in to see me and maybe we can get him on some medication to treat his psychotic symptoms so you two can be totally happy. I can get a little job for him. In fact, there's one in this very building. They want a couple to clean rooms four hours a day, during the evening, and the starting pay is $22.50 per hour for each of the workers."

"I'll ask him, but no promises will be made. I would take it, if they only wanted one person."

"No, they want a couple."

"Let me check with Stan when he gets home."

"Marsha, I don't mean this in a bad way, but you look like an orphan girl."

She was trying to be polite. I looked like hell, but she didn't put it that way. She was tactful and kind about it. I knew my face was bloated from drinking and drugs and I wore no make-up because I didn't have any. We couldn't even afford to eat, much less buy make-up. And I remembered how I used to wear only the best from the best department stores.

"Dr. Cynthia, I have a bad feeling. I don't know what it is. I thought things were bad at home with Ben and my mother. And I thought things were bad with Carl. Damn. If only I had stayed. He has helped me out with money, and all I have to do is call him and he comes to my rescue. Can you keep a secret? He wants me back, Dr. Cynthia. I still love him. Why did I promise to be Stan's Guardian Angel? But I love Stan. I really do. He is my precious husband. Damn." I was so mixed up, and she wrote things down, as I talked.

"Dr. Cynthia, I just want to die. But now, I have your wedding to look forward to so thank you for giving me a reason to live. I don't want to die after all. You will be such a beautiful bride."

"Here I go again, skipping around to different subjects. I wanted my Mother to come live with me as I didn't like the nursing home she was in. But you know what? There is no way I could have taken care of her. I know that now. I can't even take care of myself. Maybe she can come next spring, if things are better. It will give me a while to improve myself."

"Dr. Cynthia, I don't tell Stan everything. I think all wives have little secrets. Maybe they tell their Mothers, but not their husbands. All I know is that I am on the way to being a street drinker. I buy the cheap stuff now and drink it alone, and if Stanley is with me, he takes it and drinks it up before I even have a taste. Is that terrible? I drink the cheap wine, the very cheap wine, and hide it under different bushes in the park where we live. One night I was going after a bottle and a strange man was alongside me and all of a sudden, he tried to rape me. I called out to Stan and he didn't answer because he was "out of it" from drinking. It didn't matter where he was; if he felt like drinking, he would. He doesn't treat me like shit anymore, but he still drinks and does drugs. Mostly marijuana, but on occasion, he does some cocaine and little reds. He also takes my tranquilizers and mixes them with alcohol. I just don't know."

"You know, I am not religious, but I do believe in God. I am a Guardian Angel and tolerate things and pray a lot and thank God for Stan, even if he isn't the greatest at times."

"I was so happy to leave Alabama when I was only fifteen and come to Chicago with that nice older couple, and they paid my way, bought my meals, and dropped me off on my Aunt's porch. I inherited everything when she died because I was her only relative. I loved her so much. But both of my ex-husbands worked at

St. Gilbert's and I stayed there and watched them with their new wives. I had to move, and had enough money to do so. My job was great, and I could have lived comfortably for the rest of my life. But here I am, not even two years later, flat broke, homeless, and depressed as hell."

"Marsha, would you do six little things for me. They are simple and so uncomplicated."

"Sure, if you let me count them."

"Okay."

"Stop drinking, Cold Turkey." "1"

"Stop looking for men, as you have one." "2"

"Be nice to yourself." "3"

"Take this $500.00 and get your hair done and buy a new outfit. "4"

"Go out to a fancy restaurant and have dinner with Stan." "5"

"Come see me in two weeks and show me the new "Old Marsha." "6"

"I can't take that money."

"Yes you can."

"No I can't."

"Yes you can."

"Yes, I will."

She hugged me and we both cried. There were mixed emotions floating around that room. There were tears of happiness, thankfulness, joy, anxiety, uncertainty and love, plus feelings of hope, trust, and a fresh start for me.

~~~~~
~~~~~

CHAPTER THIRTY

April 5, 2004

I don't remember what I did after leaving the office. I blanked out temporarily. I'd been doing that lately and of course I forgot to tell the doctor. I believe I went for a walk in the park, as I did just about every day that I could to see the changing colors and the children playing in the different seasons. But I couldn't understand why everyone was staring at me. Were they staring at my clothes, my messy hair, the dark circles under my eyes, or was there toilet tissue handing out from my panties? I felt as though I looked just like the woman I used to see in the bathroom mirror and in the toilet bowl. I felt miserable. Even the little children looked at me.

One feels terrible when they think or know they look shitty, and I told myself that I'd begin to take better care of myself

What would I prepare for Carl's dinner that night? It must be something simple but good as my ironing had piled up and I didn't want him getting upset. Then I remembered that was long ago, not now, but I didn't know how many years ago it was.

I was married to Stan now and didn't have an ironing board or iron at home to iron. "I am married to Stan." I said this out loud and two women walking by me began laughing and whispering. I didn't care. Nothing mattered.

"Fuck off, both of you." I said to them. I began dancing and singing.

I had to get going. There was something on my list of things to do but I couldn't remember what it was. I sang as I skipped down the sidewalk to the road. "Seven-eight-nine-ten-eleven—I want to go to heaven."

Why was everyone watching me? They probably liked my act so I began dancing, right in the middle of the streets. Cars honked at me, and children laughed. I laughed with them.

April 6, 2004

I went to meet Stan at Bud's. He held and kissed me and said, "Oh honey, I missed you. You were gone so long." He didn't care who saw us, he kissed me passionately. We sat, having two beers each and I told Stan that I was going to quit drinking after these two beers. We finished our hot dogs. Bud looked different somehow, and was on the quiet side.

When walking out of the bar and onto the sidewalk, we ran right into Connie, who was definitely pregnant. Looking at her hurt and made me jealous. I thought that I would be having a baby too, but it turned out to be a false alarm. I could never have children. She probably could have as many as she wanted. She was definitely advertising the fact that she was pregnant and going to have Stanley's baby at any moment.

Maybe it was my imagination but she seemed to push her stomach forward, making it look larger, and she rubbed her hand over it as she looked directly at Stanley, with the biggest smile I ever saw. She didn't even look at me or acknowledge me. But that was fine. Stan was my husband and dammit, he was becoming sexually aroused for some reason just looking at that bitch and oh how that hurt. I knew he was getting aroused just by looking at his bulging crotch.

She wore the most beautiful maternity outfit that I ever saw. It was a designer dress in royal blue, with ruffles and semi-precious stones floating all over the delicate fabric. She only had extra weight in her stomach area; otherwise, she was thin and beautiful. She had on "my" royal blue sandals, and "my" jewelry, and was carrying "my" purse. Stanley had given her everything beautiful that I once had. Yes, he had been supporting her on my money.

Their eyes met and I wasn't just a casual friendship look. It was something beyond that.

"They still love each other. Stan said he loved you. He lied. You lost. You thought things were better. They weren't He was acting. We hate to have to tell you this, but Marsha, all is fair in love and war. If you want him, go after him."

No, I couldn't compete with her. She had on designer clothes, and her shoes cost $120.00. I know. Her French Manicured toe nails and finger nails and two of my favorite rings that Stan had given her put the frosting on the cake. "What good would it do to cry, Marsha? Forget it." I kept telling myself this. "No not now, No not now, No not now. No not now, No not now." I had forgotten how to count—

"Stanley." I called but he didn't answer, as he continued to stare at her, lost in another world.

"Stanley." I called again and he still didn't look over at me. He kissed her and grabbed her arm and for a second I thought he was going to lead her away, and leave me, his wife and Guardian Angel. But no. He wouldn't leave me for her, even if she was having his baby. Stan and I had shared too much and I loved him as he loved me.

"It's going to be a boy, and he will come anytime now. His name is going to be Stanley, just like his Daddy." She announced this for the whole world to hear. Bud was even looking out the window at us.

When she made her announcement, Stan hugged her and planted a big smooch on her lips and I had to turn away. I could no longer look. I could feel the beginning of stinging tears fall. This wasn't right. What was she doing to me and why? I never hurt her, and she was even wearing my jewelry.

A sudden feeling of hatred, something that rarely happens to me, began welling up inside.

I tried to convince myself that Stan loved only me but he held and kissed her then whispered something in her ear. They both giggled.

"Oh my God."

They did love each other.

"Stanley." I called again but either he didn't hear me or was ignoring me. Whichever it was, it hurt and my heart began to pound and skip beats and I felt as though I was falling. Suddenly dizzy, I had to grab the nearby building to steady myself.

He was my husband and I was his Guardian Angel and he wouldn't even look at me. Then it dawned on me. Connie was the enemy that the angels talked about on the hood of my car that day. Fireworks—sparklers—sparks—bang—pop—call it what you want. They continued, loud and clear, between Connie and Stan. Stan and "the enemy." How the hell could I ignore that fact? He evidently did love her. I could see it in their eyes. The enemy was winning this battle. I was losing

"Stan," I called again but he still didn't look at me. Oh my God. I must really look bad.

He didn't answer, either then nor did he look back which was good. I didn't want him to see my tears. He stood closer and put his arm around Connie, and whispered something in her ear once more, and she smiled. (He was doing all this right in front of me. Give me a break, God.)

How could he have forgotten already what we shared these last months?

Didn't I matter to him at all? If I had gone to his room at the Republic the first time he asked, right after we were married, and gone to bed with him, would Connie still have gotten pregnant, or would it have been me? I wondered.

Then he kissed her on the cheek. But that was okay with me. After all, she was having his baby and what the hell was a kiss on the cheek? There's quite a difference between that and the passionate kind.

I couldn't catch my breath when seeing them kiss. Her make-up was impeccable, and it surely wasn't a cheap brand from the "close out sale box" that one finds at a dollar store. I couldn't even afford to buy that. She was a picture of health. I compared my dowdy appearance plus that fact that I was almost twice her age and felt like puking. Shit. I could take no more and had to sit on the bench alongside the store. Stanley was dressing her in style, and having his fun at the same time I was working my ass off.

I tried hard to ignore those glances the two of them shared; the glances that I though would never end.

Slowly he turned and walked back to me. I dried the tears in my eyes and told myself the truth. "Dammit, I did care. Dammit, I fucking hated my crying jags."

It hurt to look at Connie and smile but I did even though she didn't smile back. I couldn't give her the satisfaction of thinking I was jealous. Needless to say, she didn't speak to me as she walked away. She turned around only once to wink at Stan.

He held my hand as we walked towards the park but I saw him glance back at her.

~~~~~
~~~~~

CHAPTER THIRTY-ONE

April 7, 2004

It could have been my imagination, but he seemed a million miles away, not at all with me, as we walked to our territory.

He was quiet and withdrawn and didn't squeeze my hand as he usually did. It felt cold and limp, like a dead fish. He didn't look at me and had a blank look on his face as he stared straight ahead and bit his lip. He didn't even have a stash of liquor for the night and didn't seem to care, which was unusual. You could see things were pressing on his mind.

He wanted to say something. All that came you was "Marsha—." "Marsha—"

Nothing else was verbalized. His hands were trembling. I didn't like what I saw, because I knew something wasn't right. I could feel it and knew it. During the night, he was restless, but since I was mentally and physically exhausted, I slept better than he did. He didn't even kiss me good-night or try to hold me and play around for a while.

April 8, 2004

I woke early the next morning to take our shower and go with Stan to Bud's for our usual cup of "Morning Brew" which was simply very strong coffee with a couple shots of Whiskey in it. It took me awhile to get used to the mixture, but once I did, it was hard to break the longing for one or two cups to start the day. (I forgot that the night before I supposedly had my last drinks.)

Yes, it was a bitter drink, but it was better bitter. The first swallow was the hardest. We loved our early morning drink as we sat and held hands and talked about our daily plans. We always held hands as we drank and Bud laughed at us. But it was a happy laugh.

Yes, I woke early, looking for that drink and reached over to hold my man, my husband. Hopefully he had forgotten all about the evening before when we ran into Connie.

But to my surprise, when I felt on the other side of the blanket, I found nothing but an empty space. His side of "our bed" beneath the bushes was empty. He was nowhere to be found.

Perhaps he was taking a shower without me, hoping I would sleep in a little as he knew how tired and upset I had been. But, I never did that. I checked the bathroom by the Goddess, and he area around it anyhow, and called, but he didn't answer. I looked around the bushes and checked to see if he was talking to a neighbor, which would be unusual for him, but I still didn't see him. I had no idea where he was.

I was lost without him. My mind was spinning like a top. The purse from my pocket was missing, along with the money from Dr. Cynthia, plus the money I made panhandling. I was penniless and my husband was gone. I had nothing once more, except an old dress and dirty shoes. I didn't even have my old panties or bra. So what was I supposed to do, walk around with my tits and ass hanging out?

Why did he have to take my money? Worse yet, why did I have to leave it where he could see it to take it.

My intentions were to buy an outfit or two and have my hair done, and then go job hunting with the extra money that was left. Then it hit me like a ton of bricks. The enemy had run away with my husband.

It took a while to calm down as I just sat and stared into space, but finally I got up and went into Bud's alone, cold and shaking, and I asked if he had seen Stan. The tears were streaming down my face. I already knew the answer. I could see it on his face, and he hesitated to speak. Finally, he said, "Marsha, he was in here earlier with Connie. She is pregnant with his baby."

I began laughing.

"Take it easy. You're not happy, so why laugh? Don't be ashamed to cry and show your unhappiness. Under the circumstances, we would be unhappy too. He's with the bitch. We all know that."

Yes, I knew that, and so did Bud.

"I think I need another drink. Here fill my cup please." I sat staring into space, looking at the ceiling. I began counting the tiles in the ceiling—ninety eight—ninety nine—fifty three—

Yes, I had forgotten how to count. Who was I? What was I drinking? Why didn't it have foam?

I thought of Dr. Cynthia and surprisingly I found myself desperately in need of talking to her but I looked so frightful and was drunk as a skunk. Shit, there was no such thing as a fucking drunk skunk.

What would Bud do if I decided to unload on him, and let it all hang out? There was so much to tell him, and through the years, I'm sure he'd gotten to know Stan quite well. I began to cry uncontrollably.

"What's wrong, honey?"

"Stan—left—me." That's all I could say.

"Why did he leave me? I don't understand. I was good to him. I took a lot from him. I never complained. I always defended him. Why did he go?"

"Why? Before Stanley left, he emptied my purse, took all the money I was given by a friend to have my hair done and get some make-up. I don't know what I'm going to do. My husband is gone, my money is gone, and I have no home. I live beneath fucking bushes in the park. How can I start a new life this way? I don't want to live anymore, Bud. I'm going now. Talk to you later."

I grabbed the top of the bar to balance myself and began to leave when Bud said, "Here. I know how much money he had, and I'm replacing it for you." He handed me $700.00. "I'm giving you a little extra to get started on."

"Bud, I can't take this."

"You'd better, or I'll never speak to you again."

Oh how I wanted to take it, but I couldn't. He insisted and I told him "no." Then we both started laughing. I took it and reached over to give him a kiss. It seems that street people aren't ashamed to take anything from anyone.

"Just promise that you'll come in and show me how pretty you are, like when I first met you, honey. You know what I mean."

"Yes, I will." He had a polite way of telling me that I looked like shit as he used the same words as Dr. Cynthia, asking me to come back to show him the improvements.

"Marsha, you're like a daughter to me. You are what Stanley needs and he didn't even appreciate you."

I was glad he gave me the money. I owed so much on Stanley's Dr. and hospital bills. If he stayed with Connie, I could even go back to the Condo and get a job. No, I could never leave him and he didn't like the Condo.

I would hide it under the blankets for the night and pay bills in the morning.

I was on my way to "our home" in the park, and on the side of a brick building near the park gate, I noticed the pay phone. Funny, I had never noticed it before. I copied down the phone number and would use it as my own, give it to people, in case they needed to call me. I only hoped vandals wouldn't mess around with this one as they had to so many others, causing an "out of order" sign to be installed over it. Gads, what if there was an emergency and I needed the phone and the damn thing didn't work?

Yes, with Stan gone, I inherited the spot under the weeping branches and the next morning I woke and automatically began looking for him, hoping he had come back, but he hadn't. The other homeless in the area became friendly, came over by my territory and started talking. I wondered what they wanted to tell me. It was as if they wanted to tell me something, but couldn't get out the proper words. They reminded me of my Mother in the nursing home. I started to laugh just then, thinking of bringing my Mother to live with me under a tree in a park!

No, I wasn't capable of taking care of her and God only knew where I'd be next spring or summer when the nursing home administrator said I might be able to have her.

As it turned out, the others wanted to teach me more things about survival on the streets. I put my mind on that subject, rather than wondering where Stanley was and what he was doing. I just couldn't think of that—the baby—her. My thoughts were spinning. Were they telling me these things about street life because they knew I'd be alone? Did they know something they weren't telling me?

I had to think of myself and survival. I had to stay alive and do a few more things before the curtain was pulled after my final act. I had to gain some positive energy, and eliminate my negative shortcomings.

April 9, 2004

My new friends told me things about survival that I never even thought about. Stan had always taken care of those things. But now I was alone. They told me about different methods of survival, which restaurants threw away freshly wrapped sandwiches that weren't sold the day before, with not a thing wrong with them except they were a day old. The bread was soft, and the filling was still good as the cold outside was equal to a refrigerator.

They told me which garbage cans held fresh fruit, sandwiches, and ones that had the best leftovers from plates that were hardly touched. I was no longer too proud to look for these places, as I had to survive. Funny, when it comes right down to survival, our way of thinking **does** change.

I also learned what corners to stand on to get the most money, the ones closest to the parking lots that executives and secretaries used. They told me where doctors and dentists had their offices and wondered why I started to cry when they mentioned the word "dentists."

They taught me where to find used clothing for the least amount of money and told me where the nearest shelters were that we could use on the coldest nights.

Sometimes it dipped way below zero and it was not pleasant to sleep outside. Of course on those nights I would visit Bud.

They took me under their wings. They also taught me effective ways to fight and kick, to protect myself and the areas that are vulnerable for men and women. I learned that the street women also fought and wouldn't hesitate to harm another female. The guys told me how to talk to men who approached and began taking advantage of me. I certainly didn't need any more men taking advantage of me in my life.

I was the only homeless woman in that entire park. There are people in this world that look down on us and avoid homeless people standing on corners here and there. Unless you have been homeless, you don't know how desperate things can get, and how thankful these people are when you drop quarters into the cups they hold. I have seen a lot in my life, and know that the homeless people are amongst the kindest, most caring, and sensitive people out there.

They are just victims of bad luck of some sort, or foolishness or some damn crazy act, as was my case.

(I remember back to when I was working, as a R.N. and standing there giving out medication while smoking. No, I didn't get caught, and when Delores came by, I said one of the residents was smoking and she believed me. She knew I smoked from time to time, never much, but I would never smoke while working. She also noticed the smell of alcohol on me, but could never prove I'd been drinking on the job. Maybe it was from the night before, but I never admitted that I would sneak a drink now and then in the bathroom.)

I was dirty and unclean like the rest of my homeless friends. The fact that we usually are dirty, and wear old clothes, and don't brush our teeth before we do go to bed is that usually we don't have tooth brushes, tooth paste, or a place to wash. I was told that if you don't have tooth brushes and tooth paste: "just eat an apple." That supposedly was the natural way to clean your teeth and freshen your breath. But how many homeless have apples? Therefore, with no toothbrushes, and no apples, many of us are losing our teeth.

Let me tell you something. The homeless don't mean to frighten people or make them walk on the other side of the sidewalk. We just need a little smile now and then, and a little bit of help to see us through the day.

But where do we go to wash our clothes with no money? How are we expected to look clean and neat if we live outdoors and are too sick or too weak to panhandle? Some seem to think that if they put money in the cups we are holding that we will reach out to grab them. It is just the opposite. People that look so innocent, then reach out and grab our partly filled cups after we stand outside to collect the money. Can you believe this?

Stan was the experienced "man on the streets" and at one time had taught those who lived in the park new things and now my new friends were teaching me, since I am his wife.

They also showed me how to set up a shelter in a cardboard box, in case of desperation and which direction to place the box so the wind wouldn't blow directly in my face. Many of these things they told me I already knew from Stan.

They told me how to arrange newspapers and cloth under and over me for warmth. I also found out which porches and store fronts wouldn't mind if you spent the night there. Also, some churches were kept open at night, in case anyone was in need of a place to sleep.

April 10, 2004

I had an appointment the very next day at the beauty shop. My hair was a beautiful blonde once again, and with the facial and make-up, including a massage, I had money left over for a beautiful two-piece suit from their boutique and then had my nails done. I felt like a million dollars and must say it improved my entire outlook on life. I hardly recognized myself when I looked into a bathroom mirror.

Oh how I hoped that when Stanley would see me, come over to me, and look at me, then kiss me and tell me that he had left Connie. Of course, that would be too good to be true. I could be such an unrealistic bitch at times.

It was difficult to keep my hair fresh, and the style didn't remain because sleeping on the damp ground wasn't conducive to beauty. I had my choice. Either sleep sitting up and look tired all day or sleep on the ground and have slightly messy hair. I had to comb it with my hands until I bought a comb and brush the following day.

(I wondered if he kissed her like he kissed me, and if he wrapped his arms around her and felt her boobs and butt while kissing. All of the others that lived in the park knew of my predicament: that I was alone because my husband had left me for another woman. A few were talking in loud voices. I even saw some leave together, casting a look in my direction, and then either coming back to squeeze my hand or put an arm around me.)

Perhaps he had brought her to "our territory" and I didn't even know. But then, I really didn't want to know.

My friends were attentive, asking if I needed anything to eat, drink or if I needed anything from a store. They were willing to panhandle to get the money to buy whatever I wanted.

It seemed that every cent I made while working was used to support Connie or buy clothes for her while I had nothing.

My homeless friends bought me a new pillow and a silk pillow case, telling me that would keep my hair fresh. They approved of my new clothing and hair style. Their concern for me was genuine, and not a day went by without them hugging me and saying, "Honey, it will be all right."

I ran into Buzz a time or two, and all he said was "Hoity-Toity Bitch—. Guess he showed you." He never offered a penny or any sort of help as he had once promised.

The voices spoke to me loud and clear:

"Marsha, that just goes to show you. Buzz is rotten as Stan was at first and now with this last act. Take care of yourself. Things will work out for you. We know that. You matter to us, and always will. Remember that."

I saw Dan for the first time in ages, when I went to the grocery store for a loaf of bread.

"Marsha, how are you?"

"I'm just fine, Dan."

"You look awesome. I like your outfit and hair. Same old girl!"

"No, not really."

"Did your wife ever come back or did you remarry?"

"No to both questions. I was still hoping to meet up with you so we could start over."

"No such thing, Dan. I love Stan more than anything in this world."

"Then would you be interested in just seeing me now and then?"

"No, I don't date. I won't get involved with anyone as I love Stan too much."

He didn't know what to say but told me he wasn't going to SCA Meetings anymore and wondered if I was.

I told him that I wasn't and he asked if we could have an innocent cup of coffee now. I explained that I had to get home but didn't include any information about where my home was or say anything negative about Stan and Connie. No way, no matter what, I would never cheat on Stanley again.

"I'm happy now, for the first time in my life and don't want to start screwing around again." I was glad however, that I looked nice when Dan saw me. Somehow, for some reason, I'm glad it wasn't a week earlier when he happened to pass me in some store or worse yet, in the street panhandling.

I left him and began walking. I thought of him and John Reynolds, and faces from the past, and was so thankful that my thinking on life had finally straightened out. Better late that never. Right?

There is no such thing as a "Mr. Perfect." They all have their faults and so do we. Each has a different print on their luggage and different problems inside, but they all carry luggage.

I thought of my shopping days on Saturdays, and thought of Oliver Twist. I laughed. I thought of being a bridesmaid soon, and would have to check again with Dr. Cynthia for the date. I hope their marriage is as happy as what Stan and I shared.

Stan, who was pretty close to being a "Mr. Perfect" in my book, would come back to me and everything would be fine. Things just had to work out. The baby he had fathered was just something that "happened" right after our marriage and he probably felt comfortable, familiar, and obligated to Connie. But I was his wife and what about me? How could a Guardian Angel wife take care of her husband, if she didn't even know where he was? Forgive me for repeating myself here, but tears are filling my eyes once more, and life is the pits. The fucking pits.

He'd been unfaithful more than once or twice, but then so had I, so forgiveness was the name of the game now. We had enjoyed life so much for such a short time and it wasn't fair. To know happiness and then have it disappear is like being able to see, then waking one day and finding yourself blind.

April 13, 2004.

I didn't hear from Stan and slowly accepted the fact that he was gone for good. It was that same feeling that usually originated in my bones—a premonition. He would never come back to me. I had this bad feeling and didn't know why.

Then later, I called the hospital to see if he was there. I explained who I was, and that he had disappeared. They told me that he had been there with his pregnant wife since he was admitted. They had been outdoors and Stan stopped breathing. She didn't have the slightest idea about what to do but did get him to the hospital somehow, and he was diagnosed with end-stage pneumonia.

There I was, his wife, and not with my man who needed me. I knew shit would hit the fan when I went to see him, because of her hatred for me, but I had the same hatred for her. I was a determined bitch.

April 14, 2004

His room was dark. The large private room had one bed, which was facing the door and all you could hear was the click-click of the medication pump and oxygen machine. The I.V. Antibiotics plus a feeding tube in his stomach, and a sleep monitor were by his bedside. He could only receive 2 liters of oxygen as he was a heavy smoker with COPD (chronic obstructive pulmonary disease.) His breathing was labored. The head of his bed was elevated and his rough and shallow breathing brought tears to this "easy-to-cry-person." The nurse came in and raised one side rail. I introduced myself as his wife.

"His wife is with him now."

"No, that's his girl friend."

"Honey, you come to the nursing station to talk to us before you leave today."

One side rail of the bed was up and I only hoped the nurses there were observing things. Connie entered the room, she gave me a shitty sneer, and said, "What are you looking at, Mother? Don't worry. I'm watching my future husband. He doesn't need you. You may leave now, Mother."

Thinking back, I should have punched her out. But I was so happy that two nurses alongside me heard how she talked to me. They actually heard her! They actually were waiting for this confrontation.

I was told by the nurses when I left, "She has been by him day and night. If we chase her away, it would cause him to be upset. And that would mean a massive heart attack. He would fall out of bed, but she does watch him. At least we know now who the real wife is."

Being a nurse, I explained the situation to the head nurse. We as nurses hear all sorts of things, so she didn't even bat an eyelash. She promised to call me if there were any changes. But she also told me that his breathing and heartbeat were irregular and he was having some gurgling in his chest. I knew for sure, that no way was my husband going to return to me as a man, and husband, and just that thought made me want to die.

I left, barely able to see where I was walking. On the way out, I gave my phone number to the head nurse and once again she ascertained me that they would call me immediately if there was any change. And then I said a prayer that the phone would be in working order to receive the call I didn't want to receive.

"Are you leaving now?" I was asked by the nurse.

"Yes, since his girl friend is here. He doesn't need me. But I'm his wife and love him too much to watch this going on. Sorry I have to leave but it's making me crazy to stay here. I feel like screaming. Don't forget to call me—if—anything—changes." I could hardly talk anymore.

April 15, 2004

It was two days before Stan's birthday, and I wanted to bring him something special, something he could hold and think of me. But how would I get it to him with Connie by him full time. I was stubborn. I'd find a way! I wanted to give him a big teddy bear with a bright red heart with our names embroidered on the heart. I panhandled to get the money for the material for the heart, needles, and embroidery thread to sew the heart on and also for our names. I managed to get enough money and also embroidered, "I love you Honey." It was perfect. I put a baseball cap on him, one like Stanley wore that I picked up in the thrift store. I was going to see him again, come hell or high water.

I walked into the room and Connie told me, "Get out, Bitch. He wants me." I didn't argue. Trouble in that room was all I needed. I just wanted Stan to rest.

I left the teddy bear with a new nurse, explaining that Stanley's birthday was April 17, and I wanted him to have the teddy bear. I told her that I was his wife and insisted that he have it, and that the woman with him was just his girl friend. She apologized, and promised to do just as I said. I listened, and heard her tell Connie "his wife wants him to have this teddy bear so you make sure it stays with him."

Connie didn't like the idea but promised that she would leave it. It had been placed in his arms, and he was able to see it and see the writing on it. In fact, the nurse came in later and told him that his wife brought it and told him what it said. She told me later that he smiled briefly but also told me Connie had left the room after she read the words and saw Stan smile.

I gave them Dr. Connors' phone number and went to see her as I promised. I had on my new outfit and my hair was freshly washed and set by a beautician. Dr. Connors approved, and told me the wedding would be at Christmas time, and hoped I would stay as pretty as I was. "Such an improvement this makes, Marsha. I can't believe how pretty you are."

Dr. Connors asked why I looked so upset. I explained that my husband was dying and Connie was by his side and wouldn't allow me in the room. I told her the entire story and also that the nurses thought if we chased Connie out, he would have a massive heart attack. That's why she is still there.

Dr. Cynthia told me that they both must have wanted it that way, and told me that it would all work out.

Dr. Cynthia motivated me, removed me from my temporary slump, and we talked about the weather, diets, eating, and our conversation was cheerful."

I asked Dr. Cynthia if she thought I would be schizophrenic some day and she said that was the least of my worries now. "You are a beautiful woman, and you must take care of yourself. Remember that."

We didn't talk about Ben, and mentioned that he was the one to blame for all my problems. She told me that I was the kind that would be able to handle anything that came up, no matter what it was." She had confidence in me. It felt so good to hear those words.

"Dr. Connors, what will I do without Stan? Where will I live? How will I get a job?"

"Marsha, you start by thinking of yourself, putting yourself first, taking better care of yourself as a person, and quitting the drinking and drugs. You need to get a job outside of the psychiatric world and raise your self-image a few notches. Get away from all sickness, depression, and mental illness. Do geriatric or orthopedic nursing, or become a travel agent while you're still young enough. Work with flowers. And who knows? Probably some of your mother and stepfather's behavior allowed you to grow up in a negative environment. Together we will work to bring positive feelings for you. But we are taking a breather for now. Just take care of yourself and help Stan. Remember that I'll call you every day, and check on you and I will send best wishes along with you for Stanley." I did give her the number of the phone on the back of the building by the park.

We talked for quite a while and I promised to visit in one month to tell her how things were going. She wished me well and promised to give me $50.00 each week until I landed a job, and then I could pay back part of it. At first I hesitated, but finally agreed to take her up on it.

~~~~~
~~~~~

CHAPTER THIRTY-TWO

April 16, 2004
Afternoon

I don't know what the reason was, but after that visit with Dr. Connors, my hands shook. Her office had been a temporary escape from life, but even so, I was claustrophobic and kept looking behind me as I walked. The thunder outside grew louder, but there was no rain. In fact, I didn't know for sure if it was thunder or drums. The voices in my head grew louder, too.

"It's about time. It's about to happen. It's about to end. Rush to him."

I didn't know what those voices meant. They grew louder and louder and I only hoped they didn't mean what I thought they meant.

I had to get back to the problem at hand. I had to get back to my real world and kept walking. Where, I didn't know. I envisioned angels flying close to the ground, but this time they were carrying shovels full of fresh, black dirt. I was probably hallucinating this time, thinking Stanley was dying and I wasn't with him.

April 17, 2004

Everything was blank in my mind. I was on my way to the park, forgot everything and walked one block north, then one block south, turned around, totally forgetting where I should be. I wanted to be near the pay phone, but somehow thought I was supposed to meet Stanley at Bud's so I headed for Bud's and then realized Stanley wasn't going to be there as he was in the hospital. It was his birthday.

Later that day

Night passed but the day dragged on. It grew later and later and began to get dark again. I headed for the park, after sitting outside Stan's hospital room all afternoon. I must pay those bills, but I will do it tomorrow, I checked and still was carrying the money. Stanley's condition remained the same.

I expected the phone to ring. It didn't. I went to the washroom, thinking I missed the call. I sat, as tiredness overtook my body. I had to get back to the hospital.

I thumbed a lift to the hospital, and it didn't take long for someone to pick me up and I couldn't help but notice how well-dressed the woman was. She had long blonde hair, and was driving a new Lexus, the same color as I had somewhere. But I didn't remember if I still had it or where it was parked.

"Where are you going, honey?"

"To St. Gilbert's Hospital."

"Let me give you a lift."

Then I remembered that I couldn't go to that hospital and see that bitch at Stanley's bed again. I just couldn't handle it. Yes, I wanted to see my husband, to be near him, but thinking about her being there made me feel as though I was cracking.

"No, No. Please take me home. I can't go to the hospital now. I'll just go home and wait for a phone call from the hospital."

The driver became impatient with me and said, "I picked you up as a favor. I was headed in another direction and you don't even know where the hell you are going? Make up your fucking mind. I don't know where you live. I don't know your situation. What the fuck is going on with you?"

"Madam, I once had a hair style like you, and drove a Lexus and had anything in life I wanted. But now, my husband is in the hospital dying. His pregnant girl friend is in bed with him and I don't want to see her face. I am homeless now. Take me to the park over there. I live there."

"Wait a minute. I am sorry." She was looking at me in the rear view mirror and not only heard me sobbing but saw me.

"What can I do to help? I feel so sorry." Her voice changed drastically. It was now sweet and somehow at that moment, she looked motherly.

(God, I want my little Mother now.)

"Okay honey, where do you live?"

"Under a tree."

"Come on young lady, we have to go have a cup of coffee and talk."

"I can't. I'm waiting for a phone call from the hospital."

"Don't you have a cell phone in your purse?

"No, I don't have a cell phone. I don't even have a purse."

"I have nothing. Nothing at all. I have one dress now, no underwear and tennis shoes plus this outfit. I also have a dying husband and I have just a few months to live. I have nothing to look forward to. Do you understand my situation now?"

I didn't mean to start crying again, but I did. "There's a pay phone—on the building—next to the gate—next to the bench. I will sit there and wait for that call."

I sat and talked. I would still hear the phone. "Yes, I once had a $350,000 home in the western suburbs, a beautiful condo on Lake Shore Drive, which cost me more than my home. I had a job as Assistant Director of Nursing, and a part-time job to support my fourth husband who spent all my money on his pregnant girl friend, twenty years younger than me. Yes, I had four husbands, took the wrong path in life and believe me it could happen to you or anyone else. And once I chose that wrong path, everything changed. It's so easy to happen, so gradual that you don't even notice it. When the road of life ahead comes to a fork, you might not know which way to go either."

"I'd like to get to know and help you. I am alone and need a friend. In the meantime, I want to give you a little something." She gave me her name, address and phone numbers at home and her cell phone number and then handed me two fifty-dollar bills. She instructed me to call her if I needed anything. "Call me anytime, don't hesitate. My name is Cindy Childs. Please call me."

"Thank you." I reached over the front seat and hugged her. I dried my eyes and tucked the information and money in my pocket, and then left her car and proceeded to walk trough the gate at the park to sit on the bench—and hope the phone wouldn't ring, even though I was certain it would.

It is surprising how many wonderful people are out there, people that you have yet to meet: helping, friendly, people ready and willing to help. I prayed to God. "Please God, I'm going through a hard time now. Please know how I appreciate all you are doing for me, allowing me to meet helping people and being able to with Stan as much as possible, and please help me to keep on keeping on."

Of course I had to ask for something! "Dear God. It looks hopeless, so don't let Stan suffer more than necessary."

I had a call from the hospital. They increased his pain medicine given I.V. and began giving injections of Morphine and something else. I asked but they wouldn't say. Now my new worry was: when would it happen, how much would he suffer near the end, and how would I get there. "Please God, help him in all ways possible."

I got up from the bench to walk around and it started to rain. Without realizing it was raining, I got up on stage and began to sing and dance. My audience of homeless in the bushes, probably thought I had gone crazy from the stress, and I was ready to do just that. I twirled, did the polka, did the twist, and did the mashed potatoes. Suddenly I was a ballet dancer and then I sang like Carly Simon. The entire world was watching me. Their applause didn't stop.

April 17, 2004
Morning

I smiled for all to see, then laughed and then began to scream. It was at that moment. That very moment when I heard the sound of a telephone ringing and wished it would stop. I waited. It didn't stop. I picked it up on the tenth ring and held it upside down on my ear, dropped it, then turned it the right way and said,

"Hello."

"Mrs. Stevens?"

"Yes."

"We need you here right away. He doesn't have more than a few minutes left. Hurry."

I ran to the street, and then I danced, and began chanting. There were no cars in sight to take me to the hospital and I didn't have money to call a taxi. No quarters, dimes, or nickels. So I would pretend the call hadn't come and go back home. I danced some more right in the street.

~~~~~
~~~~~

CHAPTER THIRTY-THREE

April 17, 2004
Early a.m.

How in the world could I get to him at such an early morning hour? There were no drivers out to even see me thumbing for a ride, but I managed to run two blocks to a busy street, hoping that somewhere, somehow, a car would come by to take me to my Stanley.

There wasn't a single vehicle on the road. I began laughing and singing. I was crazy. Then the tears started and the voices were telling me:

"Hurry. Hurry. It's now. Get to him."

Just as I was about to start running to him, a car appeared and stopped. I don't know if it meant to pick me up or if it stopped to avoid hitting me as I was in the middle of the road. I didn't know who the driver was, nor did I care. I opened the door and got in the back seat uninvited.

"Please take me to St. Gilbert's Hospital."

"Do you have any money?"

"Here." I handed him one of my $50.00 bills and he blinked twice then pushed the gas pedal to the floor and we made it to St. Gilbert in less than three minutes.

I ran in and up to his room. I couldn't even feel the steps. Once there, I wondered why I had come and had a strong urge to turn around and go back out, but my feet continued towards his room. My mind was blank. I didn't want to see "her" but "he" was mine. And I added "And me is me." With that I laughed my head off.

They say at the end of your loved one's life, visions of your whole life come back to you. I thought of all my loves, and everything in me hurt and the pain was spreading. I couldn't see because my eyes were clouded and my bones and joints were aching so, I could hardly stand up.

Stress is a killer. A fucking killer. All my pain was of little importance, as Stanley lay there dying.

I said, "Oh God, don't punish me like this. I know I have been a bad wife. I know I have been negligent. I know I took the wrong path, but I didn't know any better. I don't even know when it happened."

Two minutes later

I knew the symptoms too well and he was fighting. I know my man, and I knew he was waiting for something. He was waiting for me.

Connie had her arms around him and she was crying. Her arms were squeezing him so tightly, he probably couldn't breathe. He gasped, but then his eyes wandered over towards me. He opened his eyes, I smiled, and Connie surprised me by getting up and saying, "Go to him. He's been asking for you. He smiled again, and I knew it was to be his last smile.

Thank God. He knew I was there. His eyes said, "I'm sorry Marsha. I love only you. I really do. Please forgive me."

His arm extended out towards me and it seemed as if he was trying to reach me but no way could he move. He had the teddy bear, still in his arms. I listened to his moaning, watched his squirming, and noticed his change in breathing. He had "the death rattle" which echoed throughout the room. It came from deep within his chest.

That death sound—

Dr. Black came in the room and put his arm around me and called me to come with him into the hallway in a few minutes. He wanted to talk to me.

I stayed at Stan's side. His grasp was weak. But I made up for it when I held his hand firmly. He evidently recognized the grasp, as he, with eyes closed said, "Marsha."

"Stan don't try to talk. I love you more than anything in the world and I do forgive you. I just want you to forgive yourself."

Did I see a tear in his eye? I don't know. But I do know he breathed his last breath at that instant. I stood there, staring at him. Helpless. I had seen his last smile, held his hand until the end and was with him when he took his last breath. It was his birthday. I cried.

His chest wasn't moving. His lips weren't moving, but his eyes were wide open as Connie walked back into the room. She whispered in his ear, "Stanley, I love you so much, just as Marsha does. We both love you." Connie then embraced me.

Suddenly I saw her in a different light. She was also a woman in love, and it just happened to be with my husband, and now she would have to raise their baby alone. She did anything and everything for him just as I did. She loved him so much she had to stay with him.

Connie held her stomach and flinched as if labor were starting. Someone from labor and delivery hurried in to take her to have little Stanley.

The room filled with Angels, and I head screaming, but didn't know if it was me or the voices within.

Later, I left and Dr. Black was waiting for me in the hall. "His vital signs were not normal. His temperature remained at 103, and his pulse ox (how they measure oxygen in your blood) was only 2. The normal is 100. His blood pressure was inaudible and we didn't get a pulse those last few minutes before you arrived. I am so happy you made it here and Connie seems to have grown up with this experience."

"Oh Dr. Black, what will I do?"

"Let me just tell you that at the end he didn't suffer much. We gave him all the pain medicine we could. Your husband was a fighter!"

"I know it."

"They were both consenting adults, and neither would budge an inch up until the end. God you're a brave lady."

Who was I? Where was I? What had happened? My feet guided me out of his room, down the steps, and out the front door. My feel led me, because I couldn't think and couldn't remember a thing about getting out of St. Gilberts. But when I saw the hospital name, I remembered everything. Oh my God!

As I left the building, Angels surrounded me, saying, "You did a fine job, Marsha. You tried to protect him from the enemy, but he made it impossible for you. You are not to be blamed."

At this point, I just had to ask. "Just what was the enemy that I was protecting him from?"

"The evil was pneumonia, which began as a child, and lingered like a black cloud over his head, ready to reach out and squeeze the life out of this man. It finally did kill him. You tried everything but he continued to love the outdoors like no person we ever knew. That was his craziness in life. We are just thankful to you for extending his life for a few more months.

I wanted to scream at the realistic visions I had of my life. Visions of cheating. Cheating on my husbands. "Oh Carl, What I did to you? If only I had waited for you. Oh Carl, I never did stop loving you. Why didn't I give us a chance?"

Why was I thinking of Carl when my husband had just died? I don't know. I didn't know anything. Thoughts of Bud, and music on the juke box, and the drums in my head increased their beat. Louder and louder. I tried to think. I must call Bud. I had to call Bud.

I found a nearby pay phone, searched in my pockets for some coins, but some kind woman passing by handed me money for the phone.

"Bud, this is Marsha. I have to talk to you." I paused, not being able to talk for a few moments.

"What is it honey?"

As hard as I tried, the words didn't come out.

"Bud, Stanley just passed away. In the hospital. I was with him. So was Connie. I wanted you to know this."

There was complete silence at the on the other end and then Bud began to sob.

"My son. My only child. I loved him so. I loved his mother and he was my only child. Marsha. Marsha. I loved my boy and I love you so much. I can't live without him. What will we do? Thank God he had someone like you for a while in his lifetime. Oh Stan. My only son," He cried hysterically.

~~~~~
~~~~~

CHAPTER THIRTY-FOUR

April 17, 2004
Later in the day

I wonder if San knew that Bud was his father. Stan's death was really hitting Bud hard. I could just see this grown man with tears running down his face. I heard a thump, and thought maybe his head fell forward, hitting the counter, and suddenly there was dead silence.

Soon Bud said, "I was so happy he found you, even if I was for a short time. You were perfect for him; he just didn't know that. You are my daughter. Please be my daughter. After all, you were married to my son. I'll give you everything and anything you desire. You'll have a place to live in my apartment building as long as you want. You will have your choice of five apartments, rent free. I'll even buy your groceries and pay the utilities. Please say yes."

I said "yes."

I was shocked at what Bud admitted, but then was I really? No one knows of another person's secrets. Quite a few things were answered with that statement from Bud. I loved this man, as Stan did.

"Oh by the way, I have a message for you. Wait a minute. I put it somewhere. I can't find it. I'm all shook up, babes."

Bud couldn't understand why I sobbed when he called me by that name. I told him that's what Stan used to call me and we both were silent. My eyes were ready to fall out and too sore to cry anymore.

"Here I am, back and I have a wrinkled piece of paper inside a wrinkled envelope here. Should I open it?"

"Yes, please, Dad."

"Let me see. He read it to me:

> Sale of Condominium
> $400,000.00
> Cashier's Check enclosed."

I was speechless. Suddenly I had something to do.

"Bud, I'll be right there. Wait for me."

I thumbed a ride to the bar and hugged my new Father and told him, "I have some business to take care of. Please give me the paper about the sale of the condominium and the check and I'll be right back."

He did, and I thanked him.

I hurried to my lawyer's office. In spite of my tiredness and the day's happenings, I had to make a Will before anything else happened. The paper was on a legal form, signed by a lawyer, with two witnesses. The Will would insure that Bud, my Mother, Connie, and little Stanley would have no worries in life, for a while, anyhow.

As I left the lawyer's office, the silence, was interrupted by a churning sound and I walked across the street saying, "I fucked up my life. I did it all by myself."

I didn't care who heard me talking. Now there was no one to help me. I was completely alone and almost broke. It was not entirely Stan's fault, and I should have tried harder to control this problem. I should have insisted he sleep indoors. But then I remember the old saying, "Only one person, the person involved, can control his or her own actions. No one can force you to do something you don't want to do."

But I couldn't control my own actions or addictions throughout my life, no matter how hard I tried. Wrong choices were made and I didn't even know if I was completely to blame.

Bad decisions. Failures.

A passer-by stopped and gave me more money. I called Dr. Cynthia. "It happened, Dr. Cynthia." That was all I could say. "I'll see you soon. Good-bye and thanks for everything."

I was in no condition to go home to my husband. I had to walk, to do something. I didn't have my car, so I couldn't drive. Then I remembered, I had no husband. I heard the noise come from my throat the loud crying and choking.

I beat my head on the ground as curious onlookers watched. Once again, I had to choose a path. I did, and it crossed over to a gravel trail. My eyes seemed to glaze up and I lost my vision. I couldn't see at all. Everything was malfunctioning and bees were surrounding me, but the angels chased them away. Angels, all over. I tripped over a plate of food, and fell flat on my face. I was able to see and walk once more. Rabbits, thousands of them, running up to me, climbing and crawling on me.

It didn't matter where I was going. I didn't care. I didn't have a husband, couldn't be with my mother. I had no job no money, nothing. That was true. I did give all of the money from the condominium sale away. I don't remember keeping a single cent for myself.

It grew later and I was hungry and thirsty, but that didn't matter. I couldn't stop to eat or drink. The hell with it. I had to reason to eat or drink, as I didn't care if I lived or died. He was gone. My best friend and partner in life was taken away from me.

I had taken a path that was leading me into a dark forest, winding around, through clumps of bushes and between trees.

Daylight had disappeared and the night was suddenly pitch black. This reminded me of my life.

I heard the sound. It was a train whistle and it wasn't that far away. Then I stumbled on the tracks and just stood there. Between the two rails. I just stood. and suddenly the bright light of the train was only fifteen or twenty feet away. "Hit me. Hit me." I screamed to the train as I stood directly in front of it on the tracks as the whistle sounded once more. I was extending both arms and laughing. Another shrill whistle blew.

Then someone grabbed me. Someone with strong arms. He pulled me off the tracks and we both fell to the ground, three feet from the rails and I felt the strong breeze as the train passed us. If I had remained, where I was, only five seconds longer, the train would have hit me.

"I've made a mess out of my life and just want to die. Leave me alone. I'm all fucked up. You had no business stopping me from what I wanted to do."

He sat alongside me and kissed my cheek, and then took a cell phone from his pocked and called the police.

It didn't take long before I heard the sirens. Two officers arrived and helped me into the squad car. I was handcuffed and taken to the precinct where they questioned me, and filled out papers and one officer made calls from another room. I couldn't quite understand what he was saying. I just heard one word: "committed."

He returned to the room where I waited and told me that I would be taken to a safe place, where I would have good food, medication and the proper care. I barely heard their words as they told me attempted suicide called for being taken away for protection. I didn't know what that meant. Hell, I didn't even know who I was.

"I have something to do first. I must finish it. Then I will go with you."

"What do you have to finish?"

"Something that I feel is very important."

"How long will it take?"

"Just one night, maybe part of the morning."

"We know where you live, and we'll be by in the morning about 8:00 o'clock. Will that give you enough time? Will that be okay with you?"

They knew me and my tale of woe and knew I didn't have the energy or means to skip town, and they were right. They gave me some food to hold me over and said, "Take care of yourself." They helped me into the car, and took me to my home in the park.

Quite a few of my homeless neighbors watched, but no questions were asked.

My question is? What happens to some people and why?" I heard the officers talking and I began writing. I had to finish this Diary. I couldn't write in the park and needed more paper. I went along the streets and collected scraps of paper, a total of 99 scraps and wrote frantically on them. I had run out of space to write in my little diary. I would have to get Saundra to finish it for me. She would do it. I know she would.

Something was driving me on and I had a compelling urge, a necessity and secret drive to finish this task, and dammit, I would do it.

There are so many people out there like me, and this will help them. Actually, it should help everyone.

I beg of all of you not to make the same mistakes in life as I did. Do you realize how hard it was for me to write in the darkness. I had to think back to some days earlier in time and fill in blanks here. I won't have a chance to proof read this. Please forgive me for everything. Forgive me for my writing errors and errors in spelling, and forgive me my jumbled thoughts. Oh God, forgive me for everything. Forgive me for causing so much misery to so many people.

April 18, 2004
The next morning,
8:00a.m.

The police car arrived to pick me up at 8:00a.m. "We have a long drive ahead of us," they said as they handed me a cardboard tray with some breakfast. They then double-secured the back doors, as if I'd try to get away! Shit! They were kind, caring and concerned. My entire body ached, and I noticed this more while sitting still. It was kidney and bladder pain, and pain in my entire stomach. But when did it get this bad? I had been so busy that I didn't seem to notice. I was constantly on the go.

"You are going to a new home for people like you. It is one that has the record of being the best in Illinois." They told me the name of the facility, and I knew at least I wouldn't have to sleep on the ground anymore and was certain I would have good food.

I sang "Oh not now. Oh not now. Oh not now." I sang it to the tune of "Three Blind mice."

They took turns driving and it seemed like forever until they pulled into the driveway leading to the large, rambling brick facility, with white trim, and the police officers helped me out of the car, each holding one arm as they walked me in.

I handed the taxi driver a $50.00 bill and told him it was a "thank you for the blankets payment." Then I told them I wouldn't be needing it.

I remember talking to someone in an office, but don't know what we talked about. She filled out some papers and looked over a folder of my medical history. I had no idea where that thick folder came from. Lastly, she asked me three questions:

> "What does it mean when they say the rolling stone gathers no moss?"
>
> "What does it mean when they say people in glass houses shouldn't throw stones?"
>
> "What does it mean when they say a bird in the hand is worth two in the bush?"

I laughed my head off and they couldn't figure out why. I just couldn't stop laughing.

She looked at me and asked why I was laughing.

I laughed some more, unable to stop.

I had the following admitting diagnoses: Schizophrenia secondary to Schizotypal Disorder with psychotic features, Alzheimer's Disease, Syphilis, Ovarian Cancer, metastasized to kidneys, liver, and lungs. No wonder I hadn't felt good and no doctor would tell me these things. Now it was too late. Would it have been too late two years ago?

I was escorted to a room that I would share with another woman about my age, and she sat on the bed rocking, in just a nightgown. She had no teeth, but was neat and clean. Even though she was crying, I heard her meek. Little voice say, “Hello.” She offered a pleasant smile.

“Hello,” I answered back with a smile.

~~~~~
~~~~~

CHAPTER THIRTY-FIVE

April 18, 2004

I was to learn again, things that I had forgotten. I learned to brush my teeth and even had my own toothbrush, comb and hair brush. I was able to have my hair done every week. I forgot what dinner plates and bowls looked like, and the silverware matched.

There were napkins at each table, and people actually served you a meal while you sat. Only once in a while did we have hot dogs, thank goodness! They served good meat, potatoes, vegetables and desserts.

I had sanitary pads, and toilet tissue, my own soap, my own toilet, and my own shower.

I even had a dresser and they filled it with new clothing they bought me. I had real shoes and slippers with plenty of underclothes that fit and stockings.

I had real, soft, warm blankets. I cried.

"Thank you God. Thank you so much."

I silently said, "I love you, Stanley."

That night my room mate and I sat in bed and smiled again. "How was your first day?" she asked.

"Just great. Thank you."

We did rock, and we did shed a few tears.

Then I called, "Mother. Mother. Mother."

But she didn't answer.

~~~~~
~~~~~

EPILOGUE

To the best of my ability, I have copied Marsha's words exactly as written. I was with her on a few occasions, so I know what she went through. This is her Biography and she changed only names and places, to protect the guilty. The rest of it is true, as her eyes saw things, and as things happened in her world.

She asked me to finish it for her as she was too sick. I read those ninety-nine pages over and over, but I did it! She was my best friend, no matter what.

Marsha has a roof over her head and everything she wants, including wonderful care. She has all the medication she needs.

Bud tells Marsha that her Mother is in one of the finest nursing facilities in Northern Illinois. Bud visits her and on occasion has even brings beer for her. The staff approves. Lori Lee is happy.

Bud has a new room added to his bar, which features live music and many Blues Bands. The room has a dancing floor and booths, with fresh flowers. It is called "***Stan's Room.***"

Connie and little Stanley are doing well. He was born nine hours after his father died. He is healthy and weighed 9 lbs. 14 oz. at birth and Connie has a little apartment and a job as a receptionist in a clinic. She is taking Nursing classes during the evening hours. She wants to be a R.N. She doesn't date.

The other day Connie visited Marsha and she had little Stanley dressed in a blue suit with a tie. His tennis shoes had laces! Connie walks on the vast grounds with Marsha frequently, and they are best friends and talk of everything. They embrace, they cry. They have much in common.

One day Marsha remembered about the money in the bank and the "bill money" still in her purse. She kissed Connie on the cheek and gave her the money in her purse and authorized her to with withdraw the money in the savings account for herself. Her hands were shaky as she wrote that note. Both of them say that after knowing Stanley, they will never date or marry again. And I know they mean it. The warmly embrace at the end of each visit.

Little Stanley calls Marsha, "Grandma"—she Marsha loves it.

Carl waits patiently for Marsha. John waits patiently for Marsha, Dan waits patiently for Marsha, and two other men who won't give names also wait patiently.

~~~~~

Marsha died ten days later, peacefully, in her sleep. She is buried next to Stan. The grave is perpetually decorated.

Saundra Stone
~~~~~